TOM GRAVES
# Louise Brooks, Frank Zappa,
& other charmers & dreamers

**DEVAULT-GRAVES**
**DIGITAL EDITIONS**
www.devault-gravesagency.com
Memphis, Tennessee

*My Afternoon with Louise Brooks*, copyright © 2011 by Tom Graves. *Blonde Shadow: The Brief Career and Mysterious Disappearance of Actress Linda Haynes*, copyright © 2011 by Tom Graves. *Meat Eaters, Killers, and Suckers of Blood: Mano a Mano with Harry Crews* was first published in that form in the anthology *Getting Naked with Harry Crews*, copyright © 1999 by Tom Graves. *Natural Born Elvis: The Story of Bill Haney, the First Elvis Impersonator* was originally published in *The Oxford American* magazine in 1998, copyright © 1998 by Tom Graves. *The Cajun Hank Williams* was originally published as *The Back Door Frontman* in *The Oxford American* magazine in 1999, copyright © 1999 by Tom Graves. *In the Midnight Aisle: The Story of the Blackwood Brothers Quartet*, copyright © 2011 by Tom Graves. *Sympathy for the Devil: A Kind Word for Albert Goldman*, copyright © 2009 by Tom Graves. *Ten LPs You Probably Don't Have (But Should)*, copyright © 2009 by Tom Graves. *When the Sex Pistols Came to Memphis*, copyright © 2010 by Tom Graves. *Guilty Pleasures: Tennessee Ernie Ford* was originally published in 1991 in *Rock & Roll Disc* magazine, copyright © 1991 by Tom Graves. *Woodstock Revisited* was originally published in *American History* magazine, copyright © 1996 by Tom Graves. *Interview: Frank Zappa* was originally published in 1987 in *Rock & Roll Disc* magazine, copyright © 1987 by Tom Graves. *Interview: Mick Taylor* was originally published in 1988 in *Rock & Roll Disc* magazine, copyright © 1988 by Tom Graves. *Have Mersey: An Interview with the La's Driving Force and Angriest Member, Lee Mavers* was originally published in 1991 in *Rock & Roll Disc* magazine, copyright © 1991 by Tom Graves. *Take Me Seriously!: An Interview with Mark Lindsay of Paul Revere and the Raiders* was originally published in 1991 in *Rock & Roll Disc* magazine, copyright © 1991 by Tom Graves. *Louise Brooks, Frank Zappa, & Other Charmers & Dreamers*, copyright © 2015 by The Devault-Graves Agency, LLC. All rights reserved. No part of this publication may be reproduced, stored in a retrieval system, or transmitted in any form or by any means, electronic, mechanical, photocopying, microfilming, recording, or otherwise, without permission of the publisher.

Print Edition ISBN: 978-1-942531-08-1
Ebook ISBN: 978-1-942531-07-4
Cover design: Martina Voríšková
Title page design: Martina Voríšková
Layout: Patrick Alley

# DEVAULT-GRAVES
## DIGITAL EDITIONS
www.devault-gravesagency.com

Devault-Graves Digital Editions is an imprint of
The Devault-Graves Agency, LLC.
Memphis, Tennessee.
The names Devault-Graves Digital Editions, Lasso Books,
and Chalk Line Books are all imprints and
trademarks of The Devault-Graves Agency.
www.devault-gravesagency.com

*"Without obsession,
life is nothing.*
—John Waters

# Table of Contents

Author's Preface .................................................................. 11

**Film**

*My Afternoon with Louise Brooks* ............................................. 17
    Chapter One – Lulu ..................................................... 19
    Chapter Two – Naked on My Goat ............................ 21
    Chapter Three – Kansas .............................................. 27
    Chapter Four – Rochester ........................................... 31
    Chapter Five – Secrets ................................................. 39
    Chapter Six – Finis ...................................................... 43
*Fallen Angel* (aborted biography of Louise Brooks) ........... 47
    Author's Disclaimer .................................................... 49
    Chapter One – Kansas ................................................ 53
*Blonde Shadow: The Brief Career and Mysterious Disappearance of Actress Linda Haynes* .................................... 75

**Literature**

*Meat Eaters, Killers, and Suckers of Blood: Mano a Mano with Harry Crews* ..................................................................... 119

**Music**

*Natural Born Elvis: The Story of Bill Haney, the First Elvis Impersonator* ........................................................................... 161
*The Cajun Hank Williams: D.L. Menard* ............................... 187
*In the Midnight Aisle: The Story of the Blackwood Brothers Quartet* ....................................................................... 203
    Prologue ...................................................................... 205

Chapter One – Ring of Fire ........................................... 207
Chapter Two – Alpha and Omega ............................... 215
Chapter Three – Aftermath .......................................... 223
Chapter Four – Daddy (Sumner) Sang Bass ............. 225
Chapter Five – Gospel Music into Praise Music ........ 231
Afterword ...................................................................... 237

*Sympathy for the Devil: A Kind Word For Albert Goldman* .... 243
*Ten LPs You Probably Don't Have (But Should)* ....................... 251
*When the Sex Pistols Came to Memphis* .................................... 273
*Guilty Pleasures: Tennessee Ernie Ford* ..................................... 283
*Woodstock Revisited* .................................................................... 289
*Interview: Frank Zappa* ................................................................ 297
*Interview: Mick Taylor* .................................................................. 331
*Have Mersey: An Interview with the La's Driving Force and Angriest Member, Lee Mavers* ............................................ 361
*Take Me Seriously! An Interview with Mark Lindsay of Paul Revere & the Raiders* ....................................................... 375

# Author's Preface

I WAS BOTH BLESSED and cursed to have been born and raised in the South. In fact, I've lived the whole of my 60 years in Memphis and it's highly possible that I will run out my string here in the Bluff City. My parents, however, were both from the backwoods of Sulphur Springs, Arkansas just outside the town of Pine Bluff. They both lived in poverty and struggled through, first, the Great Depression, and second, World War II. My father and four of his brothers fought in the war and all of them returned home, more or less, in one piece. Dad thought this was a miracle and it cemented his certainty that a higher power was behind the survival of this notoriously roughhouse gang of Graves.

My mother's side of the family, the Rogers, were the master storytellers. Out in the country, where television reception was a rumor, Saturday night entertainment consisted of sitting around and swapping stories, many of which had been heard several times. I have never understood the rudeness of people who will stop you when telling a story and say, "Yeah, you've told that one before." Knowing the quirks, the punch lines, and the build-ups to these classic family yarns made them screamingly funny. I have never laughed so hard in my life as at the repeat stories of my Granddaddy, Uncle Joe, Uncle Glenn, Uncle Benard (correct spelling), and Aunt Katy.

Not all the stories were funny. I'll never forget how my Granddad's stories of panthers roaming the woods of Arkansas would keep me wide awake at night, listening for the sound of a woman screaming, which is how my Granddad described the yowl of a panther. In the front yard, when the women were away telling their own stories, the men would relate some of their war experiences, careful to watch their language with a boy (me) hanging on every word.

I was fortunate enough to inherit this gift for storytelling, although I'm nowhere as good as my family, all of whom now are slapping their knees in the Great Beyond. When I decided to become a writer, my relatives never could quite get a handle on it. Why not use my gift of gab for something that could earn me a good living? They universally thought I should be a lawyer. They had a point. But I had learned—slowly, very slowly—to transfer that wonderful oral tradition onto paper, where other people might read my stories.

I graduated from Memphis State University with a bachelor's degree in journalism. I not only wanted to tell my stories, I wanted to tell other people's stories too. I was particularly taken with people who courted both fame and obscurity. Those who had tasted fame and celebrity and ran the other way drew me as a moth to flame—and just like that moth I often got my wings singed.

It took me the better part of 30 years to come to grips with Louise Brooks, the legendary silent film beauty who had a second career as a writer and recluse. I had such mixed feelings about my dealings with her that every time I tried to write the story I found myself locked in the same mental Rubik's Cube. Age and distance finally allowed me to tell the story. And here it is in this collection.

This book collects what I think is my best journalism,

and when I look back over the decades I have been working as a writer I am somewhat surprised with the widescreen lens of my muse. This also has been a bit of a problem. There is a lust for categorization in the world of arts and letters, and exactly how can you categorize a book on Louise Brooks, Frank Zappa, Harry Crews, and the Sex Pistols? Well, you can't, but they were all passions of mine at one time or another.

As a journalism undergraduate I saw right away that the work of the New Journalists—Tom Wolfe, Hunter S. Thompson, Truman Capote, Norman Mailer, and even Rex Reed (who was the best celebrity profile writer of them all)—would serve as major inspirations. My first book, a novel, which surprised everyone who thought I only wrote nonfiction, was compared to Thompson. This pleased me to no end. My next book, *Crossroads: The Life and Afterlife of Blues Legend Robert Johnson*, had a prose style intentionally very different from anything I had previously written. Hemingway's iceberg technique of saying less and implying more I felt was totally suited to the mystery of the largely unknowable Robert Johnson, and it worked well, enough to earn me the Keeping the Blues Alive Award in 2010 (formerly known as the Handy Awards) for Literature.

When one of my students occasionally asks me the biggest thing I've ever done (I'm a professor at LeMoyne-Owen College in Memphis) I don't have to think but a split second: my publication of the first J.D. Salinger book in 50 years, *Three Early Stories*. That eclipses anything else I have done or will ever likely do in the future. As a co-owner of what one industry insider has called "the most gonzo indie publisher in the U.S.," The Devault-Graves Agency, my life has taken yet another curious turn.

But in this book I wanted to bring back the jewels of my writing life, which have been floating in the ether of the internet to be stumbled across on occasion by intrepid readers and fellow writers. Yes, I was the last journalist admitted to Louise Brooks's bedside. I talked with Frank Zappa shortly after he appeared before Congress. I was in the audience and sober as a Utah judge when the Sex Pistols played Memphis. I found the first Elvis impersonator completely by accident. Quentin Tarantino provided me the phone number for one of the best and most obscure actresses ever to flee Hollywood, Linda Haynes.

So, if you have this book in your hands, kick back and let me tell you a few of my stories.

# My Afternoon with Louise Brooks

# Chapter One – Lulu

[A scene from the 1928 silent film classic, *Pandora's Box*]

Dr. Ludwig Schoen, a German newspaper magnate, takes a key from his immaculately tailored trousers and opens the door to the love nest that has become the scandal of Berlin. Inside, waiting for him, is his lover, Lulu. She is wearing a clinging white chiffon dress and her hair, black as an arctic night, is worn in the latest fashion, a dutch bob cropped close to the face revealing the full curvature of her long, splendid neck.

Schoen does not embrace her. Instead he paces toward the fireplace mantel and sits dejectedly on the arm of a chair. After removing a cigarette from a silver case and lighting it, he finally looks Lulu in the eye and says, "I'm going to be married."

She does not register the hurt he expects. Instead she laughs gaily and asks, "And because you're going to be married you won't kiss me?"

"The whole city is talking about us," he answers. "It is ruining my career."

She walks to her day bed and lies upon it, her arms outstretched to him. He sits next to her, still consumed by his sullen mood. Lulu tilts her head back in a repose of seduction, her white neck an open invitation.

"Don't you realize it's got to be finished between us?" he pleads.

Lulu entwines her arms around Schoen's neck and pulls herself to him.

"You'll have to kill me if you want to get away from me," she whispers as she presses her lips to his.

# Chapter Two – Naked on My Goat

THE MOMENT I FIRST clapped eyes on Louise Brooks in her portrayal of Lulu, I too would have sold my soul for a moment of such intimacy with her. It was 1980, five years before her death, and I sat by myself at the first ever Memphis screening of the silent classic *Pandora's Box*, the film that cemented Louise Brooks's cult status as the most beautiful and ruinous femme fatale ever to leave scorch marks on a silver screen. When I watched her, the glistening raven hair, luminous, deceitful eyes, and thin ever-so-parted lips that smirked over every life she wrecked, I was reminded of those Saturday mornings of childhood visions watching cartoons on television and the evil, seductive black widow spider who lured the good little cartoon flies into her web of death. A sleek and shimmering dominatrix in black leather, she made my breath short and pulse quicken on those chilly mornings in my pajamas and slippers.

Two decades later, as I leaned forward in my auditorium seat transfixed by Louise Brooks as Lulu in *Pandora's Box*, I saw once again that black widow, a breathtaking, mesmerizing chanteuse who spread her poison without remorse and utterly destroyed every man she pleasured. Louise Brooks's portrayal of Lulu wasn't merely a performance, it was a possession. After seeing the film in Paris decades ago, Henri Langlois, founding director of the Cinemateque Francaise, declared to the world, "There is no Garbo! There is no Dietrich! There is only Louise Brooks!" Louise Brooks as Lulu was an exquisite, haunting apparition, a vision in black and white as ethereal and disturbing as a deeply erotic dream.

In that final moment, when the last frame of film had slipped past the lens and the projector was silenced, I knew … I had to meet her.

The events that led up to my spending an afternoon with the most reclusive, perplexing star in the history of cinema actually began a year earlier than my epiphany watching *Pandora's Box*, on one of those routine weeknights when television beckons. Kenneth Tynan, the esteemed British drama critic and playwright, was the guest on *The Dick Cavett Show*. Tynan was discussing his *New Yorker* profile of a silent film actress, Louise Brooks, singling out for lavish praise Brooks's appearance in the German silent film *Pandora's Box*. It was a title that echoed in the memory. I also vaguely recalled something about a Louise Brooks cult in Europe.

It was not long after that night that I saw Lulu for myself at the Memphis screening of *Pandora's Box*. From Tynan's *New Yorker* profile, I was aware that Brooks was living in an efficiency apartment in Rochester, New York, where she was in declining health, confined to her bed with arthritic hips. Although she had for years been an almost total recluse, turning away all strangers and answering no fan mail, she had met with Tynan and they had developed an intimate, perhaps even sexual, relationship. She had admitted few others to her bedside.

It was more than beauty that made Louise Brooks so appealing. In one of film history's more curious twists, Brooks, who had been stereotyped by Hollywood as a scheming jazz baby, had become a writer and wit of some renown in her later years, penning brilliant, idiosyncratic essays on film for respected journals such as England's *Sight and Sound* and France's *Positif*.

In 1982, I was an advertising writer for a large medical firm in Memphis, working after hours as a freelancer. I was 28, happily married, a mortgage holder, and the proud father of a six-month-old daughter. Yet, somehow it all just didn't seem to add up to enough. The walls of my office cubicle—a depressing shade of corporate orange—grew more suffocating by the day. A satisfying paycheck in no way equaled a satisfying life, and I was determined to restore some semblance of meaning from a regimented, barnacled career. Louise Brooks was a way out.

I had decided that Louise Brooks was worthy of a full-length biography and I wanted to be the one to write it. The notion loomed larger at the approach of every ad deadline and the demand of every blank page. When the company WATS line was open and available I used it, ferreting out obscure magazine articles in far-flung libraries, chatting with a few of the sage New York film critics who had written admiring pieces on Miss Brooks, and finally seeking out those hallowed places where one could actually see an archival print of Louise Brooks films other than *Pandora's Box*. (Keep in mind that the videotape revolution was barely underway in 1982 and obscure films were virtually impossible to screen unless you were in the business.)

My inquiries to those in charge of the George Eastman House film archives in Rochester, New York, who reportedly had convinced Brooks to move to Rochester to be near the world's largest collection of her films, were met with yawns and polite refusals. No, they could not help me get in touch with Louise Brooks, and yes, they would be happy to screen all the Louise Brooks films for me—at a fee that roughly equaled a year's salary.

I next turned to James Card, the retired film curator of the Eastman House, the man credited with discovering Louise Brooks's whereabouts in New York City in the 1950s, where she had lived for well over a decade in isolation and near-destitution, surviving by means that are even today the grist of gossip and speculation. Brooks would speak of those years only in the most circumspect fashion, expertly dodging the issue of exactly how she was able to afford a Manhattan apartment.

Card, an imperious and imposing man—at least that's the image he conveyed in telephone conversation—was initially polite but aloof.

"Yes, Miss Brooks and I are very close friends, but I'm afraid I can't help you at all in regards to a biography," Card said in his thunderhead of a voice. "She doesn't approve at all, you know."

"You mean she knows about me and my efforts to begin this biography?"

"But of course. She wishes for you to stop at once. Did you know," he added conspiratorially, "that I have in my possession the only copy of her autobiography?"

"Do you mean those articles she published that are going into this new book, *Lulu in Hollywood*?"

"Oh no. I mean her autobiography, *Naked on My Goat*. The one she supposedly threw into an incinerator. I am in possession of the only copy and it's under lock and key," he said, conjuring for me a mental image of Vincent Price with a mad gleam in his eye.

"And," he added, "we plan on publishing it."

I soon discovered that *Naked on My Goat* was a book as elusive as J.D. Salinger's rumored unpublished novels. I began to suspect that Card might have personal reasons for keeping me away from his prairie blossom.

## Chapter Three – Kansas

I WAS NOT TO be deterred. It seemed logical to me when laying out the plans for the biography to begin at Louise's beginning in Kansas. I began to solicit and collect information on Louise Brooks's family background in Cherryvale and Independence, Kansas. A great deal of impressive research already had been completed by Charles Cagle at Pittsburg State University in Pittsburg, Kansas and two ambitious high school students from Topeka who had made Louise Brooks the subject of their senior project.

I traveled by automobile from Memphis to the flatlands of Kansas to meet and interview all the townspeople who recalled anything about the former silent screen beauty and her family. The portrait of the Brookses that began to emerge from the long conversations with these unpretentious, no-bull folk often was at odds with the glowing tributes from the cult of admirers.

Brooks's maternal grandfather, a country doctor named Doc Tom Rude, had a hatchet buried in his face during a drunken brawl. His father, Havilas Rude, also a country doctor, was deeply addicted to morphine. Madness and eccentricity twined like malignant vines through the family tree. Tales of strange, erratic behavior by Louise began to surface also. As a child she had severe fits of temper that went far beyond the machinations of a spoiled child. She took up dance at an early age, but was considered unmanageable by most instructors.

In a side trip to Wichita, I interviewed a dance partner of Louise's, Hal McCoy, who had worked with her after her film career came to its bitter end in the mid-1930s. She had returned to her home state of Kansas for a brief, miserable period in which she attempted to start a school of dance. She had formed a partnership with McCoy and they performed as a dance duo at numerous local society gatherings.

"I wasn't a trained dancer like Louise," said the genial McCoy at his home. "I was just a better than average hoofer who was introduced to Louise through her sister, June. Louise was very precise in choreographing our dance steps. She had been one of the Denishawn Dancers at one time, which was a dance troupe famous throughout the country. Later she was a chorus girl for the Ziegfeld Follies. I was nowhere near her equal, and I would occasionally miss a step and try to cover it with something ad-libbed. This would send her into an absolute frenzy; she would explode if the least little thing went wrong.

"The last time I saw Louise Brooks was after a performance of ours. I had flubbed a few steps again and in the cab ride afterwards she literally screamed at me the whole time. I made up my mind on the spot that I would never work with this woman again. She was acting positively insane with rage. Then she totally threw me off-balance when we pulled up to her door. She said, 'I know what it is you've been wanting all this time. Come on in and I'll give it to you.' Then and there I knew she was crazy. I was engaged to my future wife and wanted no part of Louise Brooks."

I also contacted Louise's relatives. Most of them refused to talk to me. One who didn't was Louise's nephew, Robert Brooks. Louise had doted on him when he was a child, reading to him and preparing him, in his words, "big, awful meals." When talking about his aunt, Robert was frequently overcome with emotion. He finally said to me, "You know you should talk to her yourself."

"I'm afraid I don't have her phone number," I replied honestly.

"Well, let me give it to you," Robert replied to my astonishment.

I held my breath and dialed. After two rings a woman's voice answered "Hel-*lo*" in a voice as musical as a violin's.

"May I speak to Miss Brooks?" I asked.

"Who's calling?" she demanded emphatically.

I explained who I was and why I was calling. She was wary and obviously caught off-guard. She suggested that I write down any questions I had and send them to her. I knew, of course, that she never responded to any such written requests.

I decided to tell her about my travels to Cherryvale, Kansas and the childhood friends of hers I had met and spoken to. As hoped, this changed the tenor of the conversation. She began to ask me questions.

She recalled one of the girls she had gone to school with, a Morna Wagstaff, and laughed like a delighted child when I told her I had only recently spoken with the lady.

As we continued to talk, her voice began to weaken. She told me she had emphysema and said that she would be recording an acceptance speech in her apartment the next day for the prestigious George Eastman Award from the Eastman House Museum. She said she was afraid to talk anymore for fear she would ruin her voice and wouldn't be able to make the recording.

I later learned that she could make her voice hoarse at will. It was a ruse she used frequently to get off the phone. The acceptance speech she recorded the next day for the George Eastman Award, which was played for the audience at the awards ceremony, was clear as crystal.

The awards presentation was only weeks away. Myrna Loy, Maureen O'Sullivan, Luise Rainer, Sylvia Sidney, and Louise Brooks were all to be honored at the black tie ceremony, which was to be followed by a gala reception. I couldn't help but wonder if the sound of all that applause wouldn't seduce Louise out of her tiny apartment. Even if she refused to attend due to her health, I felt sure she would be receiving, at the very least, a few visitors. The timing seemed right for my visit.

# Chapter Four – Rochester

ROCHESTER, NEW YORK WAS stark, gray, and whipped by bitter cold that November day. The taxi cab windows were tinged with frost. I asked the cab driver to stop at a liquor store and went inside to buy a gift bottle of wine. When I told the clerk on duty the wine was to be a gift he slapped on a tiny red bow.

Set and on the way, we drove by several bruised automobiles parked on the street that seemed to have the same dead pallor as the row upon row of apartment buildings we passed. The city was disturbingly quiet. The cab stopped at a grim, slate-colored apartment building barely distinguishable from the others. I could see no movement behind the rows of small, begrimed windows that stared out like so many clouded eyes.

After paying my fare, I stood for a moment taking stock of myself. I could see the faint reflection of myself in the apartment building's outer glass door. I thought I looked like one of the explorers in Peary's expedition to the North Pole. At six feet four inches and 250 pounds, covered thigh to jowl in a screaming blue down coat, I wondered if I might look a little, well, intimidating to a 75-year-old recluse.

Nah, I thought to myself, Louise Brooks has handled a lot worse than me.

I entered the cramped vestibule and found the address tag that said L. BROOKS. With a ball of snakes twisting in my stomach I found the buzzer and pressed twice.

There was a moment's hesitation, then I heard the unmistakable voice. "Yes? Who's there?"

In one rush the words came spilling out. "Miss Brooks, it's Tom Graves from Memphis. I'm on my way to the George Eastman Awards tonight and I brought you a gift bottle of wine. I also have some photographs of your childhood friends. I thought you might like to take a look."

For the longest few seconds of my life I heard only dry, dead, cold air.

"Well, come on up then," she finally answered in a surprisingly loud and clear voice.

She activated the buzzer to the security door and I went through it to the elevator. I heard her shout into the intercom again, "I said come on up! Did you hear me? COME ON UP!"

When I stepped off the balky elevator at the third floor, I noticed a door directly across the hall cracked open about six inches with two hard, round eyes staring needles through me.

"Miss Brooks?" I said.

"Tom?" she said.

She smiled the thinnest of Mona Lisa smiles. "Well, don't just stand there."

The door slowly opened and a reed, a mere quill of an old woman, a woman who looked well into her 90s but in fact was 20 years younger, ushered me in. Her skin wasn't merely white, it was translucent, and a roadmap of tiny blue veins sketched her face like fine marble. She could not have weighed over 80 pounds.

The room we entered, a combination kitchen and living room, was as simple and orderly as an army foot locker. There wasn't an errant dish, spoon, or sponge in sight. She had me take off my coat and lay it across one of the matching chairs of her aluminum dinette. I noticed a couple of bookshelves filled mostly with film books (no Proust) such as Ephraim Katz's *Film Encyclopedia*, David Thomson's *A Biographical Dictionary of Film*, and a European edition of *Hollywood Babylon*. Paperclips marked each book, at the precise spots where I estimated there were references to Louise Brooks. On the wall was a gaily-colored painting of a tropical bird which reminded me of the crushed velvet paintings found in Mexican border towns. The painting was signed Luisa. I asked, "By any chance did you paint this?"

"Uh-huh, I used to paint, but I don't anymore now that I'm old. I'll have to show you the painting I did of St. Therese. It's in the bedroom."

"Oh, before I forget, I brought a gift for you." I held out the bottle of wine.

"I don't drink!" Louise's eyebrows clamped together and her pupils narrowed to two pencil leads.

"Well, what kind of wine is it?" she asked irritably. I looked at the gift bottle I held in my hands and stammered, "It's a red wine, actually."

"No!" she snapped. "What *kind* of wine is it?"

"Oh, a Bordeaux," I answered flushing, and read a few

lines from the label.

Louise's scowl softened. "A Bordeaux ... hmmm." The words floated, carrying her to some other time, some other place.

I wasn't by any means the first young man to bring the former screen siren a bottle of wine. What I couldn't know at the time, in 1982, was that I would be the last.

"I can't drink anymore," she said abruptly. "My doctors won't let me touch a drop. Take the bottle back home with you and enjoy it yourself. I can't smoke anymore either, you know. *Emphysema*. I'm dying from it. Sylvia Sidney was in here the other day with that agent, John Springer, and they both smoked like chimneys. I thought I was going to choke to death. I almost had to throw the two of them out.

"Well, I can't stand here all day. My hip's killing me. We can talk in the bedroom."

She slowly felt her way toward the bedroom with the help of a heavy four-pronged orthopedic cane. Stopping at a closet, she motioned me to help her remove her bed jacket. As I placed the bed jacket on a hanger in her closet, I could not help but notice her nakedness beneath the thin veneer of a nightgown she kept on. Here was the naked flesh for which, half a century before, men had fought, swooned, and paid dearly. Where I come from, a man, if he has any manners, doesn't stare, and so I averted my eyes. What I had seen out of the corner of my eye was enough.

Once she had settled into bed, it became even more apparent she was highly suspicious of my visit. Her fixed stare further unnerved me. No one ever stared down an unwelcome man harder than Louise Brooks.

To break the ice I asked her about the awards ceremony that night and if she had reconsidered attending.

"Hell no!" she fired back, her long, gray ponytail doing a crazy jig around her pipe cleaner of a neck. She pulled a tattered electric blanket tighter around her waist. "I hated all that Hollywood bullshit. I see no reason to get mixed up with that mob again. That's why I left Hollywood, you know. It was all so stupid and phony, and most of what they were turning out was such crap. I still can't stand to see myself in those Hollywood movies. When I went to Europe and worked under G.W. Pabst, it was so different. He was an artist. I never knew anyone in Hollywood who ever read a book. The whole town was stupid."

I asked her if, by chance, she knew the actor Brian Aherne, who was to be master of ceremonies at the awards presentation.

"I know *of* him," she said. "Remind me what he has done."

I ran down a list of films that I remembered. "I hope to meet him tonight," I said. "I just bought a book he wrote about his friend, the actor George Sanders, and it's actually quite well-written."

"Isn't George Sanders dead?" she asked.

"Yes, he killed himself a few years back."

"How?" she asked.

"Pills, I believe."

"What kind?"

I took Aherne's book from my briefcase and found the passage. Louise sat poised with a pen and writing pad.

"Five bottles of Nembutal," I read.

"Spell that."

"N-e-m-b-u-t-a-l."

She wrote it down in a jagged scrawl.

"How many bottles?"

"Five," I answered as the hairs on my neck began to stand.

"What kind of drug is Nembutal anyway?"

"A barbiturate, I'm pretty sure. A heavy downer."

"I wonder if it's a painless way to kill yourself. For your information, Tom, I plan to kill myself and I'm trying to figure out the best way to do it.

"I'm sick of living like this. My hip's killing me all the time and I'm dying of emphysema. I refuse to let them put me on oxygen to prolong the agony. I'm in pain all the time now and can't do a damn thing anymore. See this pad? I have to write down everything or I'll forget it. I can't remember anything anybody tells me. As long as I have this," she pointed to the pad, "I can get along. But what if I get worse? I've begged some of my friends to bring me a gun, but dammit, I guess they love me too much. They won't do it."

I excused myself to go to the bathroom and as soon as I closed the bathroom door I heard Louise pick up the phone and peck frantically at the dial pad.

"Tom Graves is here. What am I supposed to do?"

(Pause)

"Well, yes, he seems nice enough I suppose. He's not trying to interview me or anything and he has been polite. He brought me a bottle of Bordeaux."

(Pause)

"No, you're right. I can't very well just throw him out on the street. Wait, I hear him coming …"

She hung up the phone and smiled coyly as I entered the room.

Hoping to get the visit on a better tack, I offered to show her the photos I had brought. As I passed them to her, she studied each one minutely, frowning at some, laughing at others.

At one point she paused long enough to ask, "Tom, just what is it you plan to do with all these photographs and this research on me?"

"I had hoped to write a biography," I explained.

"Of *me*?"

"Yes ma'am."

"Well, I'm flattered, but I've already authorized Jack Garner, the film critic here in Rochester, to do it."

I had spoken with Garner several times and knew for fact that the project was as good as dead. He believed Louise would be impossible to work with.

"I've completed a sample chapter," I added. "Just out of curiosity, would you like me to read you a few pages of it?"

"I don't suppose it could hurt."

I took the manuscript from my briefcase and read the opening scene that led to her grandfather's barroom brawl and a hatchet buried into his face. When I finished I was met with a long, strained silence. Louise's eyes fixed upon mine and did not look away.

"That was good. That was *damn* good," she said.

She picked up the phone and began dialing.

"I'm calling Jack Garner," she whispered to me. "Jack, Tom Graves is here and I want to authorize him to write my biography. I don't want you to do it. Okay? All right then, it's settled," she said and hung up.

"I like your writing style," she added.

# Chapter Five – Secrets

AN AUTHORIZED LOUISE BROOKS biography! My mind raced toward book signings, talk shows, articles, interviews, foreign language editions. It took exactly two weeks for the pin to touch the bubble and for Louise to de-authorize me as her biographer. I refused to drop the project and let her know, and her housedogs too, that I intended to go forward with or without her authorization. Her literary agent wrote a caustic letter forbidding me from contacting anyone in Rochester. I wrote him back explicitly telling him that if I received so much as one more nasty word from him I would call everyone in the Rochester phone book. I never heard from him again.

James Card, the retired film curator for the Eastman House and, I soon discovered, one of Louise's many secret lovers, rattled long sabers. "Let me assure you," he blustered, "that there are very powerful people who will not allow you to write this book."

"Oh yeah, who?" I asked as a loud click rattled in my ear.

His threats, however, had an unforeseen consequence. None of the New York gaggle with whom I had to deal understood the Southern character. They didn't realize that turning up the heat and raising their voices would only make me dig in deeper and scratch all the harder. Card's arrogance and condescension in particular galled me. I wondered who was old enough to have been a friend or lover of Louise Brooks's still powerful and proprietary enough to do me harm? I drew up a very short list and immediately crossed out Card's name. Bob Hope was one of the first names I came up with, but I had trouble placing them together in any kind of time frame. They also just seemed too opposite in personality. The name at the top of my list was William S. Paley, long-time head of CBS. I knew Brooks had worked at CBS radio for a time and sensed there might be a connection. By sheer happenstance, I saw an article on Paley in that month's *Esquire* magazine which included a mention of the Paleys having a private screening of *Pandora's Box*.

It all began to click.

I called one of Louise's closest confidants and the only person in her inner circle with whom I had a rapport. "What's the story about Louise and William Paley?" I asked, casting the bait.

"Oh my God! How did you find out?" he answered in a near faint.

So it was that I uncovered Louise Brooks's Big Secret. She and Paley had briefly been lovers in the 1930s and Louise lived on a confidential 400-dollar-a-month writing stipend she managed to arm-twist out of the Paley Foundation. Paley got his bragging rights of having bedded one of cinema's most ravishing beauties and she got the hard cash. Her single worst fear, according to my source, was that word of the grant would leak to the press and embarrass Paley, who might or might not cut off the money pipeline.

Although she had received a $30,000 advance for her book *Lulu in Hollywood* and undoubtedly received some form of Social Security or government assistance, the extra 400 dollars a month was a sum she regarded as life or death. I became the centerpiece of Louise's paranoia. My source in Rochester told me she had become so worried about what I would write about her that she could neither eat nor sleep. She made call after call to her Rochester friends begging them to do something about me. My source said that she was not only making all her friends' lives miserable, but the situation was getting critical enough that they feared for her health. After receiving all manner of threats from Rochester short of broken legs, someone finally wised up and approached me gentleman-to-gentleman, the way we do things down here in Memphis. I was politely asked if I would please consider dropping the project, at least in Louise Brooks's lifetime, for the sake of her well-being.

I took stock. Without her authorization, I doubted I could find a publisher for a biography. I also knew that I would get little to no cooperation from her friends and family. My prayer had been answered—I had met Louise Brooks. As the saying goes though, tears fall harder over answered prayers than the unanswered ones. I learned early enough in my career that movie stars and cult factotums are depressingly human, just like the rest of us. I was tired of the hostility, the accusations, the petty snubs, and finally just tired of Louise Brooks herself. I also didn't want to be blamed if something bad happened to Louise. I didn't want her leaving some suicide note with my name underlined in it. I didn't want my name to be a dirty word to some future biographer.

So I told them I would drop the project.

A few days later I received a handwritten thank-you note from Louise, a final gesture.

## Chapter Six – Finis

LOUISE BROOKS DIED IN 1985, not of emphysema, arthritis, or Tom Graves, but of a heart attack as she made her way to the bathroom. No one from Rochester called to tell me. I read it in my local newspaper.

By the time of her death, my memories had turned acidic. It would be years before I could look back on my visit to Rochester without bitterness or regret. All earlier attempts to write about her bogged down in disgust and conflicting emotions. With the comforts and distance of age, however, I can at last remember and laugh. A little.

Back in that apartment that cold day in November the room was warm and the laughter easier as the afternoon lengthened.

"Now, where did you say you were from? The South you say?"

"Yes ma'am. I'm from Memphis, Tennessee. I'm sure you can hear it in my accent."

"Heavens yes!" she said and rolled her silver screen eyes. "It's preposterous!" She chuckled and set her mouth in the half-smirk I recognized from the film I had watched in the darkness of that theater auditorium in Memphis. It was at that moment that I could finally see the younger Louise, the raven-haired flapper who had broken a million hearts.

"I had a terrible Midwestern accent, you know. When I first came to New York everyone made such fun of my Kansas accent that I paid someone to help me speak properly. It was the wisest money I probably ever spent."

The sunlight had softened and there was a knock at the door.

"Oh, I forgot. It's Jack Garner with that actress, Luise Rainer. He's bringing her over to meet me. Could you go to the door for me?"

I went to the door and finally met Garner, the film critic, who only hours earlier had lost his job as Louise Brooks's biographer. As we shook hands he shot me a hard, sidelong look and then introduced me to the former screen beauty and double Oscar winner, Luise Rainer. Miss Rainer, a tiny sparrow of a woman, was swallowed-up in an enormous fur coat. Her lipstick, flaming orange, detoured far outside the natural boundaries of her lips. She could have passed for any number of old ladies at an opera soiree.

I thought it best that I take my leave and began to gather my belongings as Garner and Miss Rainer settled themselves into Louise's cramped bedroom. Louise called out to me, "Tom, you'll call me tomorrow won't you? Don't forget."

"I won't."

I walked out of Louise Brooks's apartment building, found a phone booth a couple of blocks away, and called a cab. An hour later the cab arrived. As I climbed into the back seat, I glanced over my shoulder in the vain hope of catching a parting glimpse of a former celebrated beauty. I was the last writer ever admitted, even for one brief afternoon, into her world.

# LULU IN HOLLYWOOD

*To Tom Graves
with love
Louise Brooks
5 Nov 1982*

# Fallen Angel
(an aborted biography of Louise Brooks)

# Author's Disclaimer

PRIOR TO THE AFTERNOON I spent with Louise Brooks on November 5, 1982, I had begun the first chapters of what I had hoped would become the definitive biography of this elusive, compelling figure. My plan, at the time, was to research her childhood and write a chapter or two for both potential publishers and to have something to show Louise that might seduce her out of her seclusion to authorize the book. I had traveled to Kansas and retraced the paths of Brooks's early life, interviewing scores of people who had known the Brookses during those years.

Even at the age of 28, I had been writing and publishing my work for nearly a decade, and my day job since obtaining a journalism degree was as an advertising and public relations writer. None of that, however, had fully prepared me for the arduous task of such a sustained work as a biography of someone who didn't want her past revealed. I had read Kenneth Tynan's brilliant *New Yorker* profile, "The Girl in the Black Helmet," and was left wanting more. I thought, why not me?

The more I researched the life of Louise Brooks, the

more of a problem I had with Tynan's article, elegantly written though it was. The issue? Lies. Particularly the sin of omission.

Tynan is far from being the only master stylist I know of who plays footloose with the facts. (Aside: A music writer of some renown who is in possession of the most musical prose this side of Truman Capote and who has written legendary articles for major publications once sent me an unforgettable review he had written of a book on barbecue. In this review he told the story of a barbecue joint in Memphis so serious about its cuisine that it had 10 levels of hot sauce, the last of which had to be prepared with industrial rubber gloves. He also mentioned that dental floss was placed on every table. Memphis is my hometown and I'm a barbecue fanatic, so I immediately hopped in my car and barreled over to Cozy Corner Bar-B-Q. Not a string of floss was to be found in the place and only two sauces: mild and hot. When I asked about the 10 levels of hot sauce, the owners looked at me as if I had lost my white boy mind.) Tynan left out virtually everything about his own relationship with Louise, which was far more involved than either of them ever let on, her affair with and subsequent monetary support from William Paley, the long-term affair she had with James Card, which was the real reason she moved to Rochester, and her mid-life years of living in Manhattan with no traceable means of support.

Tynan also propagated the company line that Louise Brooks was too brilliant for Hollywood and therefore was misunderstood, misused, and ultimately abandoned. Only the Europeans, who understood a truly great perverse artist—There is no Garbo! There is no Dietrich! There is only Louise

Brooks!—captured her essence. But as I began to research her life I uncovered many disturbing instances of what I can only call mental imbalance. They occurred early on. I heard story after story from people in Rochester as well, stories Kenneth Tynan must have heard too but chose not to report because they would interfere with the Louise Brooks he was attempting, with some success, to resurrect.

I originally developed two chapters on Louise's life in Kansas and later combined them into a single chapter. I cannot vouch for the literary merit of this chapter—it was my first attempt at that Great Beyond that is writing a book. Subsequently, I overcame this obstacle and wrote a nicely-reviewed novel, *Pullers*, and an award-winning biography of bluesman Robert Johnson, *Crossroads*. After Louise Brooks de-authorized my biography in a collect phone call she made to me just weeks after my visit to Rochester, and the ill-treatment from just about everyone in her small circle of protectors, I quit the project in disgust and for nearly 30 years could not bring myself to ferret through the boxes in my attic to revive any writing about her. It was the thrill of possibility of a whole new world of writing and readership with eBooks that brought this book about.

*My Afternoon with Louise Brooks* set out to do something virtually no one else could: describe in intimate detail precisely what it was like to visit Louise Brooks in her apartment before she died. This long-form journalism article in no way had the same objectives as Tynan's "The Girl in the Black Helmet." If you are determined to compare the two, however, I will say just one thing: my article is 100 percent true.

If you desire a full-length and comprehensive biography of Louise Brooks, you can do no better than Barry Paris's expertly written and documented book, which I wholeheartedly endorse. Paris did not meet Louise Brooks and that is the only thing I bring to the table that he does not. This chapter from my aborted bio was added to this book at the request of early readers who asked for it. Like *My Afternoon with Louise Brooks*, the one thing I can with a clear conscience vouch for in this chapter of *Fallen Angel* is that it is the truth.

## Chapter One – Kansas

THE LARGE, BROWN BARREL was addressed to John Doe in care of Burden, Kansas. No return address was marked or stamped on the wood. The Wells Fargo clerk who had kept watch for the barrel got word to the German butcher at the meat market that his "package" had arrived at the train depot. The butcher then told his friends, who in turn told their friends, and before long half the town knew that the new keg of beer had arrived.

Those who were in on it were invited to the butcher's party that night. Those who were not kept their mouths shut and accepted the drunken parties as a small price to pay for the state of Kansas's prohibition of liquor 10 years earlier in 1880.

Doc Tom Rude, as always, was smack in the middle of the sawdust and broken glass late that night. Had he not been such a good and kindhearted country doctor, who performed minor miracles almost daily for everyone in Cowley County, the temperance ladies might have run him out of town. He blistered many an ear with his swearing and frequently drank himself into crying jags, but he set the bones and sewed the flesh as no one else in those parts could. All too often, he performed his duties without pay, so his faults were overlooked and the good people of Burden, Kansas turned their backs on the quirks and foibles of Doc Tom Rude.

The men had drained off the last of the keg but were far from calling it a night. One of the group suggested they all go to Ben Franklin's Restaurant for a late-night bite to eat. The others shouted agreement.

At three in the morning, Ben Franklin was awakened by the sound of a mob of drunken revelers hammering at his door. As Ben unlatched the door, several of the party forced themselves in and demanded food and drink.

Doc Tom had laughed himself hoarse. Franklin tried to reason with the men, pointing to the late hour and reminding them all that the kitchen had been long closed. His refusals turned things ugly. Several of the mob warned Ben to feed them or else. When one man threatened to kill him, Franklin picked up a sharp, sturdy hatchet and threw it at him. The intended target ducked and the hatchet found its way deep into the cheekbone of a very surprised Doc Tom Rude.

Nearly faint from pain and shock, his friends carried him miles away to Winfield where another doctor sewed up his face and gave him medicine for the pain. In later years, Doc Tom affected a beard, so it was said, to cover the ugly scar that remained from that ugly night.

Doc Tom's eldest daughter by his second marriage, Myra, had been sensitive to her family's reputation since she was a child. It was widely known in that part of Kansas that Doc Tom Rude was an alcoholic who also had a bad habit of gambling away his money. Even worse were the lingering memories of Doc Tom Rude's father, Dr. Havilas B. Rude, who was also a country doctor. Old Doc Havilas suffered from one of the most common of occupational hazards for a doctor in the mid-1800s—morphine addiction.

It was a common sight for the old doctor to stagger into the back of the town drugstore and slump over in a chair. The local pharmacist, J.M. Henderson, without a word would uncork a quarter-ounce bottle of morphine and pour half of it into the doctor's open palm. Doc Havilas would lick up all the morphine solution in his hand and fall back into his chair. Presently, his body and neck would twitch spasmodically and after several minutes he would straighten up, smooth his clothes, and walk out—a new man.

Myra Rude was desperate to overcome the shame and stigma of her father's and grandfather's excesses. She was the eldest of six children—four others had died—and was called upon under the circumstances to perpetually care for her younger brothers and sisters. Myra hated domestic servitude and vowed to someday be rid of it. In rebellion she drove herself passionately in her piano playing, working tirelessly on a Mozart or Haydn piece until she felt she had perfected it.

For a young woman born in the Kansas of 1884, Myra Rude was unusually devoted to matters of the intellect and society indulgences in the arts. Although not known to be particularly religious in nature, Myra attended church regularly to sing and to listen to her mother, Mary, play the organ for the congregation. More than her educated parents, Myra was absorbed in books, which formed an escape for her from the mediocrity of life in small town America. Her ambitions lay far beyond the rolling farmlands of Kansas and the town of Burden, which for her was aptly named.

Theater, opera, poetry, ballet, evenings spent with the ladies discussing the latest books: these were what Myra most wanted to be a part of. Shortly after her 19th birthday, Myra began receiving calls from a gentleman 20 years her senior. The man, Leonard Porter Brooks, was a young attorney she had known from childhood who had only recently moved from Burden to Cherryvale, a small but growing community some 80 miles away that had a reputation as being more upscale than the surrounding towns. Leonard was a small, bespectacled, retiring, serious man who aspired to nothing more than a respectable career in law.

As a child Leonard had traveled by covered wagon from Grainger County, Tennessee, over a thousand treacherous miles to the wilderness of Burden, Kansas. The Brookses were typical prairie homesteaders, eeking out a hard, unprofitable living from the soil. Those pioneers died by the hundreds from disease, hunger, pestilence, and Indians, and those who survived latched onto their homesteaded acres and worked ceaselessly for subsistence yields from their meager crops.

Leonard was one of seven sons born to Martin Luther Brooks, a hard-toiling dirt farmer who tolerated little foolishness from his boys. Martin Luther, a Civil War veteran, had joined the Union Army and fought in the battles of Shiloh and Missionary Ridge. He moved from Tennessee after the war to raise corn in Kansas, a crop not always suited to the pasturelands topography of that part of the state. Leonard grew up loathing farmwork and the sometimes frantic, nose-to-the-grindstone nature of his father. Like Myra, he too had retreated into the world of letters, refusing to root himself into the demanding and demeaning rigors of farm life.

Many of the townsfolk regarded Leonard as a queer sort because he had no interest in baseball, the favorite pastime of the locals, or any other form of athletics. Instead, he chose to sharpen his mind by burying it in books. Law books, history books, the great books of literature, even algebra books. Didn't matter, as long as they were books. Although Leonard was not without a sense of humor and a dry wit, his serious, earnest nature did not endear him to a lot of people in his hometown. Or to women for that matter. A higher education seemed to Leonard the only way out of what for him had become a prison.

L.P., as he was known, was eager to get into the law profession and entered the University of Kansas law school in Wichita when he was in his early 20s. Upon graduation in 1897, he set up practice back in Burden. Business was so poor, however, that L.P. astutely transplanted his practice to the more thriving burg of Cherryvale.

With his more stable income, he began to travel more and decided to pay visits to the young Myra Rude, who had flowered into one of the prettiest and most refined ladies in Cowley County. L.P. must have seemed a godsend to Myra. She had not been receiving the company of men for very long, having only turned 19 and still having to care for her siblings. Compared to most of the yokels and plowboys who had come a-courtin', Leonard Porter Brooks must have seemed the epitome of refinement. He didn't smoke, use coarse language, drink, or, heaven forbid, play baseball. Instead, he read philosophy and took a fancy to the arts. He could engagingly converse on almost any subject a dilettante like Myra could suggest, and he even liked serious "long-hair" music—the classics.

L.P. had taken up, yet failed to master, the violin. How perfect! He was nearly twice her age and was already a pillar of Cherryvale, a town that seemed to Myra like a metropolis. L.P. also commingled with the upper-crust of Cherryvale society, as finite as that group was. But best of all, Leonard was a Rock of Gibraltar with money and finances. He saved and invested money. He never gambled and was not about to risk his finances on any shaky scheme or investment. He was the cultured father figure Myra had always desired but never had in her kind but crude and alcoholic father.

When L.P. asked for her hand in marriage, Myra almost certainly saw an inroads into polite society. She accepted his proposal with two conditions: that no matter what she would never be bothered with the care of children again, and that Leonard try to provide her with the creature comforts she never had. Like Culture with a capital C.

The two were married at the Rude home at an early eight o'clock morning service in May of 1904. A few relatives were in attendance. The local newspaper stoically summed up the event by saying it was "a pretty wedding." In retrospect, it seems remarkable that Myra did not insist on a lavish church wedding attended by all in the community. It is likely that many of Myra's friends felt she and L.P., a much older man, made too odd a couple. However, a small, intimate wedding seems at odds with Myra's ofttimes flamboyant tastes and undisguised social climbing.

That very morning they were off by East-bound passenger train 80 miles away to Cherryvale, a teeming city of 7,000. Cherryvale in the early 1900s was, in fact, a boomtown. The population had doubled in its last 10 years and new homes were sprouting everywhere. The Edgar Zinc Company, one of the largest and foulest zinc smelters in the U.S., was the town's major employer. Many of the new homes were for the scores of workers hired by the company. The deposits of oil and gas found in the area also added to the town's prosperity, as did two brickyards.

L.P. brought Myra to his home and office, a small white frame house at 531 East Seventh Street. Within weeks Myra had joined a ladies club and L.P. had moved what little there was of his office to a new location on West Main Street. Myra also announced that she was pregnant.

L.P., at 37 years of age, was getting no younger and was eager to start a proper family. Myra, who was 20, also wanted a proper family simply because she felt that was the proper thing for a proper lady to do. In only her first months in Cherryvale, her star in local social circles was clearly on the rise. She was often seen in the company of Tot Strickler, the fun-loving wife of the local oil baron, Tom Strickler. In later years, the two ladies often startled local farmers and their animals by driving Cherryvale's first automobile, an electric car steered by a handle and owned by the Stricklers, out of the town and onto the backroads. A vase with fresh-cut flowers was affixed to the running board.

It is very likely that Myra wanted her firstborn to be a daughter. Nature had other plans, and in 1905, barely a year after marriage, Myra gave birth to a handsome black-haired boy they named Martin, after L.P.'s father.

L.P.'s practice was fairing much better in Cherryvale, an industrial town, than it had in the farming community of Burden. He often did work for the city government and had a small but steady group of clients. In the short time he had been in practice, L.P. Brooks had become a highly-regarded man in almost all circles. He was honest to a fault and immersed himself in the practice of law with the same ardor that Myra expended on her piano practice. His intellectual bearing and noble demeanor helped make him one of the most trusted men in the community. Unlike many attorneys of the day, L.P. did not care for politics or running for political office.

A year after the birth of Martin, Myra bore another child on November 14, 1906–this time a daughter as she had hoped. The baby was small with a full head of her mother's jet-black hair and her soft, rounded features. She was named Mary Louise.

*The Cherryvale News* announced the birth in a page one squib:

*A Girl*

*Attorney L.P. Brooks is stepping around today like a blind horse in a clover patch all on account of a young lady who came to his home this morning where she will reside in the future. All concerned are doing nicely.*

Myra was overjoyed at the prospect of raising a daughter as she herself had wanted to be raised—with books and ideas, opera and dance, song and verse, society and teas. She was to teach her daughter etiquette and refined ways. Her Louise would be well-mannered, well-educated, and well-liked.

In a studio portrait of Myra taken when Louise was a child, one can see the studied grace of an ambitious woman struggling to overcome the background of being the daughter of a poor and drunken country doctor. Myra's Mona Lisa smile and considered pose, her wrist and hand gracefully curled upward in her lap, belie a woman desperate to alter her life—to the point of marrying an older man whose temperament and dreams had little in common with her own.

Everyone who remembers Louise Brooks as a child remarks on how happy and full of life she was. Indeed, she had almost everything a child born near the turn of the century could want—a doting mother who provided her everything she herself did not have when she was growing up, and a father who never lost his temper no matter how much she and her brother fought or misbehaved. Although apparently the Brookses did not hire a nursemaid, Myra kept good her promise that she would not be a slave to her children. She maintained all her social commitments and practiced the piano, without interruption, daily. Myra refused to let the niggling details of keeping house interfere with doing the things she considered important. The children were frequently left with L.P. while Myra played the role of the *grande dame* to be.

Shortly after Louise was born, the Brookses moved into

a larger and more comfortable home on Main Street, right in the middle of the town action. It was a move that placed the Brookses more prominently into the thick of Cherryvale society. Six years later Myra would give birth to another son, Theodore, in this new home to be followed by the birth of June in 1914. The four children would complete the Brooks family.

As Louise grew year by year, her mother began to imbue her with the arts, culture, and fashion, the way to walk, to sit, to speak, to politely respond to an adult's question. When Louise was about five years old, Myra altered her daughter's appearance in a way that nearly 70 years later would cause critic Kenneth Tynan to write of her hairstyle, "(it) rings such a peal of bells in my subconscious." This change became the trademark of Louise Brooks, later celebrated in such divergent media as Jean Luc Godard's film, *Vivre Sa Vie*, and the Dixie Dugan comic strip.

Myra was a faithful subscriber to *Vanity Fair* and *Harper's Bazaar* magazines. She imitated their fashions in the clothes she made for herself and her children and, as did many other upwardly mobile ladies of the day, regarded them as the twin bibles of taste and style. One of the new and more celebrated hairstyles was the dutch-bob, a cut similar to that of Buster Brown of advertising fame. The hair was cropped close to the nape of the neck and worn straight with bangs and spit curls. Often a type of gloss was added to give the hair a "sheen." Although silent film star Colleen Moore took credit for popularizing the dutch-bob hairdo, Louise Brooks wore this same cut nearly all the years of her childhood and in her early career as a dancer.

The dutch-bob seemed a perfect accent to Louise's features, even as a small child. The bangs helped mask and detract from a high and broad forehead and gave balance to her thin, black eyebrows that were spaced far apart. Most importantly, the short style displayed to stunning effect what writer Christopher Isherwood would dub, "that unique and imperious neck of hers."

No other girl in Cherryvale wore her hair in a dutch-bob. So even at the early age of five, Louise Brooks was a striking stand-out, someone apart from the other girls. Myra loved to show off Louise to her circle of friends, who thought she was a darling in Myra's fashionable little clothes and her dutch-bob. Most of the society ladies were impressed with the worldly manners and airs Louise would affect in their presence. They could see that Myra was definitely rubbing off on her little girl.

Several of the society matrons, however, felt Myra went overboard in her ambitions for her daughter. One lady remembers an elaborate birthday party Myra gave for Louise when she turned seven. Nearly all of the better-off children of Cherryvale were invited and enjoyed one of the most painstakingly orchestrated affairs of their youth. Myra served dainty little finger sandwiches, an hors d'oeuvre common at the ladies soirees, but quite unusual for a children's get-together.

The birthday cupcakes contained dime-store jewelry, and the children squealed with delight as they bit into their little treasures. The boys and girls then played party games for additional prizes. Nearly 70 years later the Cherryvale girl who so well remembered this birthday party would remark,

"I definitely think that Mrs. Brooks was too ambitious for Louise."

In spite of Myra's over-attentions and spoiling, Louise got on fairly well with the other children in Cherryvale at this stage of her childhood. She and the other girls in the neighborhood enjoyed roller skating in the evenings on the sidewalks down Main Street. Louise also liked to outfit herself and her girlfriends in her mother's hoopskirts and blouses and preen and play grown-up in front of the mirror. Many times the children would go together to the local theater to see the latest of those flickering images they had begun to call movies. Children were frequently admitted into the Saturday matinees by paying the only price many of the farm children could afford—an apple or a potato. Louise only had to pop into the Avey Grocery two doors down from her house for the necessary fruit or vegetable.

Across the street from the Brooks home were row after row of tombstones on display in the lot adjoining the local monument works. Venus Jones and her baby sister, Vivian, were two playmates Louise romped with among the many grave markers. Louise often walked down Main Street after finishing supper and called the two Jones girls out to play. Venus had to wash and dry dishes before the girls were allowed outside, and Louise many times pitched in to speed up the work. Vivian Jones later became known as Vivian Vance, the comedienne who played Ethel Mertz opposite William Frawley in the much-beloved *I Love Lucy* television series. Vance would remain the local favorite, considered by all the Cherryvale residents as the girl who rose highest in the climb for stardom. Unlike Louise in her later years, Vivian never turned her back on the people back in Kansas. As a result of this love, they never forgot her.

Louise and the other girls in town all walked every day to McKinley School, just blocks from the Brooks home. Louise was never outstanding academically but had clear cut preferences for English and social studies. From first grade on Louise was the envy of the other schoolgirls for her pretty looks, her dutch-bob hairdo, and her grown-up manner.

A middle-aged bachelor in Cherryvale who Louise later referred to as "Mr. Feathers," was a favorite of all the kids. He bought them treats and candies and often took an entire group with him for an afternoon's entertainment at the Liberty or Gem movie houses to watch the newest two-reel comedies or cartoons. "Mr. Feathers" was considered by all an amiable and harmless man who, because he had no children of his own, compensated by befriending all the children in town.

About the time Louise turned nine, "Mr. Feathers" began to take a special shine to the pretty little black-haired girl with the freckles and creamy complexion. He made a special effort to please the fickle Louise, taking her to her favorite movies and plying her with all the soda pop and candy she wanted. "Mr. Feathers" also sexually molested her.

When Louise told her mother that "Mr. Feathers" was doing "funny" things to her, Myra turned on her and accused her daughter of leading the man on. Other than that, the incident was dismissed. Perhaps the whole idea of sexual abuse was too repugnant a reality for a dreamer like Myra. She may have feared being ostracized by her society friends if they found out and deemed it all distasteful.

Louise claimed to have repressed the memory of this man for nearly 40 years until a former neighbor reminded her of "Mr. Feathers." She later confessed to Kenneth Tynan, "I've often wondered what effect Mr. Feathers had on my life. He must have had a great deal to do with forming my attitude toward sexual pleasure. For me, nice, soft, easy men were never enough—there had to be an element of domination—and I'm sure that's all tied up with Mr. Feathers."

A year later, when Louise was 10, she was to experience another pleasure that would permanently alter her life—dance. Myra had long been interested in what was being called "modern dance." The pages of *Vanity Fair* and *Harper's Bazaar* were full of articles and glamorous photographs of the innovative dancers of the day such as Isadora Duncan, Martha Graham, and Ruth St. Denis.

Independence, Kansas, another fast-growing boomtown, located a mere eight miles south of Cherryvale, was considered the center of culture for the entire Southeastern portion of the state. At one time in the 1920s, Independence reportedly boasted more millionaires per square mile than any other locale in the United States. Driving through Independence today one can see the wealth of the oil dollars in the stately homes in well-tended neighborhoods. The architecture is all pre-1930. There is little evidence of wealth after the local banks crashed in the 1930s.

The Brookses did much of their shopping in Independence for everything from clothes in the dress shops to books in the bookstores. Entertainment was plentiful in the town also.

John Philip Sousa played at the Beldorf Theater, as did the popular Denishawn dance troupe, headed by the husband-wife team of Ted Shawn and Ruth St. Denis.

Mischief on Halloween had so alarmed the residents of Independence that the town elders decided on a new tack. Instead of Halloween, they would celebrate Neewollah (Halloween spelled backwards), a week-long gala of parades, parties, dances, and music. Once the children became involved, the tomfoolery ceased, and the adults enjoyed the celebrations as much as the youngsters. Neewollah now attracts thousands of people from every corner of Kansas as well as many bordering states. The Brookses are sure to have been involved in Neewollah activities.

Several of the daughters from the wealthier families of Independence took dancing lessons from a stern, no-nonsense instructor, Mrs. Mae Argue Buckpitt. Mrs. Buckpitt was a divorcee who had schooled herself in the art, from general ballroom dancing to the more inventive forms of modern dance. Mrs. Buckpitt has been described by former students as a tall, dignified, cultured woman with a modulated, forceful voice that commanded respect from her pupils. She took her work very seriously and limited her enrollment to about 50 students, mostly girls of some means. Mrs. Buckpitt was the type of older single woman who focuses all her time and love on her work when her marriage has failed. She left a lasting imprint on every student she taught.

Shortly after Louise turned 10, Myra paid Mrs. Buckpitt to ride the Inter-urban trolley car once a week from Independence to Cherryvale to give her daughter dance lessons. Myra accompanied the teacher and student on piano.

For the first time in her life, Louise was commanded to a rigid discipline. The small, diminutive build of Louise adapted easily to the physical requirements of dance. It became obvious to Mrs. Buckpitt and especially to Myra that Louise was a born dancer. Even at this early age, Louise had with ease acquired the mental and physical stamina that enabled her to find expression through movement.

Dancing quickly became an obsession with Louise. When dancing, a side of Louise emerged that many of her girlfriends had not seen before. She became selfish, unruly, and given to terrible temper tantrums when things did not go to her liking. If one of the costumes Myra made for her did not allow her enough freedom of movement, an entire afternoon could be ruined by Louise's crying fits. If she flubbed a new dance step she could become so miffed that Mrs. Buckpitt would be dismissed by Myra. Louise was never punished or scolded for even her most impertinent behavior. Myra believed that these tantrums were simply a part of the creative process. It wasn't long before Louise had developed an insufferably self-indulgent character. In later years she would snatch the cigar from a visitor's mouth and throw it into the backyard without a word. With her kewpie doll looks and occasional charm, she got away with murder. Louise later admitted, "I came to think my mother had implanted in me an idea of liberty that was entirely Utopic and a source of delusion."

In addition to dance, Louise began to develop an appreciation for another art—literature—that would remain with her a lifetime. Both L.P. and Myra were compulsive readers, and Louise later wrote that at an early age she was exposed to such writers and thinkers as Charles Darwin, Charles Dickens, Mark Twain, and her favorite, Goethe. Although she claimed she understood little of what she read, there is ample evidence to suggest she was an astute, sometimes introverted, reader who would mull over a passage in a book for days. In later years she developed a deep, even exhaustive appreciation for the works of Proust and Goethe.

Myra is certain to have influenced Louise in literary matters as one of her major social preoccupations was to review books for the ladies clubs she belonged to. Louise would later wittily remember, "Mother herself laughed at literature. For her book reviews, she selected such books as *Nijinsky*, written by the dancer's wife, Romola. Its strange sexual overtones set up a pleasurable creaking of the respectable matrons' chairs. Behind their backs, putting on her club-member's face, Mother would coo unctuously, 'Myra Brooks is *so* cultured.'" Louise suggests that Myra took a cavalier attitude toward her book reviews and ladies clubs; however, nothing could be further from the truth. Myra, in fact, continued to lecture to women's groups on books and a variety of other subjects until she died in 1944.

In 1919, Myra prodded her husband into moving the eight miles south to Independence, where he re-established his law practice. Cherryvale no longer held interest for Myra. She wanted a bigger slice of the high society pie than she was getting in the small town. Independence with its oil bucks and support of the arts seemed the best opportunity for the Brookses. Also, Louise would be nearer Mrs. Buckpitt's studio and could continue her dancing.

Louise turned 13 and for the first time was forced to compete with the other girls for the attentions of Mrs. Buckpitt. Louise had become accustomed to dancing in public, at Elks Club meetings, local talent revues at the Opera House, and the like in Cherryvale. Her experience, dedication, and natural ability easily made her the standout pupil of her class in Independence.

Mrs. Buckpitt lorded over her girls with an iron will and a single-minded purpose. They practiced over and over the latest choreography of such as Louis Chalif, a well-regarded Russian-born choreographer who had relocated to New York. Hundreds of dance instructors such as Mae Buckpitt taught folk dances and short ballets from Chalif's popular instruction books.

The Brookses stayed in Independence only a matter of months, but Louise remained locked into the memories of her schoolmates. Over 65 years later many of them described her singular looks and the effect she had on the local boys. Several remembered her as a kind of sophisticated flapper long before the roaring '20s had even growled. Her dutch-bob hairdo was still the envy of the other girls. Louise, even at this early age, was the town beauty the others wanted to emulate. She emulated no one.

The future Vivian Vance had also moved to Independence. In years to come Vivian would be hitting her stride on Broadway in *Hooray for What!* as Louise began her plummet into obscurity. Playwright William Inge, author of *Bus Stop, Picnic,* and *Come Back Little Sheba,* also grew up in Independence. He would also later remember the slender, jet-haired mystery that was Louise Brooks.

Just months after settling into Independence, L.P. accepted a position with the Sterling Oil and Refining Company in Wichita as a corporate lawyer. Myra had again pushed L.P. for bigger and better things. Wichita was the best move they could make in Kansas. By playing their cards right, they would be thrust into the high society of the entire Midwest.

In just months Myra fit right in with the ladies auxiliaries and afternoon teas and book reviews in Wichita. For the most part she ignored her husband and his career to pursue her own interests and those of her eldest daughter.

In May of 1921 Louise returned once again to Independence as the featured dancer in a program produced by Mae Buckpitt. The recital, titled "The Pageant of Childhood," was presented at the Beldorf Theater to a sold-out crowd. Billed as "Miss Brooks and Company," Louise was the star performer of the show and was featured in two different dances. One of her numbers, "The Balloon Dance," was a ballet-like choreography that called for the use of many multi-colored balloons to heighten the impact of the dance. Those who saw Louise in "The Balloon Dance" would never forget her performance.

The show was received enthusiastically by the audience, and the families had flowers brought to the girls on stage as each was introduced at the end of the show. Although stern L.P. had always thought of Louise's dancing as "silly," Myra is sure to have been deeply moved as her daughter brought the house down.

One girl who danced onstage with Louise remembered

her as being unusually "aloof" that night and "to herself." But Myra was more than satisfied and had even grander things in mind for this talented and beautiful daughter.

Myra enrolled Louise at the Wichita College of Music to continue her study of dance. Her new instructor was Alice Campbell, whom Louise would regard with contempt and scorn because she felt she knew more than her teacher. Louise's bad humors and temper fits soon brought Miss Campbell to the point where she could no longer tolerate her impossible behavior. And so Louise was dismissed.

Myra pleaded with Miss Campbell to keep her daughter in class by saying (in Louise's telling), "Yes, Louise is hard on everyone, but she is *much* harder on herself." Whether true or not, the pleas did not budge Campbell. She refused her admittance back into her class. It was only the first of many such blacklistings.

Louise wrote about the experience in her diary in a style that would portend her future writings: "Although Mother has gone to everybody, weeping and telling the tale, it has left me with a curiously relieved feeling. I must study, and that means away to broader fields. I've had enough of teaching my teacher what to teach me."

In November, 1921, Ted Shawn with Martha Graham and Charles Weidman, appeared in Wichita at the Crawford Theater. Every hopeful dancer in the area attended including Louise and her Svengali, Myra. In a move that paved the way for her daughter's future career on Broadway and in the *Ziegfeld Follies*, Myra brazened her way backstage to meet Shawn with her dark-haired ticket to fame in tow. Shawn, it so happened, was opening a dance studio in New York, and seeing another pretty amateur worth 300 dollars tuition, asked Louise to enroll in the summer course the next year.

From that moment, Myra was dead set on Louise going to New York. L.P. was unusually resistant about sending his daughter halfway across the country to New York City, and could well-imagine the horrors that awaited his 15-year-old. But Myra was adamant. L.P. loved his wife and daughter too much to refuse them. He asked only that an appropriate chaperone live and study dance with Louise.

Although Louise later wrote that a chaperon was found—one Mrs. Alice Mills, a 36-year-old housewife who had "fallen idiotically in love with the beautiful Ted Shawn"—it was Myra who accompanied and stayed with Louise much of the time in New York. Sixty years later many of the ordinary folk in Kansas would recall with clucking tongues and wagging heads Myra Brooks for all practical purposes abandoning her other three children when she took Louise to the big city.

But Louise took it all in stride like another young Kansan, Dorothy of *The Wizard of Oz*. She clicked her heels and was off forever on her happy and troubled voyage down the yellow brick road.

# Blonde Shadow: The Brief Career and Mysterious Disappearance of Actress Linda Haynes

"MY MESSAGE IS FOR Mr. Tarantino. My name is Tom Graves, I'm a writer from Memphis, and the reason I'm calling is that I'm on a mission from God. I've been trying to track down Linda Haynes for at least five years, and I swear to God I'm getting this weird ESP vibe that you've been trying to find her too. I know you know the Linda Haynes I'm talking about. Maybe I'm completely wrong about this, and if I am, well man, I liked your movies. But if I'm right—and I think I am right—why don't we pool our resources and try to find her?"

It had taken about a dozen calls before I finally reached Quentin Tarantino's private office. One contact led to another contact that led to a friend of Tarantino's that led to a writer in L.A. that led to the magic number. Naturally, there wasn't a human being on the end of the line, just an answering machine with a crisp, businesslike announcement left by his personal secretary. After leaving my message, I waited by the phone for two or three days, fidgeting and doing busywork, playing computer Solitaire, before it dawned on me that I was a damned fool. There was no way any bigshot Hollywood director would have time for my obsession with an obscure actress who disappeared into the celluloid mist after her last film, *Guyana Tragedy,* in 1980. I would shrug the phone call off as another dead end in a long series of dead ends with only another bulging phone bill to show for my efforts.

Three weeks later the phone rings: "Mr. Graves, this is Quentin Tarantino's personal assistant. Quentin asked me to call and give you Linda Haynes' phone number. You were right that he had been looking for her. Well, he found her."

Probably not one in a hundred trivia masters could tell you who Linda Haynes is. But that hardcore little group can tell you in great detail what the film world missed when she left Hollywood in 1980, never to be heard from again.

Linda made only nine films, including those in which she played only bit parts. Two of those nine films, including *Guyana Tragedy,* her last performance, were made for television. She made two commercials, one for Mountain Dew and the other for a mouthwash that was never marketed. She starred in one episode of *Room 222*, one episode of *My Three Sons*, one episode of the TV series *Paper Moon*, and one episode of an obscure drama series, *This Is the Life*. These are mere footnotes, however. She was never nominated for a major award, didn't appear on a single talk show, and sat for only a handful of brief newspaper interviews that clearly revealed the enigmatic, brooding persona that seemed so apparent on screen.

She spent over a decade in the glare of the fill lights, yet only one major Hollywood figure (Melanie Griffith) can claim to have really known her, and that friendship, like her movies, ended abruptly in 1980. Even so, the memory of Linda Haynes and the mystery of the blonde shadow she cast in disturbing and ultra-gritty films such as *Rolling Thunder* (1977), the film for which she has become a legend to a miniscule but obsessive cult that includes people like rogue actor/director Vincent Gallo, and the basis for my own obsession, have lingered years after her proverbial 15 minutes of fame and subsequent, self-ignited flame-out.

Long before Jennifer Jason Leigh rather extravagantly portrayed a succession of emotionally-crippled low-lifes and losers in films such as *Last Exit to Brooklyn* and *Rush*—hell, maybe even before Leigh was *born*—Linda Haynes was giving unblinking, nail-hard performances that transcended type, defining the character of the small-town beauty born into a hardscrabble world and turned out onto the streets at entirely too early an age. She was the woman who walked the edge between prostitution and respectability, fighting to keep her dignity as a whore or kept woman, determined to eventually triumph over her circumstances. Despite the health and great beauty Linda radiated on screen, she also carried an internal suffering like a dead mental weight. One look at her lovely face, as she narrowed her eyes to slits to size up a situation, told you she'd been to places few men would willingly go.

Her great beauty, which often had to be toned down for her roles, presented her characters with a dichotomy—her beauty seemed an abnormality in those situations, not the product of good breeding or gentility that one typically associates with those so blessed, but something wildly out of place in a hard, ugly world. Out of Linda's nine films—*Latitude Zero* (1969), *Coffy* (1973), *The Nickel Ride* (1974), *Judgment: The Court Martial of Lieutenant William Calley* (1975), *The Drowning Pool* (1975), *Rolling Thunder* (1977), *Human Experiments* (1979), *Brubaker* (1980), and *Guyana*

*Tragedy* (1980)—she played a woman on the fringes of society in all but one, her first credited role in *Latitude Zero*, a Japanese/American production directed by Ishiro Honda, renowned in horror film circles as the creator of Godzilla. In the characters she would develop after this first film, her blonde good looks were always an out, a means to an end, and she certainly wasn't above using them. These characters were also smart enough to realize that being beautiful, in and of itself, was an answer to nothing. It was, at best for a woman at the bottom of the social heap, a temporary fix.

Linda's own comments about her blonde looks make for a curious parallel to the screen persona she created. "I've relied on my looks most of my life," she said in 1996. "It's been a real waste. Being good-looking is *crippling*.

"Being beautiful will get you to a lot of places, but the problem is you don't necessarily feel you deserve to be there, and you haven't gone through all the steps of developing yourself in order to get there. So it's almost a hollowness that results. You know, you look great, and people, they *look* at you. People don't hesitate to come right up and kind of look at you as though you're a freak and ask you questions that ordinarily I don't think they would ask. Men *and* women. You do end up feeling weird; it's almost like having a defect. You are a point of attention because of the way you look instead of maybe who you *are*. You become stunted in certain ways. I've said before that it's like having a handicap."

I once had the ironic opportunity to play these words, which I had recorded on cassette tape, for a writing class presided over by Lucy Grealy, author of *Autobiography of a*

*Face*, the heart-wrenching account of her excruciating treatments and surgeries for facial cancer, which had often left her face looking like the distortion in a funhouse mirror. Everyone sitting in the room was fully aware of Lucy's years-long ordeal and could see for themselves that her face was a long way from looking even remotely normal. As soon as Linda's words flew out of the tiny recorder's speaker, every eye in the room slid over to Lucy to see how she would respond to a beautiful woman complaining of being beautiful. She blithely replied, "Tom, I think it sounded better when you quoted her than when she said it herself." Rimshot! However, as the discussion continued it became clear that one could never truly know another person's pain. Even a beautiful woman's.

There was no question that Linda Haynes, with her sculpted goddess curves and blonde hair that curled insinuatingly around her shoulders, and her almost balletic use of body language, was an outstanding beauty. But on screen it was a fractured, offbeat beauty, what one person I know called "white trash beautiful." Her distinctive eyes, almond-shaped, betrayed a wariness, an aloofness, that immediately dispelled the notion of a dumb blonde. The color of those eyes was equally striking, a blazing turquoise as liquid and inviting as a tropical tide pool. I later learned why the camera was so taken with them; one eye is predominantly blue, the other predominantly green.

The first time I saw Linda, in the film *Rolling Thunder* in 1977, I thought, *I know this woman*. Her particular type of beauty, although unusual for the silver screen because it avoided stereotypical glamour, was as familiar to me as the good-looking gal down the street in the tough Memphis suburb where I grew up, the one who enjoyed raising hell and cruising in your Mustang, would laugh at your dirty jokes, and for the right lucky guy might even let him get to second base. A woman any man would be proud to show off in his bass boat. A touchable beauty.

Linda's unusual good looks and equally distinctive voice, with her odd, lazy way of rolling vowels and flattening consonants, undoubtedly the result of Swedish being her first language, were both a drawback and an enticement to acting jobs. Other than her two commercials, she had only done a smattering of theater work and played uncredited bit parts in films such as *In Like Flynt* until 1969 when she landed her first starring role in the Japanese-American production *Latitude Zero*. In this piece of sci-fi silliness starring Cesar Romero and Joseph Cotton and directed by Ishiro Honda, Linda played a beautiful but emotionless physician on board a futuristic submarine. She is almost robotic in her movements and the implication is that she is sexually unresponsive. As one might expect, one of the male shipmates makes it his responsibility to thaw her out.

Because the film was directed by Ishiro Honda, creator of Godzilla and director of many other Japanese sci-fi/horror classics such as *Rodan* and *The Mysterians*, it has developed quite a cult reputation and Linda is revered among this subcult for her performance. However, it took years for this cult to form and Linda did not get another speaking role until four years later in the legendary blaxploitation film *Coffy* starring the iconic Pam Grier, another one of Quentin Tarantino's comeback miracles. In *Coffy*, Linda played the prize white prostitute of a cut-throat black pimp played with finesse by Robert Doqui. Released in 1973, the film is one of the first to exploit mixed-race sexual relationships, and although there were no sex scenes with Haynes and Doqui, there was a lingering kiss that was more than a little shocking in its day.

Even though the part was barely credited, Linda's performance was indelible. Her character, beautiful and deadly, had a sleazy charm and vulnerability that elevated what could have been a cartoonish role into something far grittier. Her subservience to her pimp boyfriend masked a deep jealousy and a cunning malice. As a part of her machinations against Doqui, she orchestrates a fur-flying, body-slamming cat fight with the film's star, Pam Grier. But the Grier character, fearing some kind of trap, has laced her sizeable afro with razor blades. When Linda grabs Grier's hair during the cat fight sequence, she screams and draws back bloodied hands. The scene did not go unnoticed, particularly with some of Hollywood's young, maverick filmmakers.

After the box office success of *Coffy*, Linda was asked to screen test for 20th Century Fox, which was considering putting her under contract. Unlike most film actors, she did not have her teeth capped. A large part of her screen appeal was her natural, unaffected beauty, which included her all-natural smile. Looking closely, one can see that one incisor slightly overlaps another. Hollywood legend Mervyn LeRoy, then still very active in the business, is reported to have remarked, "Tell her to get her teeth fixed." In the last generation, so many Hollywood figures have acquired teeth of such super-perfection that they look entirely artificial and unbecoming. The pendulum has swung back so hard that actors such as Steve Buscemi and Anna Paquin make a point of celebrating their dental imperfections. With Linda, though, as one dentist once remarked of my teeth, "you've got good configuration." Linda never needed her teeth fixed.

This same year Linda received an invitation to audition for the renowned Actors Studio, the Mecca of method acting, the intense, personalized acting style made famous by Marlon Brando, James Dean, Montgomery Clift, and Paul Newman among many others. Even with her slender résumé, particularly in theater, she had nonetheless impressed some important people. She auditioned for a panel that included the Studio's grand master, Lee Strasberg. Based on this one audition, Linda was given a Life membership to the Actors Studio, something that was virtually unheard of. This credential ushered in a series of roles for Linda that would define her as an actress.

Almost immediately she was signed to *The Nickel Ride* for 20th Century Fox, which was calculated to give her budding career a quantum boost. The film was to be directed by Hollywood royalty Robert Mulligan, whose straightforward, workmanlike style had won him an Academy Award for his direction of *To Kill a Mockingbird*. He was responsible for such other fondly remembered films as *Fear Strikes Out*, *Summer of '42*, and later *Clara's Heart* and *Man in the Moon*. The film starred playwright Jason Miller, then hot from the success of his award-winning play *That Championship Season* and his role as Father Karras in the blockbuster horror film *The Exorcist*.

In the film Miller plays a mid-level Mafioso who is double-crossed by the Mob; Linda plays his girlfriend. Unfortunately, *The Nickel Ride* is filmed in an impressionistic, Altmanesque manner that is virtually incomprehensible. The '70s were a decade of great experimentation in American cinema; some stream-of-consciousness films worked and some did not. *The Nickel Ride* is a seemingly endless series of disjointed conversations that are nearly inaudible and garbled enough to need subtitles. The worst offender is our heroine, Linda, who was directed to adopt a Southern accent on top of her already unusual speech. It didn't work. Even though Mafia movies were cleaning up at the box office in the '70s, *The Nickel Ride* sank without a ripple and even today it is difficult to find a copy (it is reportedly coming out on DVD). The director, Robert Mulligan, returned to his more traditional narrative style in subsequent films. Quentin Tarantino, that great archivist, is a fan of the film and has shown it at one of his periodic screenings of his favorite movie obscurities. His stamp of approval almost assuredly is responsible for its upcoming re-release.

The next year, 1975, is when Linda finally broke into the big leagues with key scenes opposite a bona fide superstar, Paul Newman, in *The Drowning Pool*, a sequel to Newman's popular '60s film, *Harper*. Cast once again as a prostitute, Linda, in the film has information that private eye Lew Harper needs. To get the information, Newman gets Linda drunk and feigns being drunk himself. He squires her away to her house trailer for sex. But after smooth-talking the information he needs out of her, he abruptly leaves. At the end of the film, Harper brings the golden-hearted prostitute, Linda, an envelope full of money, which is not the last time Linda's screen persona gets money instead of love.

As interesting as Linda was in her previous work, the film that defines her screen persona and the one mentioned most often by her intense but small core of fans is *Rolling Thunder.* Tarantino admired the 1977 thriller enough to name his film distribution company after it. A brutal, violent film about a returning P.O.W. of the Vietnam War who seeks bloody revenge against Dixie Mafia thugs who have killed his wife and son, *Rolling Thunder* was in part scripted by Paul Schrader who made his name two years earlier with the screenplay for *Taxi Driver*, a tour de force about another alienated, disturbed Vietnam vet.

Tight-jawed actor William Devane played the returning P.O.W., Major Charles Rane, a walking bottle of nitroglycerine who predictably explodes in violence when things go wrong. Upon returning home, Rane finds himself a ghost to his family. His young son has no memory of him and seems much more attached to the local sheriff, who Rane quickly surmises has become his wife's lover in his absence. At a brass-band ceremony, the major is given a new Cadillac and a box of silver dollars, with one silver dollar for every day he spent in captivity. The town beauty who gives him the keys to the Cadillac along with a hug and suggestive kiss is Linda, who has worn his P.O.W. bracelet while he was held prisoner in Vietnam.

Dixie Mafia thugs break into the major's home to steal the stash of silver dollars. When Rane and his son enter their home, they are held at gunpoint and ordered to give up the money. Rane, however, is nearly immune to such torture, having been conditioned to it as a prisoner of war to the point that such pain becomes a masochistic pleasure. Because he refuses to talk, just as he did in Vietnam, his family is shot to death in front of him and his hand is sickeningly mutilated in a garbage disposal.

The major recovers in a hospital and is fitted with an artificial limb, a hook, which he sharpens on a grindstone before setting out from San Antonio, Texas for Mexico with a car full of guns and ammo. His only companion is the small-town beauty, named Linda Forchet in the film, who works as a cocktail waitress in a low-rent, noisy bar. Although beautiful, one look at her tells you she's had too many bad men and a lifetime of hard knocks. She is a picture of heartache. Her image of the P.O.W., whose bracelet she has worn faithfully for many years, feeds her rescue fantasies. She has day-dreamed of Major Rane's return to Texas and of her loyalty rewarded by being taken away from it all—but to where?

When Rane is ready to go on a manhunt to avenge his family's killers, he stops by the bar where Linda is working and asks if she wants to go on a trip with him, no questions asked. In one of the film's more riveting scenes, she answers his request to come with him to Mexico sarcastically while carrying a tray of cocktails, "Do you want me to just *drop* everything?" The major doesn't answer her and turns to walk away when Linda drops the tray of cocktails crashing to the floor and leaves with him.

Linda quickly finds out that the major is simply using her as a pawn in his deadly game of vigilanteism. At first she resists, but after a violent quarrel she slowly begins to accept her role as his accomplice. In her most memorable scene, Linda is awakened after sleeping in the major's Cadillac by the sound of gunfire. She and the major had pulled off the highway during the night to catch some sleep by the roadside. That morning Rane is target practicing, perfecting his ability to shoot with an artificial hand. Linda joins in the target practice, picking up a shotgun, racking a shell, and blowing the target to kingdom come. Her expertise suggests she has handled firearms her entire life. (I later learned that Linda was completely inexperienced with guns and that the shotgun kicked so violently that it left a purple bruise on her shoulder for weeks.)

A heartbreaking moment in an otherwise ultra-violent film occurs when Linda has finally coaxed Major Rane into making love. It isn't so much a seduction as a nursing of the major's wounded spirit; he *needs* love. The next morning the major dresses in his military uniform while Linda sleeps. When she awakens, he is gone, off on his private war. The only thing left behind is a wad of hundred-dollar bills on the nightstand. The reward for her love is cold cash and abandonment in a motel room. The look of quiet pain on Linda's face when she realizes what has happened is alone worth the price of my obsession with her.

"I thought Linda Haynes was a wonderful, terrific actress," says the director of *Rolling Thunder,* John Flynn, who has subsequently worked with many major Hollywood stars such as Sylvester Stallone and Steven Seagal. I interviewed Flynn by phone in 1996 and he was still enthusiastic those many years later about Linda and her work in the film. "I had seen her work in *Coffy* and in *The Drowning Pool* with Paul Newman and thought she had something really different. Linda seemed to perfectly fit the part of the character Linda Forchet, who was a certain type of woman we've all seen or known, a good-looking woman who leaves home too early, drifts from place to place, works in massage parlors to make ends meet, or at best winds up as a hairdresser—that was the girl. The character desperately wanted stability in her life and someone to love and be with. She was a lonely woman with many bad men in her past. She even has a line to that effect in the film. To me, Linda Haynes seemed the embodiment of this woman.

"I agree that she was a standout in this film. Linda was in no way a typical actress. Everything about her seemed slightly off-center. There was a great mystery about her, something that always made you want more. She always held something back from the viewer, kept something in reserve. There was always a subtext, a layering to her performance, and there are few actors who can get across that sort of complexity in so little time.

"She had an oblique approach to the part. She got inside the woman and played her in a heartbreakingly accurate way. In real life Linda struck me as being somewhat shy and reticent. She never discussed her role—she just went and did it. Some days she was very up, and other days she was quiet and to herself. In real life she was a bit of a mystery as well."

With only a few exceptions, the critics savaged *Rolling Thunder* for its relentless, realisitic violence. There were those, however, who for the first time discovered an unusually talented blonde actress. *People* magazine stated, "The real sneak attack in this film is the marvelously gritty performance of Linda Haynes as the girl who goes along for the ride." Bruce Cook writing in *The Wall Street Journal* said about her, "(Linda Haynes is a) blonde with a slightly wacky, offbeat manner (who) came across with unexpected force in a Robert Mulligan movie that nobody saw called *The Nickel Ride*…she showed up last year in *Rolling Thunder*, a movie generally reviled by critics but one that found favor with some audiences. As usual, she did a first-rate job in it and was more than able to hold her own with William Devane and Tommy Lee Jones, her co-stars."

One of those in the movie industry who took special notice of her talents was a young screenwriter named Greg Goodell who was slated to direct a low-budget horror feature titled *Human Experiments*. "I was very aware of Linda from her work in *The Drowning Pool* and *Rolling Thunder*," said Goodell in an interview with me a few years ago. "I was terribly impressed with her and her work. The thing that is so wonderful about her is that she is so real on screen; her acting comes across as something totally natural.

"In spite of the good work she had done, I had to fight very hard to get the producers of *Human Experiments* to accept her as the lead, and the lead role is exactly what I wanted for her. The producers complained about her funny way of talking, that marbles-in-her-mouth thing she has that is so compelling. It's a natural quirk of Linda's that makes her voice distinctive and unique; you hang onto every word she says. Very few people in film have that kind of vocal quality. But the producers didn't know what to make of it and they didn't think she was pretty enough. Well, I thought that was just totally wrong. It's just that she didn't have a lot of make-up on in *Rolling Thunder* and some of her other films. So I arranged a photo session for her with Douglas Kirkland, one of Hollywood's best glamour photographers. That put her over. Kirkland really did a great job of showcasing her natural beauty."

Linda's star certainly seemed to be ascending. She had secured the lead, liked the script, and was prepared to give the creepy film her best performance. *Human Experiments* was the type of film that had "cult" stamped all over it. The script cleverly and with tongue-in-cheek weaves together plot elements and clichés from various slasher and psycho movies, chicks-in-prison films, mad doctor movies, as well as a few touches from the *Living Dead* pics. A horror film for all tastes.

In the film Linda plays an itinerant bar singer, obviously fallen on hard times, who must play every rural dive she can to make a buck. After being run off the road while driving to her next gig, she goes to the closest house to use the phone. The house seems empty, but when she enters it she finds a bloodbath. A young boy holding a rifle sits in a chair staring vacantly. When he points his rifle at Linda, she picks up a nearby weapon and shoots first. She is convicted of murdering the entire family and sent off to a women's prison.

Once in prison, the viewer encounters the usual *Caged Heat* clichés: tough bitches, sadistic bull dykes, corrupt turnkeys, a degrading strip search scene, and a plan to break out. Geoffrey Lewis, the rubber-faced character actor familiar from numerous Clint Eastwood films, plays the prison shrink, mild-mannered on the outside, a murderous, brainwashing madman on the inside. When Linda discovers the truth about the prison—that it is a laboratory for evil experiments and that she was set up by the prison officials on her murder charges—she is determined to escape before she is killed.

In the film's key scream scene, Linda tries to escape through a labyrinth of underground passageways and stumbles across the reanimated bodies of several prisoners who had disappeared. As she screams and flees in horror she encounters bugs, *lots* of bugs.

"Literally thousands of bugs—ants, roaches, crickets, and spiders—were dumped on Linda for that scene," said director Greg Goodell. "We needed to do three different shots with all the bugs to edit together into one scene. We shot the first take and everything went as planned. We dumped huge garbage cans full of bugs on her, she screamed and went nuts on cue, like she was supposed to, and the shot was great. We went to work immediately to set up the second shot and Linda went back to her trailer.

"When we were ready to shoot, a crew member told me she wouldn't come out of her trailer, that the bugs had freaked her out so bad that she was huddled in her trailer shaking like a leaf. So I went to her trailer and tried to calm her down. I said, 'Linda, we really need at least one more shot. If you can't do it, I'll understand, but if you can, I promise it will be the last time.' She was still shaking and reluctant, but she did it. We dropped all the bugs and roaches again, and when I said 'cut!' she brushed the bugs off and said, 'I'll do it again if you want.' The first part of what you see on film is Linda literally going berserk with fright. It really is something to see."

*Human Experiments* nosedived at the box office. It was the type of low-budget potboiler that typically played as the second-billed horror feature at drive-ins. Overall, the film is good more for laughs and Linda's earnest performance than anything, with some odd cameos by actors such as Jackie Coogan and John Travolta's sister Ellen also livening things up. Linda's performance in this horror vehicle is typically tough, gritty, natural, and revealing. The strip search scene in the film called for her to remove all her prison clothes and stand totally naked in front of the prison nurse who sprays her for lice. Obviously the scene is meant to titillate the drive-in crowd, especially when the nurse instructs Linda to hold up her breasts to spray under them. However, Linda invests the scene with such shame and degradation—here again her body language and facial expressions are minimal but powerfully telling—that the effect is anything but erotic. She is a woman figuratively raped by the prison system and her nudity an expression of helplessness.

In another scene, after lights out, Linda touches herself tentatively, seemingly checking to see if she still has sexual feelings. As she begins to experience the first stirrings of pleasure, the lights come on and it is obvious she was being watched. Enraged, she screams and throws things at the cell door. This was a scene she wasn't particularly eager to perform. She thought it too intimate and many years later wasn't pleased when asked to rehash the details for cinema's latest madman, Vincent Gallo.

*Human Experiments* was the only film in which Linda Haynes received top billing. Although largely forgotten today and rarely mentioned, even in horror references, there were those at the time who paid notice. In 1979 she won her only acting award, Best Actress, for her performance in *Human Experiments* at the Science Fiction, Fantasy, and Horror Film Awards held that year in France. The award plaque today hangs on the wall of her office, which is covered with other remnants of her brief movie life.

Stuart Rosenberg, who had directed Linda in *The Drowning Pool* with Paul Newman, cast her in 1980 in *Brubaker*, a Robert Redford vehicle in which he plays a reformist prison warden trying to straighten out a corrupt prison system in Arkansas. Linda plays a local whore who is shacked-up with one of the sleazier prison trustees. When the warden, Redford, goes to the shack, which has also been used to stockpile supplies stolen from the prison, Linda comes to the door and gives Redford a piece of her mind. Frankly, it's not much of a part, and it is a performance that Linda thought her worst. After playing the lead in *Human Experiments*, even though it was clearly a B movie, it surely must have seemed a step backward to be playing yet another common whore, even opposite Redford. There was very little in the film to hang a good performance on.

Her last film, the made-for-television *Guyana Tragedy,* at least saw Linda's career end on a high note. Originally shown in two parts on CBS, *Guyana Tragedy,* which was about the mass suicide of the Peoples Temple cult in Jonestown, Guyana, boasted a stellar cast largely comprised of up-and-coming talent such as Powers Boothe as the Reverend Jim Jones, Veronica Cartwright as his wife, Brad Dourif as one of Jones's sexually-conflicted disciples, and Ned Beatty as Congressman Leo Ryans.

Linda played, yet again, a woman of the streets who finds in Jim Jones a fellow con artist and sugar daddy. She collaborates on a faith healing scam with the Reverend and in one memorable scene fakes a cure disguised as a 70-year-old cripple who is miraculously made to walk again. In the film's climactic scene at Jonestown, Linda's character ladles out cyanide-laced Kool-Aid to other members. When nearly everyone else is dead, she steals a briefcase full of cash and tries to escape into the jungle. She is spotted by one of Jones's remaining snipers and is quickly gunned down. As she falls to the ground, the briefcase breaks open and the money sails into the air. In Linda Haynes's final shot in cinema, her body twitches as she dies.

After that, Linda Haynes disappeared forever from the silver screen.

I first saw *Rolling Thunder* in 1977 in Memphis during the film's first run. What separated *Rolling Thunder* from many of the other contemporary thrillers was its sharp turn from the stylized violence that had become the norm. Sam Peckinpah's films, for example, were infamous for their highly orchestrated, slow-motion bloodletting. Even *Taxi Driver's* truly disturbing violence, particularly the shootout ending, was stylized and presented in a sort of manic hyper-reality meant to get inside Travis Bickle's madness. Even the blood looked unreal, almost milky.

There were no such impediments to the mayhem in *Rolling Thunder*. It was fast, frenetic, and all-too-real, and it left an aftertaste of shock and terror.

Perhaps it was the adrenaline buzz from cortisone shots I had taken to clear up a stubborn bout of poison ivy, maybe it was just the boredom of an eventless summer, but finding Linda Haynes became an obsession for me in 1995 as I waited for a book contract that never materialized and I became impatient to find a new project. I had caught a showing of *Rolling Thunder* on TV that same summer which reawakened my curiosity about what had happened to Linda Haynes, an actress who to me and a handful of others seemed destined for the kind of greatness Meryl Streep was soon to find. Why had her career come to such an abrupt, clueless end? No one seemed to know anything.

I began my search by contacting the notoriously uncooperative Screen Actors Guild whose flak catchers told me without pause that they had no listing for her. I didn't believe them, so I called again. Then again. Probably to get rid of me for good, they told me they could forward a letter to her, this person they had no record of. So I sent one. The letter was returned "Address Unknown."

I called the editors of *Film Comment*, fanzines such as *Femme Fatale* and *The Psychotronic Guide*, consulted the *Reader's Guide to Periodical Literature* for clues as well as countless other texts. I conducted a Nexis/Lexis search. Nothing. Nada.

I contacted Celebrity Search, a company that keeps active files on thousands of celebrities. There was not a single item on Linda Haynes past 1977. As a last resort I called an executive friend in charge of the Investigative Division of a nationally renowned security firm. Linda Haynes had not left a trace, a smear, a smudge, a print.

But I had. Several hundred dollars' worth in fact. All in long distance charges.

I had read several interviews with the young director of *Reservoir Dogs* and *Pulp Fiction*, and in one lengthy article Quentin Tarantino discussed about 50 films that had influenced him. Among them was a passing mention of *Rolling Thunder* with no reference at all to any of the film's actors. I knew that Tarantino had named his production company Rolling Thunder and felt in my gut that it was because of the movie. Sitting at my desk one day all this came together in an explosive moment of clarity and the name of Tarantino kept pounding in my head like a voodoo drumbeat. As a long-time writer, I've learned you do not ignore such feelings. So, I put the receiver to my ear and started dialing. Three weeks later his personal assistant called with Linda Haynes's phone number. Even though I don't believe in ESP, it worked well enough for me to be absolutely right that Tarantino had been searching for Linda at the exact same time I was. That's a mighty strange coincidence no matter how skeptical one claims to be.

*"I never wanted to be an actress. That just came to me. I never wanted to be in the spotlight at all. If anything, I wanted to be obscure."* – Linda Haynes, 1996

The days I first spoke to Linda Haynes on the phone, I found out from her that I was only the second person to call her about her career in the nearly 20 years since she had left Hollywood. A week earlier a casting director for the television drama *E.R.* had called on behalf of Tarantino. Tarantino had long wanted to direct an episode of *E.R.*—it was his favorite television show—but because he had refused to join the Director's Guild, which is more or less a Hollywood requirement, he had to be granted a waiver. He was in a time crunch and wanted Linda to play Cookie Lewis, the mother of the character Dr. Susan Lewis played by Sherry Stringfield. But no one had seen Linda for 20 years, had no idea what she looked like, how she may have aged, or whether she could or would act again. The casting director asked if she would come to California and test for the role. What I learned in 2011 that Linda had not told me previously was that she stubbornly refused to test for the role. She didn't know Quentin Tarantino from Adam and felt that her acting in the '70s, although 20 years old at this point, should suffice.

I was to discover that this kind of split attitude about her acting—on one hand she was fiercely proud of her work yet she was convinced that it wasn't good enough to merit lasting attention—and the resulting years of silence from the film industry only confirmed her fears that it had all been a gigantic waste. This sudden attention from Tarantino to be followed only weeks later by inquiries from a writer from Memphis came as a profound shock to Linda who fully believed Hollywood had turned its back on her. She believed that she had tried hard in her time there but had failed. The whole movie thing was like a blip, a stain, an annoyance, something to run away from. And yet. And yet at rock bottom she wanted recognition for what she did. Her acting style was different from all the others and she damn well knew it. She created something on screen that was real, that people could feel. And if no one else ever praised her for it she knew to the bottom of her soul that she had created something that approached art. Although she laughed at the idea that some called her a female James Dean, she recognized that there was more than a little truth to it.

Linda and I clicked immediately. Trust was almost immediately established between us and to this day we are the best of friends and confidants. After the initial conversation with her there were several lengthy phone calls between us over the next several months as we got to know one another. I was always pleasantly surprised by her candor and heartfelt replies to my questions about her career, even if at times she struggled to remember names, dates, and details. I later learned why her memory at times was so befogged.

I also learned the following basics of her biography: Linda was born as Linda Sylvander in Miami, Florida to Sten and Eivor Sylvander, both of whom were Swedish immigrants. Her father was a licensed sea captain whose job and business ventures took him all over the world. Both her mother and father were matinee-idol good-looking and the pictures of them from early in their marriage show a couple that could have been having cocktails at the Brown Derby with other celebrity pairs. By the time Linda was 10 years old she had seen all the lights and cameras she would ever care to. Until that time, when she was beginning to show just the faintest signs of pre-adolescent chubbiness, Linda was the number one child model in South Florida, a seasoned professional who appeared in innumerable print ads, catalog pages, and brochures. She had been seen by millions of Americans on the front covers of *Parade* and *Look* magazines, a beautiful platinum blonde child with a practiced million-watt smile. When asked how she felt about all the attention and photographs she replies without further comment, "I did what I was told."

When Linda was seven, her mother gave birth to identical twin daughters who were almost carbon copies of her. The twins, Yvonne and Yvette, like Linda, inherited their mother's Swedish beauty and they followed in Linda's footsteps as successful child models. In later years the Sylvander Twins, as they would be known professionally, would famously grace the cover of the *Sports Illustrated* swimsuit issue of 1979 and dabble briefly in a very few obscure films before settling into marriage and careers as a massage therapist (Yvette) and a dental hygienist (Yvonne).

There was a restless spirit in Linda and she was bored in school and bored with the whole local Miami scene. Her father's lengthy absences—he lived much of the time in Venezuela attending to a fiberglass coffin business when he wasn't at sea—and the marital tensions that resulted fueled Linda's rebellious streak. At 16 Linda met an older boy in his 20s named Jay Handelman with whom she became infatuated, as teenaged girls do. Handelman received a modest inheritance and talked Linda into running away from Florida and eloping with him. The couple fled to Los Angeles to escape an assemblage of outraged parents who did everything in their power to dissolve the marriage. Linda and her new husband quickly discovered married life was no Utopia. Without marketable skills or a high school diploma, Linda could not find a job in the competitive L.A. market where good looks did not confer automatic employment status. Handelman found employment on an assembly line in a mattress factory.

In one of those it-could-only-happen-in-Hollywood stories, Linda and Jay were walking their dog down Beverly Drive when a gleaming Cadillac pulled up next to them. "Here's my card," the driver said to the attractive young couple. "Would you two be interested in coming to acting classes?" The man was Ben Bard who had acted in silent films and held acting classes at his studio. Linda, who had nothing better to do, decided to give it a try.

Stagelights, rehearsals, direction, make-up—these were things Linda could easily relate to from her childhood modeling career, although she never grew comfortable performing in front of a live audience. "Those people were *looking* at me," she told me later. The camera, a silent, undemanding anonymous partner that nonetheless understood everything she was trying to convey, *that* became her audience. "That's my secret," she said to me in casual conversation one evening. "I played to the camera and no one else. The camera and I understood each other."

The night Linda was scheduled to give her first stage performance in a showcase for prospective clients, her teacher told her she needed to change her last name. The implication was clear; Handelman was too Jewish. "Let's change the name to Haynes, something simple and easy." The name stuck even though she never particularly liked it. Practically the minute her Hollywood days were over she changed her last name again, which is one of the reasons she was so hard to find.

Linda's decade-long film career consisted mostly of years of frustration, auditions, rejection, and surprising small-scale accomplishments such as her key scenes opposite Paul Newman in *The Drowning Pool* and opposite Robert Redford in *Brubaker*. In the mid-'70s, long after she had divorced Jay Handelman (who went on to manage show business personalities such as comedian John Byner), Linda met a wealthy West Coast businessman 20 years her senior, Saul Zukerman, who, according to Linda, was widely known as "The Car Wash King." Zukerman was a broker for almost every car wash bought or sold in Southern California, which was and remains the car wash capital of the world.

Linda married Saul in 1977 during the height of her film career. Although she was only able to earn a modest income from her film parts, her marriage to Zukerman placed her in the top percentile of American wealth. They owned a multi-million dollar home on Ambassadors Row, had a his Rolls Royce and a hers Bentley, had bragging rights on a Russian wolfhound given to them by Melanie Griffith, and were surrounded by all the material things equated with success in Southern California. But instead of enjoying the good life, Linda was growing increasingly despondent, depressed, and dependent—dependent on a flow of alcohol and drugs, particularly Quaaludes, which were legal by prescription at the time. Her life with the autocratic Saul combined with the white-hot pressures of Hollywood caused her to slowly unravel.

"Linda was a total professional on the set," director Greg Goodell confirmed of the time he worked with her. "She was terrific to work with, easygoing and friendly, and always on time with her lines down. The crew really loved working with her too. But I started hearing gossip that she was drinking heavily off the set, even in the morning. I couldn't tell it, but several of the crew members had seen her belting back a few.

"As I came to know Linda and kept in touch with her after the movie, I began to have some serious concerns about her. She seemed to be hovering on a state of deep depression, and I was afraid her life was getting way out of control and she could be heading off in a tragic direction. I think her relationship with her husband, Saul Zukerman, isolated her and insulated her from Hollywood as well. He struck me as a very jealous, domineering man, almost a Svengali figure. And I can't help but wonder if Saul wasn't some sort of father substitute that was the result of things from her childhood, her father being gone so much and all.

"Linda definitely had the goods in every way. All the opportunities were there for her to take. The personal demons are what kept her from being a star. Some people want success at any price and others realize it ain't worth it. If Linda would have stayed she probably would have died."

Although Linda seldom voiced any complaints about her career, deep inside things gnawed. All along she believed her hard work had been undervalued by the power players in Hollywood, and she wasn't sure how many more years of auditions and rejections she could take. In 1979 she gave the only published indication of her disappointment to *Wall Street Journal* reporter Bruce Cook:

"I've been on maybe 30 interviews since *[Human Experiments]*. I know I'm weird, the kind of readings I do, so

I'm not going to please everyone. But even at this point it still hurts. When they turn me down, I cry afterward. Rejection hurts me. Certain people in the business have enough confidence to go with me. They know what they want, and every once in awhile I'm it.

"To be honest, sometimes, when I think about the future, I'm severely tempted to quit. But every time I've felt this way in the past I've gotten a job. And that's really what it's all about isn't it? Work? Basically, I'm real proud of myself, proud of my acting. I give them what they want. I can do the job."

While filming her last movie, the Emmy-winning made-for-television account of the Jim Jones Peoples Temple massacre, *Guyana Tragedy*, Linda realized she was in trouble. Always a total professional on the set, her lines well-rehearsed and her movements practiced and ready, she delayed filming by blowing her lines during several takes. Word spread quickly on the set that Linda was drinking and that it was affecting her performance. Although she realized what was happening and sobered up for the remaining filming and turned in some of her best work, she felt the time had come to make a decision. Her marriage was in shambles, she was profoundly depressed and at times thinking of suicide, her career seemed to be in a stalling pattern, and the only things that temporarily stopped the pain were alcohol and 'ludes. She knew it was just a matter of time before she was dead, either intentionally or unintentionally.

She went into rehab, as all Hollywood seems to do at one time or another. However, she managed to avoid the drug-cure spas that so many confuse with real treatment.

The tough love she got there revealed to her two things: if she went back to Hollywood the whole process would inevitably start all over again and she would probably end up beautiful and dead, and if she didn't get rid of Saul Zukerman the end might come even sooner. She believed them.

So Linda packed her bags and left without looking back. She spent time alone in the quiet hills of Vermont, trying to restore her peace of mind, getting the booze and pills out of her head, and deciding what to do with the rest of her life. She knew it was all over for Hollywood.

Sober and back in good health, she moved to Miami to be close to family. Her beautiful twin sisters had also found Hollywood and modeling and being the objects of men's fantasies a dead end. When the Ford Modeling Agency told the Sylvander Twins, whose bodies were perfect enough to make Greek sculptors weep for joy, to each lose 10 pounds they told them they could go to hell. It was the world's loss. Linda, who had not finished high school and was self-conscious about her lack of formal education, went to a local college and earned a degree that allowed her to become a licensed legal assistant. She had long wanted a family and during this time she gave birth to a son, Leif, whom she chose to raise by herself and upon whom she obviously doted. In Leif, Linda found the personal happiness that had so long eluded her. Hollywood never noticed she was gone. To this day Linda claims she never received another call from Hollywood until Quentin Tarantino's people tracked her down. However, Linda had also perversely told the Screen Actors Guild not to forward messages to her. Perhaps this was instigated to prevent unwanted suitors from her past to find her in South Florida. This action, combined with her changing her last name, prevented all but the most dedicated and deep pocketed—Tarantino—from finding her.

Even with these preventive measures, Linda and Saul Zukerman reconnected after he retired from the car wash business and they remarried in the mid-'90s. Once again Linda was a lady of means, but as one acquaintance of hers told me, "Linda never was a Rodeo Drive sort of gal. She was more Levi's and a work shirt and that's what so many people liked about her. She was totally unpretentious." Linda, Saul, and Leif were able to island hop in the Florida Keys and the Caribbean from Zukerman's island retreat on Staniel Cay in the Exumas, near Nassau. Linda was happiest fishing or snorkeling with her family. Being near water gave her the peace of mind agents and auditions and retakes never had. She didn't mind that she was seldom, if ever, recognized on the streets.

I had first contacted her during the summer of 1995. We had made tentative plans for me to visit her for an interview the following spring. During this time period she and Zukerman had broken up for a second time. She would be getting a divorce she informed me. She continued to work as a legal assistant, pleased that her work in film had, after all, amounted to something. She held out the hope that Tarantino's people might call again, but, in retrospect, after her earlier refusal to audition for him, it is doubtful that the Quentin lightning will strike twice.

Two weeks after a ValuJet airliner crashed in the Florida Everglades in May, 1996, killing every passenger on board, I was 10,000 feet over the exact same swampland—also on a ValuJet airliner–destined for Ft. Myers, Florida. The butterflies in my stomach had grown wings the size of bats. I was to be met at the airport by the object of my years-long search, Linda Haynes. What would she look like? After all, no one had seen her in 20 years. She was now in her late 40s, and who knew if the years had been kind? She had confessed to me over the phone that she had put on a little weight; in her film years she dieted to keep down to a size five, eating lettuce with mustard on it and pretending it was something tastier. Now, she said, she was a size seven. Back home in Memphis I could count on one hand the middle-aged size sevens I knew.

As I reached the airport lobby, just beyond the security checkpoints, I sensed something moving parallel to me in my peripheral vision, a lithe blonde shadow. When I turned in that direction all I saw was a gorgeous mane of golden hair framed and glowing, backlit by rays from an airport skylight. When our eyes met she gave me that sly smirk. Out of 50 million women, I would have recognized Linda in an instant. True, her natural blonde hair now was obviously receiving a chemical helping hand, and it had the slight wind and sun damage one might expect of a woman who had lived near the sea her whole life. She looked almost exactly the same as in her final screen performance in *Guyana Tragedy*. There were few signs of either aging or those bleak periods when she battled addictions, stage fright, and bad marriages. She wore a long-sleeved white blouse with ruffles, blue jeans with a white belt, and white Keds. Two gold chains accented the curvature of her graceful neck. She also had a most wonderful smell; in a later correspondence she jokingly mentioned that she had drenched herself in orange blossom perfume. Whatever. It just smelled really good.

Before we had reached her home in Bonita Springs we had already fallen into heartfelt conversation. It was apparent she was taking my visit very seriously, and I could tell by her thoughtful answers to even some of my most basic small talk that this interview would be a soul-searching experience for her. I knew it had been a long time since she had given thought to her Hollywood career and films and the chain of events that had caused her to leave. I also felt that exploring why she left home and married at such a tender age would be opening old wounds, but she had assured me that she was ready and would discuss whatever was necessary.

Less than a mile from her home she looked at me and said, "Tom, there's something I didn't tell you about and I hope you don't mind. I have a boyfriend that I met here—he's a neighbor who helped me with some things after Saul left—and he moved in with us a few months back. I'll make him leave when we do our interview. My son, Leif, is playing over at some of his friends' houses."

Linda pulled into her carport under a two-level stilt home typical of South Florida. At the time her property was worth nearly half a million dollars partly because her house sat on a double lot that backed up to a narrow canal built for boaters. Two small pleasure boats were tied-up at her dock. The living quarters of her home were entirely on the upper level. The bottom level consisted of storage rooms and the carport. We walked up a long wooden staircase to a comfortable screened-in porch where Linda said she liked to sip her coffee in the quiet of the morning. Inside, the house was very tastefully appointed and filled with curios from her travels in the Caribbean such as sea shells and tribal masks. The walls featured several seascape paintings, quite accomplished, done by Linda who paints for relaxation and meditation. She is a much better artist than she lets on.

True to her word, Linda asked her boyfriend to leave us, but not before she had him bring up an old trunk from one of the storage rooms. That old trunk contained all of her Hollywood memories—letters from Melanie Griffith, references to some of her other friends, Alejandro Rey, Bo Hopkins, Sandra Dee's mother, glamour photographs by Douglas Kirkland and others, press releases, publicity stills, reviews, names, addresses. A decade's worth of film work, a life, all there in one moldy trunk.

When the house was cleared and the tape recorder turned on, Linda poured her heart out to a series of questions that meant to answer why such an uncommon talent could have left Hollywood and why Hollywood could have let her go. There were lots of funny stories—Linda has one of the world's great laughs—and anecdotes about some of her co-stars such as Robert Redford, Paul Newman, William Devane, and Powers Boothe, and then there were the tears about the difficult times, the times when she did feel like she had been turned out onto the streets at too early an age, the times when booze and pills seemed the only reasons for living even though they were killing her, the times she felt her hard work in the acting profession hadn't amounted to a damn thing.

Toward evening, Linda's boyfriend, who we will call Sam, returned from doing maintenance on Linda's boat. We sat around the table carrying on pleasant, sometimes hilarious, conversation. I asked Linda if I could take a few photographs of her (note: In my life I have lost very few things. Somewhere, somehow, these photos were lost). She didn't seem to mind, and went to fix her hair and put on some lipstick. Sam and I went outside on her wood deck and I took some preliminary light readings trying to figure out how to diminish the glare of the harsh Florida light. I snapped a few exposures and had her pose for a couple more when Sam began to offer suggestions for better poses and settings for the camera. He meant well, of course, but Linda gave him a look—*that* look, the one I had seen in several of her films—in which the blues of her eyes turned into tiny, flaming pilot lights. "Is that enough?" she asked in a way that was more an answer than a question. Sam shot me a quizzical look and shrugged his shoulders. That was that. The next day as she drove me to the airport she said, "We probably should have taken more pictures, huh?"

I had offered to take them both to dinner that night and they recommended a quaint seafood restaurant located on the water. We went in Sam's sleek boat and before we got far ominous storm clouds appeared seemingly out of nowhere and gathered almost right above the water. As Sam pulled into the boat dock at the restaurant, the skies opened and the rains, they came down. Despite the storm, we had a wonderful, memorable meal.

The next morning Linda and I were both running late. She met me at my motel dressed in a billowing sun dress with white sandals. I couldn't help but notice her toenails painted a screaming fire engine red. Because our previous boat ride had been towards evening and the sky had been streaked with a Frankenstein's inventory of lightning, Linda and Sam wanted to take me out into the Gulf to see some of the coastline sights. As a landlubber whose idea of water is the roiling Mississippi River, a river I might add that claims the life of just about every fool who attempts to swim it, I was both nervous and exhilarated as my surefootedness gave way to a rubber-legged balancing act. "This is where we come for our Sunday church," Linda said and opened her arms to all that was around her. Sam soon shot back the throttle and we bolted for the high seas, knifing through water of almost indescribable blue and green.

We passed bigger boats, smaller boats, a flotilla of jet skis, people casting lines from the banks, families picnicking and firing up their kettle grills. At a small inlet that let out into the Gulf, Sam idled the engine and I watched what appeared to be a brown carpet roll lazily under the boat. "That's a school of manta rays," Linda said, pointing. Within minutes we saw several dorsal fins surface and air spray from blow holes. A group of dolphins was herding a school of fish into the culvert for easier feeding.

The sun was high and felt good on my face. It wasn't long before we had to return; I had a plane to catch. As the Silver Stream boat glided over the lapping waves Linda took off her sandals and stood in the back of the boat, the wind whipping her sun dress nearly waist high, reminding me of Marilyn Monroe in *The Seven Year Itch*. Or was this a figment of my imagination, some film script of my own playing out in my head? Linda eventually lounged on some cushions in the boat's bow, stretching her legs out to meet the sun. Her face was profiled against the neon blue of the open sky, her blonde hair trailing like lengths of yellow ribbon. The wind continued to make her hemline dance around the top of her thighs. She was beautiful. As beautiful and mysterious as the 50-foot Linda I had encountered in that darkened theater in 1977.

Over the years our friendship deepened to the point I felt writing about her and some of the deeply personal things she had revealed to me would almost be a betrayal. Linda never voiced any such fear to me, but I was more than a little afraid to jeopardize that sense of trust. I have written about many people over the span of at least three decades yet never have I felt that way about any of my other subjects. Linda and I talked often and comforted each other through many ups and downs, particularly with relationships. Linda, to me, has been the voice of reason and sanity through my stormy marriages and at least one completely maddening relationship. She too has been through a couple of relationships that soured. Our children are close to the same age and we have seen them grow up and have children of their own.

Linda has visited me in Memphis and I have visited her in Bonita Springs. Our long into-the-night conversations are almost always the best part. She is now in her early 60s and still looks the Swedish beauty she was when she was younger. She takes her job as a legal assistant very seriously and in several instances I've watched her mind lock into some sort of legal tangle and quickly sort out what's what. Her sister Yvonne lives a short drive away and the two often spend their weekends together. They are best friends.

Health issues have become more troubling for Linda over the last decade. She has had several operations on her spine and neck, difficult surgeries all, and she battles the associated pains that plague those with back problems. Medications often leave her dizzy and off-balance and she has had some bad falls; she often walks with a cane to keep herself steady. As long as I have known her, she has been a heavy smoker and often smokes and drinks Diet Coke in the place of food. She is back down to a size five and maybe even a size four. The boat has been sold, her property has dropped in value by half, and she hasn't had a drop of alcohol in many, many years. She always told me only half-joking that she lived like a hermit and rarely socialized. Other than her sisters and her aging parents and perhaps a handful of friends that would include me, she stays mostly to herself.

The brooding, self-critical feelings she projected in character for the movies are most definitely a part of the real Linda. I cannot imagine her at a wild party. Ever.

Hollywood has occasionally knocked. The notorious actor and director Vincent Gallo coaxed Linda out of her Florida shell to interview her on camera for a proposed DVD package for *Human Experiments*. The project was shelved, which left Linda irritated and with a déjà vu all over again feeling. She was interviewed by several sci-fi and horror magazines and was pleased with how they turned out.

Recently, more DVD projects have come her way. She has been asked to be interviewed for new releases of *Rolling Thunder* and *Nickel Ride*. Due to her health concerns and the issue of having to take time off from work, she is not anxious to travel, particularly as far as California. So she has pretty much laid down the law that if anyone wants her, they can come to Florida.

Despite her statement that she wanted to be obscure, there seems to be a conspiracy afoot to make sure the spotlight shines on her at least one last time. At one of the sporadic Quentin Tarantino Film Fests he showed a print of *Rolling Thunder* and in his prefatory speech to the crowd said the following: "The performance of the film for me is Linda Haynes as Linda Forchet! She was in one of the sleepers for the first QT Fest, *The Nickel Ride* and she was in Pam Grier's *Coffy* ... she was the girl that reaches into Grier's afro when she has the razors in there and 'aaaahhhh.' But Linda Forchet is my favorite female character in a Paul Schrader movie. She looks like she's been left out in the rain one day too many. She has that look that Ava Gardner got, you know blowsy, but it took Ava years to do it, and Linda Haynes just did it naturally. And I mean that in a good way."

*Ain't It Cool News*, the popular film news website run by Harry Knowles, was invited to the QT Fest to screen *Rolling Thunder* and Knowles had the following to say about Linda: "I agree with Quentin, [Linda Haynes] is a marvel in this film. I love her dearly based on a single viewing. She has what I like to call ... 'Comfortable Beauty.' What I mean is this, today so many actresses working in Hollywood films are just plain gorgeous ... they have that unapproachable perfection about them. They seem like dolls to keep mint behind glass that you dare not touch. There's almost a fear to become intimate for fear of breaking the illusion. And there are women like [Linda] walking the earth we walk on every day. 'Comfortable Beauty' is a state of loveliness that you instantly want to engage in conversation, drinking with, watching films with, living with, spending time with. You can see no harsh lines, but an ability to adapt and swing with in life. There is an openness and ease to Linda Haynes' Forchet that is absolutely entrancing to me. I believe I fell deeply, madly for her when she picks up the revolver and shotgun and begins telling stories about her being the tomboy of the litter. She's that girl, and that's my favorite type."

To those who know the films of Linda Haynes, she is everyone's favorite type.

Linda Haynes in South Florida, 2010

# Linda Haynes's Filmography

Guyana Tragedy: The Story of Jim Jones (TV movie, 1980)
Brubaker (1980)
Human Experiments (1980)
Rolling Thunder (1977)
The Drowning Pool (1975)
Judgment: The Court Martial of Lieutenant William Calley (TV movie, 1975)
Paper Moon (TV series) – "Bonnie and Clyde" (1974)
The Nickel Ride (1974)
Coffy (1973)
My Three Sons (TV series) – "Second Banana" (1972)
Room 222 (TV series) – "Laura Fay, You're Okay!" (1971)
Latitude Zero (1969)

# Meat Eaters, Killers, and Suckers of Blood: Mano a Mano with Harry Crews

I CAME TO THE world of Harry Crews through a different path than most readers. I had read his profile of actor Robert Blake in *Esquire* magazine and had been profoundly disturbed by it. This was the mid-'70s, and I was a journalism student at Memphis State University, trying to mold myself and my writing in the style of the celebrity New Journalists of the day, such as Tom Wolfe and Hunter S. Thompson. Nothing I read had prepared me for the Blake profile. Crews used his subject more as an excuse to talk about himself than anything, cutting away from Blake's life to long autobiographical asides. The back and forth of the piece was almost dizzying, until I got the point that Harry saw Blake as a sort of doppelganger of himself. It was then that the logic of the piece fell into place.

After that, I cut a wide swath through Crews's novels and magazine work. A budding writer myself, I proposed an interview with Crews to the editors of *The Paris Review*, who agreed to consider the finished piece. A date was set with Harry to meet in Gainesville, Florida but at the last minute he seemingly disappeared and I was forced to cancel my flight. Another date was set in January 1979, and I decided to chance the flight when he told me his van was in the shop—he was stuck in Gainesville until it was repaired.

I caught up with Harry at his office at the University of Florida, and he seemed in particularly good spirits and ready to talk. The interview, I thought, went splendidly. I had no idea how close he was to a personal abyss, one that would keep him from writing another novel for nearly 10 years. *A Childhood* and *Blood and Grits* had just been released to great acclaim, and Harry Crews seemed well on his way to becoming a literary icon.

*The Paris Review* declined the interview because, I was told, George Plimpton did not appreciate Crews's "rough" sort of fiction. Thankfully, other publications saw the value in it.

**Tom Graves: In your writing there has been an inordinate interest in blood and violence. You've talked about things such as cockfighting that most people would consider to be a revolting, unpleasant part of the American underbelly, something that ought to be hidden from sight and not discussed. How did you develop your interests in these kinds of subjects?**

**Harry Crews:** I've always loved bloodsports. Cockfighting, bullfighting, dogfighting, and the rest of it. In fact, I have a piece coming out in *Esquire* about dogfighting. But this article is no defense of it. Rather it is an effort to see whether or not we tell the truth rather than being hypocritical, hippy-dippy bullshitting jack-offs about it. Whether or not we tell the truth, so that we might be able to say something about the culture we live in, the society and country we come from, which God knows has gotta be among the more bloody countries that we know in history.

I point out that when Indian Red Lopez fought David

Kotey for the featherweight championship of the world, it took 37 stitches to close Kotey's face. It took seven to close Indian Red Lopez's face. What's football if it's not a bloodsport? You know, guys getting broken legs. Leroy Jordan's played a whole goddamn season with a broken bone—a non-weight-bearing bone—in the bottom half of his leg.

**Graves: Certainly during the first half of the century, baseball was considered America's favorite pastime. It now seems that football has taken over as America's favorite sport, and I'm wondering if it's because it's a more violent sport.**

**Crews:** I'm not really sure it has, it just seems that way. If you read and look at the figures that baseball teams and ballparks draw and television audiences and so on, you'll see that it's comparable to football. I'd be the last one to say it's because we got bloodier or because we got more violent or because we see it in a microcosm of our macrocosm of the world that we live in.

It's true, however, that when a player gets hurt on the field, the camera always pans away from him. The camera goes somewhere else, or the announcer guys says something like, "Well, we see a player is down on the 30-yard line. He doesn't seem to be moving. He's not getting up. We'll be back after this message." After you come back the player's already gone, they've toted him off the field. It's the same with baseball when two dugouts empty. When they come out with baseball bats in their hands, they always pan away from it. I don't think people like that though. They wanta see the fight. They wanta see the race driver at Sebring or wherever fry in his own car. "His back end is getting loose, he's up on the wall. He's spinning, my God, he's on fire! We'll be back after this word from our announcer." Or some bullshit thing like that. Well, yeah, uh-huh. Everybody's saying, "Aw, why couldn't you pan in on him close? See him a-squirming."

**Graves: In nearly every one of your novels there is a scene of a crowd that goes on a rampage. Do you have a fascination with crowd psychology, what we as a people do when we're in a crowd together?**

**Crews:** That's true. Maybe I am fascinated or appalled or dumbfounded with them. We are a crowd society. Whatever crowds do are likely to get more news coverage, whether they be riots, whether they be sit-ins, whether they be pickets at a big company. Whether they be a whole bunch of Iranian students with paper masks over their faces trying to get rid of the Shah, which, thank God, they've already done now. The sonofabitch will never get back in there again. I don't know that that holy man's going to do much better, but at least he's not going to do as bad as the Shah did. *I don't think.* This is just my own personal opinion; one might even say bias or prejudice. Whatever.

The point is that in a crowd men and women, because of a certain anonymity, because they are less likely to be identified and held responsible for their own actions, what they are, what's back there lurking, always comes out. And what comes out, coach, I'm sorry to say it—I ain't a doomsayer, I ain't pessimistic, it doesn't matter to me. Well, it does matter to me because I'm in the world with them, and I don't want to get killed or mutilated—but what comes out inevitably is just the worst kind of that thing that we all hide. We're meat eaters, that's the thing. There are vegetarians—spiritual vegetarians, emotional vegetarians, political vegetarians, and those who are vegetarians in fact—who deny that the front teeth are cutters. A human has got in his mouth a 550 pounds per square inch bite. You don't need that kind of bite to eat asparagus. You need that kind of bite to eat meat. These are cutters and these are grinders. They pretend we are something else.

It gives me no pleasure particularly to talk about that we are not what we would seem in the world. But that we are in fact meat eaters, killers, suckers of blood, and riders of one another. But in all that, there is beauty, there is humor, there is joy, there is ecstacy. I think all my books are obviously funny, there are places in them that are funny, with the possible exception of the last one, *A Childhood*. It's not that I *meant* to put humor in there, it's just in there.

Graham Greene said that he reserved the right to depict unbelievers of the Roman Catholic faith with the same kind of power he depicted believers. Of course, that got him into a lot of trouble. By and large, people want to confirm what is weakest in them. That is, their propensity for charity, sympathy, contributions to the afflicted, smiles, happy home life. They want all that confirmed, when in point of fact that is what's weakest in them. Because it is the least substantial in them. Who's ever got close to a marriage that didn't find a rotten core, a nest of snakes at the middle of it? Okay, there's joy in it, happiness in it, and there's pleasure in raising kids that go and do something. That's cool. I'm all for that. The fact that it's a sham, the fact that it's bullshit, need not necessarily upset us too much.

They want that confirmed. As soon as you start writing about the other things, that are just as much a part of us as any of the other, when you start writing about blood and violence and the predisposition to put your foot on another man's neck and let him carry you, then everybody objects.

It takes my dear old mother as long to read a book as it does me to write one. She went through the second grade. She reads everything I write. She's never blinked at any of it. And she talks about it well. She says to me, my dear mother, "Son, why don't you write a book that's happy and nice and full of smiles?" And I told her, "Mama, when one comes to me, I will."

**Graves: Don't you think your mother knows that what you write about is a part of her as well?**

**Crews:** Naw, I don't really think so. When I used to work for *Playboy* so much, she used to always get the magazines and look in them. She didn't even know such a thing as *Playboy* existed in the world 'til I started writing in it, and God only knows what went through her poor ol' dear mind when she opened the book and saw all them naked ladies in there. I bet she thought, "They touchin' theyselves, they touchin' theyselves, godamighty, they touchin' theyselves."

**Graves:** In the beginning of your book *The Gypsy's Curse*, you quote Diane Arbus. The quote, "My favorite thing is to go where I've never been," seems doubly appropriate because it appears to echo your own life, and Arbus in her photographs portrayed a dying world much like the one you depict in the book. Would you agree that your outlook is similar to hers?

**Crews:** I don't know. I am a great admirer of Diane Arbus, dead now, as you know, of suicide. I'm a great admirer of hers for one thing you'll notice: all of Diane Arbus's people that she photographed are looking dead into the camera. Next time you look in her book, notice that. Not looking off. Lookin' dead into the camera. Every last one of them. I know her brother, Howard Nemerov, a very fine poet.

I read her preface, which was really a kind of talk she had given to a class, and they put it posthumously as an introduction to her book of photographs, where she talked about, "My favorite thing is to go where I've never been." The real point is this: Not that I feel she and I … that she's one of us, although I do feel that way. But rather that business, "My favorite thing is to go where I've never been," has to do with the fact that many writers, painters, playwrights, so on—artists of whatever kind—have said that when they become American expatriates and live in Europe, you see America so much better from Paris than you do from Alma, Georgia. You see America so much better from Munich than you do from Chicago, and it's because there is the distancing of the subject. Get back so that you can see it.

Working in carnivals, living as I did with them ... I traveled twenty-seven hundred miles with a gambler for a piece that I wrote for *Playboy*, called "Carny," being with, I don't know, what society considers outcasts or not very nice folk. Being with them, minorities of whatever sort, Chicanos, Jews, blacks, south Georgia tenant farmers, and also gamblers, pimps, prostitutes, street hustlers for smack, skag, coke, that whole sort of thing, you get a view of the world from where they are that you would never get sitting in this office in this boondoggle of a building on a multimillion-dollar university.

**Graves: There is a freak of some sort in every one of your novels except *A Feast of Snakes*. Why is this book the exception?**

**Crews:** If you are determined to find freaks, think of them in that way, obviously the sheriff with a peg leg shot off in the Vietnam war, is a freak. He rapes the black girl, she subsequently having all manner of hallucinations and distorted perceptions about snakes in her world. Her mother's hair is snakes. She sees snakes and all the rest of it. She then emasculates him with a razor out of her shoe. I suppose that if you are determined to think of it in terms of freaks, that's as freaky as anything I've done.

The thing people won't admit is that when somebody says the word "freak" you think of somebody with eight toes or three legs or something like that. But there are spiritual freaks, emotional freaks, political freaks, educational freaks, people who are distorted and asymmetrical. People whose equipment, whatever it may be, arms, legs, whatever, don't work the way they oughta work. I suppose that if I were of the mind to think that way about freaks, I would say that *A Feast of Snakes* is part and parcel of everything I've ever done. People dumping poor Joe Lon over the fence into the snake pit, and him surfacing like a swimmer with snakes hanging from his cheeks. I mean, if that ain't freak city, what is it? I'm saying this for *your* benefit. For the reader's benefit. I don't think about it that way.

**Graves: How do you answer the critics who charge that your work is filled with gratuitous violence and characters that are grotesque?**

**Crews:** I answer the charge by saying that they can't read fiction, that they don't know anything about fiction, that they don't know what fiction is. There is *nothing* gratuitous in my work. There are no descriptions of landscapes that are gratuitous, there are no descriptions of people that are gratuitous. There is nothing in my work that is not necessary and inevitable to the action, the place, and the circumstances that I'm writing about.

Faulkner once said to someone—not that I'm comparing myself to Faulkner, God forbid—but this person asked him, "Mr. Faulkner, what do you think of people who read your books and say they don't understand it?" And his response was, "Read it again." Yeah.

So, the dumbasses out there that are watching television until they are rotting in their souls, watching Walter Cronkite and *Happy Days*, who cannot read my fiction, and say that it's gratuitous, I say they have no eyes, no ears, no heart, no mouth, no sympathy, no charity for the human predicament. And they think that the human predicament and situation is living over in suburbia with a high wall around yourself and worrying about your annuities and your tax-sheltered income. That's my answer.

**Graves: What do you think of the type of violence Sam Peckinpah depicts in his films?**

**Crews:** All Sam Peckinpah ever did in his movies was show that getting hit on the chin doesn't sound like (*makes a small popping noise*). When one grown man hits another grown man in the face, it splatters like an overripe tomato. And it's not fun getting killed. It's bloody and gory and altogether unpleasant. That's all Sam Peckinpah ever did.

**Graves: What about the fact that Peckinpah's violence and death are often done in slow motion, which is usually associated in the language of film with romance and eroticism? It makes one wonder if the American public is now equating death with eroticism.**

**Crews:** Naw, the American public isn't doing anything but worrying about its tax-sheltered incomes, as far as I'm concerned. They only know slow motion from *The Bionic Man*, where the guy is supposed to be able to run—I don't know—900 miles an hour, and supposed to jump 50 feet in the air. The way the director and the producer and the writer have got around that is when he's going 900 miles an hour to put it in slow motion. And hippy-dippy America out there thinks, "Man, he's going *900 miles an hour.* Wow!" Now why Sam Peckinpah did his thing in slow motion....

**Graves: Going back to *A Feast of Snakes*, have you been to the rattlesnake roundup that they have every year in Sweetwater, Texas?**

**Crews:** No, did not. I've been to Sweetwater, Texas but not for the rodeo. I think it was in the Blake piece in *Esquire* where I said I was in a jail in Grapevine, Texas a couple of years ago. But I get in jails. All the time.

**Graves: From raising a lot of hell?**

**Crews:** Just that. Getting drunk. Whatever. It's nothing to get excited about. I'm not proud of it. I really am not. But, I'm not ashamed of it either.

**Graves: How did you become interested in rattlesnake rodeos like the one you depict in *A Feast of Snakes*?**

**Crews:** Charné, this girl who I lived with for five years, and I went to—just fucking off. I work very hard when I work and when I don't work, I don't work very hard. And she and I went to a place. I'm trying to remember the name of it. It's just down from Mystic, Georgia. There really is a Mystic,

Georgia and it was just down from there. A little town in south Georgia, just about 75 miles from where my people live. And we went up there to one. I went as a participant. You know, to catch snakes. And of course they had a big place there where you could eat it. You didn't have to buy it. They gave it away to the hunters, the rattlesnake meat cooked.

It's good stuff. I cook my own, though. They don't exactly have my recipe. My recipe that's in the book [*A Feast of Snakes*] I got off a guy in Mississippi. It's good firm meat if you don't overcook it. It's a little like fish; if you overcook it, the tissue breaks down. It's mush. Most people need a thermometer to cook fish or snake or meat, for that matter. But I can pretty much do it with my fingers. I can just reach in the oven and press it and know when it's about right.

**Graves: So you don't fry it?**

**Crews:** I fry it to begin with, then I finish up in the oven. It makes it crispier. I deep-fry it, but then I take it out of there when it's about three-quarters done, put it on a dry, flat pan and bake it, and then it gets all crispy and nice.

**Graves: Did Auntie, the old black woman you talk about in *A Childhood*, inspire your fascination with snakes?**

**Crews:** I don't know if she did or not. I suspect that Auntie inspired more than I'll ever know. 'Cause I was young. I'm convinced that those years up to the time you're six or seven years old, that's where you really get bent. That's where you get toward wherever you're going.

**Graves: Many of the characters in your work appear to be allegorical. For example, the Fat Man in *Naked in Garden Hills* seems to represent a person who is imprisoned within his own soul. Of course, he is literally imprisoned by his own flesh.**

**Crews:** The same with the Gospel Singer. The Gospel Singer was given his voice. He didn't work for it, it was a gift. His problem was, and it's as old as literature is, he did not want to be God's man of the world. He did everything he could do, possibly think of, to get rid of it. He didn't mind singing and making money, and making people happy. But he didn't want everybody's soul on his hands. Or on his conscience. Again, that's a thing that goes back about as far as we know in literature. Denying what you are, the chosen of the gods … that sounds like a marvelous thing to be, chosen of the gods or God. But it is not. It is a terrible responsibility. They end up hanging him on a tree limb when he tells the truth.

The simple fact is that I think of everything I do as being—I don't know quite how to say this—as violent and as despicable as many people find it, I think of it as all work, man's relationship to God, man's relationship to his own true nature, as opposed to what he bullshits people into thinking his own true nature is. Most of my work, almost all of it if you look at it, the novels anyway—well, there's nothing to write about except good and bad. That's all the reader's interested in. Who's at fault and who's not. It's all a moral question. Dylan

Thomas was asked why he wrote his poetry, and he said he wrote it in praise of God, "and I would have been a fool to have done otherwise." I can't really say I've written in praise of God, but certainly the thing that preoccupies me the most is affairs of the heart, which always translates into who's right and who's wrong.

As we all know, there are no black hats and white hats in the world. We're all wrong and we're all right. We're all mixed. But try to get people to admit it. I mean, some of our greatest saints, at least in the Roman Catholic view of things, the greatest saints were some of our greatest sinners, cheaters, fuckers of ladies, dicers, you name it. St. Paul, who was on the road to Damascus when he saw the burning bush, was a real son of a bitch. Before he got the word. Just a son of a bitch. And you don't suppose all that went out with him as soon as he saw the burning bush?

It's like courage. All courage is, is fear controlled. Everybody's scared when the heat starts coming down. You're terrified. Whether it's in a fight, whether it's some jack-off in the Marine Corps says you got to slide across a rope over boiling rapids or in a river or whatever it is. Sure, you'd be a fool not to be scared. It's the control of the fear. And when you look inside yourself and see that you are ... well, I give you a quote. Johann Wolfgang von Goethe said, "There is no crime of which I cannot conceive myself guilty." It seems to me that he was simply a great poet admitting his involvement with mankind. But all these people that say [*in exaggerated Southern accent*], "He's jest writin' about all them nasty thangs. You ought to do what Shakespeare did." The hell. What is

Shakespeare all about? It's about regicide, betrayal, lopping off heads, you name it."

**Graves: You and I both were raised Southern Baptists and rejected it when we came of age. Why do you think Southern Baptists have the reputation of being among the meanest, most prejudiced, most narrow-minded …?**

**Crews:** I'm not sure I can subscribe to that or do. The fact [is] that they are mean in the sense of being small, their angle of vision—what they admit into their society, into their lives, into their emotions, into their charity, into their sympathy, is very small.

Up where I come from, for instance—not to get into political or social matters—but the plight of the blacks has not changed one bit. They still go to the back door, they still live on whatever they can find. Black real estate, the shanties, is very valuable, because there is only a few places those folks can live. So, if you've got a little shanty, and you want to charge 70 dollars a month for it, and the damn thing has no running water, no electricity, and the outhouse is in the back and got cracks two inches wide in it—you can get the 70 dollars a month, 'cause they got no damn alternative. It's not as though they can go in town and rent an apartment for 70 dollars. Right around where I come from they still got everything nicely compartmentalized. And they still run in all those all things about, "Some of my best friends are …" or "I've always been good to them." Or whatever. I'm glad that they've got the burden of that on their hearts and not me. Because I don't know how the hell I'd deal with it.

**Graves: The people I've known who were the most racist, the most hawkish during the Vietnam War, the most conservative in the rankest sort of way, the ones most eager to trample on the Bill of Rights for their own personal agendas, are nearly always Southern Baptists.**

**Crews:** I suspect it has to do with the God they worship. Southern Baptists, generally if you talk to them, really think they are worshipping the God of the New Testament. They aren't at all. Matter of fact, I talked to an old guy in Georgia last time I was home and he said, "I don't know what it is everybody wantin' somethin' new, new all the time. Talk about the New Test-a-ment. What's wrong with the Old Test-a-ment?" Now here was a guy never read the damn Bible—*damn* Bible … mustn't say that … Jeez, forgive me—never read the Bible, he just carried it around in his hand. Southern Baptists worship the God of wrath, the God that gives to schemers, the God that benefits the strong and lets them walk on the weak. The New Testament God obviously is a God of forgiveness and a God of love and a God of the rest of it.

It's very curious if you really get to talking to cradle Catholics or cradle Baptists or cradle Lutherans or cradle Methodists or cradle Unitarians, or whatever, just how little they really know of their religion. They go in there, they're like a mule grinding cane. He grinds cane all day and you put him in a lot and he still walks in a circle.

There's much about myself and what I believe and what

I do that I don't know. That I can't answer for. That I can't talk rationally about. I don't apologize for that. It just happens to be the way things are.

**Graves: There seems to be an awful lot of bitterness in your writing. Several critics have called this bitterness your method of revenge toward our society. For example, Paul Zimmerman in his review of *A Feast of Snakes* in *Newsweek* says, "There is a strong smell of revenge in his writing. Behind his comic grotesquerie keens the angry cry of a man enraged that life can be so cruel, and people so victimized by the lumpen conditions of their lives.**

**Crews:** [*interrupts*] The last half of it I would agree with. The revenge part I would not agree with. If you say bitterness toward the people in my book, I have a feeling that you can't write about people that you are bitter toward, that you hate. I'm not bitter toward the people in my fiction. But, yes I am bitter, and I am angry that the human situation is what it is. That we out of hand destroy whole cultures, as the Indians were destroyed. As we have tried to destroy the Chicanos. That we destroyed the blacks. That we are busily still destroying them. For all our protestations to the contrary, that we are anti-Semitic. All the Jew jokes. The Chief of Staff of the Armed Forces saying the Jews control this and that not too long ago. If somebody sounds different than we sound—that is, the voice, accent—we are right on his back. "Southerners are obviously ignorant and dumb because of the way they talk." People from Brooklyn.

I think that the collective consciousness of America would make us all sound like disc jockeys if they could. All alike. You take a disc jockey out of Gainesville and put him in San Francisco, and he won't have any trouble. He's got those pear-shaped notes and those mellow tones. He wouldn't have any problem. It is that lust for standardization which will be the death of us all eventually. They would have us all sound like a disc jockey if they could.

**Graves: Why is the lead character in every one of your novels an alienated male?**

**Crews:** I don't know, I don't know. You see, these are questions that writers can't answer. Many times they develop convenient lies about these questions that they tell at cocktail parties. "I did this because of this, this, and the rest of it." I think my characters are men because I have grave reservations about my ability to create a woman that could sustain a novel. That's first. That's the male part of it. The alienation part of it, I have never thought of it, I've never thought about it just in those terms. But I have, of necessity, been alien to the place I have found myself since I was very, very young. I left the farm when I was 17, and I have never been back there to live.

I wrote recently that I have been in the University of Florida for more or less 20 years, but I've been *in* it, never *of* it. I have no friends in the university, as we would count friends where I came from. Not one. I don't see 'em, I don't go to the places they go, I don't go to their parties. I talk to 'em in a professional capacity if we have common problems in the university. But friends, no.

I don't suppose you could imagine a more alienated human being than a south Georgia sharecropper who must move every year from one leeched-out patch of soil to another. Never owning anything. With his back continually to the wall. Other people get medical care. He gets none. Other people get oranges and grapefruit or lemon to keep from getting trench mouth or scurvy, but he has none. Other people have children who have shoes. But his have none. I mean, if he's not alienated, who the hell is? Maybe if I write about alienated male characters, maybe this alienation comes just from my own life.

**Graves: Are Marvin Molar in *The Gypsy's Curse* and Joe Lon Mackey in *A Feast of Snakes* really the same character? Extensions of the same psyche?**

**Crews:** They have both been trained throughout their lives to do something they thought would save them. And then they had the rug jerked out from under them. How the hell was Joe Lon supposed to know he was supposed to read? Nobody ever told him. He was supposed to run over other boys, which he did with great efficiency. And then it came up all of a sudden that he wasn't able to go to college, and he had been trained for violence. Trained to run over people. Then it was all ended. What the hell was he supposed to do? That's enough to drive anybody to a breakdown or violence or murder or anything else.

**Graves: Are these characters maybe extensions of your own anger?**

**Crews:** I don't want to push this anger thing too far. I'm not *that* angry. The reason so much of what is said about me by so many people again gets back to the thing I told you when we first started. Most people can't write fiction. They don't know what fiction is about. They know nothing of craft. They're not readers. And they do not have the emotional capacity to put themselves into other people's shoes. Suck themselves out of their own skin and get into somebody else's skin for a while. If they did they would be readers of fiction, supporters of plays, and readers of poetry. They are not.

I don't pay much attention to those people who say I'm alienated, bitter, or put gratuitous violence or this or that or the other. I mean, I spent 30 years learning what I do and I take gross exception to your basic female book page editor or male book page editor who is worried about everything except books. My life is reading and writing and some few things to divert me when I'm not doing that.

**Graves: Your prose style has a power and punch to it I've seen in very little other work, but obviously you've had your literary influences. Who were they?**

**Crews:** I don't pattern my style after anybody consciously, but obviously we stand on other people's shoulders. I probably learned more from Graham Greene, the English novelist … *The End of the Affair, Brighton Rock, The Power and the Glory,* and so on. His autobiography, called *A Sort of Life*, I wrote a long thing on for *The Los Angeles Times*. I learned a lot from him. My first [hero] in letters was Somerset Maugham. But then after I got to be about 22, I began to understand why he was called, by certain writers, "that old whore of literature." So I got off him. Faulkner has influenced us all, on whatever continent. Flannery O'Connor. Currently the young writers that I admire: Cormac McCarthy, Richard Price, Thomas McGuane—not necessarily *Ninety-Two in the Shade*, but other things he has done. There's a whole bunch. Don't matter. When you ask somebody what books they learned on, or what writers they admire, it's like asking somebody which of their own novels they like the most.

**Graves: Who would you say are some contemporary writers that are overrated? Let's start with Norman Mailer. He gave you a nice little plug on *A Feast of Snakes*.**

**Crews:** Overrated? Oh, I don't know, man. Norman Mailer is a genius by anybody's accounting, but he spreads himself thin. He takes on assignments that he really shouldn't take on. Norman Mailer's willing to talk, if he's got the time, to anybody about anything. Much of it I should think—although God knows I would hope he forgives me if he sees this—because of all those wives and all those children. He has to turn about a million dollars a year before he makes a nickel himself. You know, whatever he's got, 11 or 12 kids, and three or four wives.

**Graves: What do you think about the feuds he's had with other writers?**

**Crews:** Like Gore Vidal? You take a book of Vidal's like his collection of short stories, *A Thirsty Evil*, is just a marvelous book. His first novel was *Williwaw*, which he wrote when he was about 21 and still in the service. I don't admire the things that he is best known for. I don't admire *Myron*, although I read it. I don't admire *Myra Breckinridge*, which I also read. The guy just about can do anything. He's a great researcher. He has a good mind. He's a journeyman of the language.

When James Agee died, his obituary was in the *Sewanee Review*. He went to prep school right outside of Sewanee, [Tennessee] at the Episcopalian high school called St. Andrews. When he died his obituary read, "He was born a prince of the language, and so he remained."

Well, I believe the same thing is true of Truman Capote. Capote's reputation rests primarily, well, almost exclusively among people who know, with his short stories. And with his short novels. Things like *Breakfast at Tiffany's*. Short things. Ever since *In Cold Blood*, beginning with *In Cold Blood*, starting with *In Cold Blood*, everything thereafter we can dismiss, I think.

**Graves: Such as those excerpts of *Answered Prayers* that have appeared in *Esquire*?**

**Crews:** Yeah, right. But Capote is a marvelous intellect. Has a marvelous, a most wonderful sense of perception. But he's about done for.

**Graves: It seems like he's more into that New York disco Studio 54 bullshit these days than writing.**

**Crews:** He's always been sort of a jet-setter. But he just about went apeshit on a radio program in New York not long ago. He started talking about suicide, and they cut him off the air. This was about 18 months ago.

**Graves: Is this when he was having his heavy bouts with drinking?**

**Crews:** He's always had a drinking problem. He's had a drinking problem for 20 fucking years. I felt very sorry for him. I know it's kind of clichéd to say it, and the rest of it, but my heart went out to him because I know what it is to be locked into that kind of world. Yeah, he's a class A alcoholic. I guess he's not beating it, and don't want to beat it. You know, the whole uppers and downers kind of thing. You take five milligrams Dex to get up in the morning. You take a Valium or a Quaalude, or a bootleg Quaalude, which you can get fairly easily, which will put you to sleep. Which will give you a case of, as Terry Southern calls them, "the whips and jingles" the next morning. You know, you sleep well that night and when you wake up your fucking hands are shaking, your eyes are jumping, your spine is pogo-sticking. You get into that world where you just keep doing pills and alcohol and you get into a *bad thing*, man. That's a one-way street. Won't get you anywhere.

**Graves: Can people write stoned like that?**

**Crews:** You can't write that way. You can't write messed up.

**Graves: Are there any books you think of as failures in some way?**

**Crews:** Yeah, there are books that have already been labeled as failures in many cases. *Across the River and into the Trees*, by Hemingway, I think is a failure, also in Hemingway's case *To Have and Have Not*, which was actually three separate pieces of stuff put together—that was a failure. Faulkner's *A Fable* is a failure.

**Graves: What do you think of the Beat movement? Did Kerouac or any of those writers have any impact on your work?**

**Crews:** That Beat thing was just a little ripple in a very large pond. If Jack Kerouac had only been able to keep it together, hold it together. You know he died a rank conservative about a hundred and fifty miles from where we sit, in the Tampa-St. Petersburg area, living off his mother, with a John Kennedy half dollar taped to his navel?

**Graves: A what?**

**Crews:** A John Kennedy half dollar. He wore it all the time.

**Graves: That's a new one on me. Why did he do that?**

**Crews:** He admired the guy, and he was a little nuts. He was dying and he knew it. There are some writers who, apparently, never make a false move, but they are very, very far and few between. That's why a writer wants 20 or 30 titles.

**Graves: So he can be assured of having a couple of good books under his belt?**

**Crews:** You see, you write 20 or 30 in hopes that you will have one. My life is justified if I can write *one* good book.

**Graves: Are there any of your own books that you don't like now, looking back on them?**

**Crews:** My books? No, no. I like *all* my own books. I really do. I think *Naked in Garden Hills* is probably as good as I'll ever do. I know everybody takes exception to that. I like the *Snake* book. Well, what the hell, I like the *Karate* book, the *Gypsy* book. I mean, what can I say?

**Graves: Out of curiosity, what has been your biggest seller?**

**Crews:** Far and away *The Gospel Singer* made more money than anything else.

**Graves: I know it was the first novel you published. Was it the first novel you wrote?**

**Crews:** It was the fifth novel I wrote. The other four were not published and will never be published simply because they were not good enough. They were finger exercises or something. *The Gospel Singer*, the *Karate* book, the *Snake* book, the book I just did, *A Childhood*, those have been the most successful, if you measure success in terms of money. And I like money just as much as anyone else. It buys you time. It buys you freedom. It buys you food. It helps the people you care about and have responsibilities to. So I ain't knocking money.

I don't guess any writer I know, I can't think of one that I know personally who measures the success of his work in terms of the money it makes. Any guy who tells you he don't like money up to a point … I don't mean that you have to sell your ass to get it, sell yourself to get it. But money keeps your child warm. It gives him some orange juice for breakfast, a couple of eggs, some very expensive bacon. It gives them three dollars to eat lunch on. And that night when he comes in he has a nice meat loaf, a baked chicken, or a steak or something. So, yeah, you try to raise a boy that's going to grow up with his bones right and strong and durable. You want to feed him right. You want him to sleep right. So, money's important in that way.

But in terms of the satisfaction you get from doing something or the way you feel about it, money ain't shit. Money does not count. It just simply does not. If money meant anything, then you would never become a writer anyway. You would make more money, certainly initially anyway, certainly in the first four or five or six or maybe even 10 years, you could make more money if you could get some money together and get yourself a filling station. Hire a couple of guys. Pump a little gas. Lube a few cars, change some oil. You'd make more money that way.

There are obviously exceptions. Some people who have their sensibilities tuned in to the lowest common denominator the way we were taught in school. Maybe you weren't. You're younger than I am. In the multiplication of fractions you gotta find the lowest common denominator. They got their sensibilities tuned into the lowest common denominator. They write a book that an awful lot of people buy. But one has to remember that art is not democratic, it is aristocratic.

**Graves: That is exactly what the critic John Simon has said about art and language.**

**Crews:** Well, if we went out there and looked at a motor in a car of a certain sort, maybe somebody would look in there and say, "Gee, it's all shiny and looks impressive." But somebody else looks in there and they see what the parts do and they see what they are. They see the essential nature of the machine and the parts. And to suppose that the people who can only say, "Gee, it's shiny, it looks nice," that their opinion is equal to people who know why the damn machine does what it does, is madness.

**Graves: In *Car* you hit on our American obsession with cars, particularly here in the South. Do you think there is a kind of Cadillac American dream we all buy into?**

**Crews:** I think there is a kind of Cadillac dream, a kind of

Cadillac conception of America. It does not exclusively belong to Southerners. Stock car racing and the rest of it came out of the South because of running moonshine and because a powerful, shiny car was one thing that poor people could get ahold of. I do not mean to slur black people or mean this to be pejorative, but a black that lives in a shack because he can't go anywhere else, can't know anything else, he can get himself a great big car. Those of us in the South who were tenant farmers are the same sort of folk. I didn't learn to drive a car until I was 21 years old. My brother didn't learn to drive a car until he was 25. We knew all about mules, but nothing about cars.

Talk about anger and the rest of it, the thing I got a case for is cars. Every man in this country has his car to eat. And we will, by God, eat it. Because Detroit is spewing them out one every so many minutes. They have taken over Detroit. Why would you have at various intersections, four gas stations on each of the four corners available? Do we need that many gas stations? The answer is no. No we don't. The pollutants in the air—you can check me on this in the statistical abstracts in the library, but I think one out of every six people in America works for the automobile industry or in a related job. The whole business of fat people who are out of shape and can't do anything, can't be, in prison terminology, "a stand-up guy," they step on that accelerator, squeal those tires. It's not the car so much, this powerful squealing of the wheels, it's *them*. They feel that. It's all out of that enormous thing that the novel comes.

**Graves:** What does the South represent to you?

**Crews:** The South represents to me a place, first and foremost. People who have, in Flannery O'Connor's words, "manners." Which doesn't have to do with saying thank you, or wiping your mouth, or not sneezing on your sleeve. Manners—simply to her in the sense that she used it posthumously in a book called *Mystery and Manners*—means just the way we view the world, the way we view ourselves. The way we proceed in our day-to-day activities with other people. You have to know about the manners of your people before you can write about them. The South is about the last people, the last area of the country, who have that sort of communal manners. We are among the last people who have a certain way of talking, accents.

**Graves:** Why is it that a Southerner from Florida can feel a kinship with ...

**Crews:** [*interrupts*] 'Cause I don't come from Florida, I come from Georgia. Florida's not the South. Florida's got nothing to do with the South. There's a little panhandle up there that has to do with Alabama, that should have been given to Alabama. But Florida's not the South, not the South at all. It's almost like being in exile.

**Graves:** But aren't there parts of Florida ...?

**Crews:** Up around the panhandle. This is the watermelon-growing capital of the world right through here, but no, by and large Florida's not the South.

**Graves: Okay, your point is taken. Let's say for the sake of discussion that a person from Georgia can go to Arkansas and feel a kinship simply because he's a fellow Southerner. I'm trying to get at why this is so.**

Crews: Because we are the only people in these United States that have been defeated. Had an occupying army and had tribute exacted of us. That's all. One doesn't want to be a professional Southerner. One doesn't want to hash over that stuff too much. But the fact remains that the rest of the country doesn't know what it means to have the equivalent of tanks roaring through the countryside. To having tribute exacted of it.

**Graves: What do you think of the genteel South we see depicted in so many novels and plays? The kind of writing I call "granny fiction," where we have a lot of reminiscing about sitting on the front porch swing smelling the azaleas in bloom and all that stuff. Things like some of Eudora Welty's later novels.**

Crews: I happen to like Miss Welty and her work. I've met her. I met her in New York at the American Academy of Arts and Letters. And they gave me an award which came with 3,000 dollars, which I promptly blew. But I like her work, I like her stories. I don't think there's a finer story in the language than a story like "Powerhouse." How does a little old lady in a white hat who belongs to the garden club in Jackson,

Mississippi write about a black jazz band on tour? This is in "Powerhouse." How the hell does she come up with a line like, "And it was hello and good-bye and they were all down on the first note like a waterfall?" What marvelous symmetry of sentence and language and sound and image. Now her novels are quite another matter.

**Graves: Like *The Optimist's Daughter*?**

**Crews:** I just have to beg off here and say … Well, I don't like Henry James either. I always thought that was a flaw in me somehow. I've learned a lot from his prefaces, but I can't read him.

I've got a good friend named Dan Wakefield, who's one of the contributing editors at the *Atlantic Monthly*, who wrote *Going All the Way* and *Starting Over*, and Dan told me, "I'll teach you to read Henry James if you'll teach me to read Faulkner." See, he can't read the other guy. I cannot read Miss Welty's novels. I cannot. I can start and I can struggle, but I can't finish it. But that's all right. Katherine Anne Porter, that thing on Sacco and Vanzetti that she published two years ago was a goddamned embarrassment. It was garbled and badly organized. *Ship of Fools* was a big novel that was a best-seller that nobody read. But her place in American literature is safe on the basis of *Flowering Judas* and *Leaning Tower* and other collections of short stories.

**Graves: We now have the New South to deal with and in Eudora Welty's South we had the slow, genteel,**

well-mannered place you just talked about. But the South you depict is explosive, fast, often violent, and unpredictable. Tempers flare. Is there such a thing anymore as this slow, polite South?

**Crews:** I think there probably is to some extent. I mean, I was taught to say "sir" to anybody who was older than I was, and I even say it to people who are younger than I am because I grew up saying that. I grew up not calling a man by his first name until I knew him. You just didn't do that. There is a certain restraint, a certain reticence for people who are not of our kind and of our place. There is that isolated, insular quality of the South that nobody can deny. Course, if you talk about the slow pace of the South in terms of elbows and knees and rolling eyes and shuffling along and "feets don't fail me now" kind of bullshit, then no, there is not a slow South. But anyplace where the sun shines hotter, people are going to slow down. That's just a fact.

**Graves: I'm curious—did your depiction of women such as Hard Candy in *A Feast of Snakes* or blacks such as Lummy in *A Feast of Snakes* stir up any cries from feminists or black groups?**

**Crews:** Nope. Nope. I don't have anything like that, don't get anything like that.

**Graves: Do you think it's because the people who read your books are perceptive enough …?**

**Crews:** I don't know what it is. There was a time, when I figured if I got a letter from a reader—it usually comes by way of the publisher; they send it to the publisher 'cause they don't know where you live—I assumed it was a bad letter, and generally it was. But that's all changed. The specific examples you reference—Lummy and Hard Candy—no. No fem libbers, no black groups, no black people have said things. That doesn't necessarily mean they weren't thinking it.

**Graves: There are parts, particularly in *A Feast of Snakes*, where it seems to me things could pretty easily be misconstrued.**

**Crews:** Anything that I have written could be misconstrued.

**Graves: One thing I think you've done a splendid job of getting into is the jock mystique that is so prevalent in our culture, particularly in football. Joe Lon Mackey seems to represent a certain type of dangerous jock mentality I've seen a lot of in our society. How did you go about tackling this subject?**

**Crews:** Well, a writer doesn't choose a subject. A subject chooses a writer. Physical attributes, whether of strength or swiftness or stamina or whatever, is something that is measurable and seeable. We can see it, witness it, measure it. What do you do 40 yards in? You can't fake that. We can put a watch on you, and if you do that in four or five or maybe in six, we can sign you up. If you don't, say if you're a seven, shit, you're nowhere. Just one second makes the difference. Most of the people with whom I am friends are athletes. I dedicated *A Feast of Snakes* to an All-American football player, Spider Jourdan. I like sweat, I like to put your ass on the line. There's so much fudging. So many lies. "To hell with it. Let's put a watch on him. Let's put a tape measure on him." You can't fudge with that.

I just admire that because a good friend of mine not long ago said, "Harry, I wish I could find just one thing in the world, just one, that I didn't have to cheat at." This is a guy that's got a Ph.D. This is a guy that's in the *Guinness Book of World Records*. A guy that's just a super stud jock. This is a guy that's married. What he's saying to me is, "I just wish there was just one *fucking* thing that I didn't have to cheat at." I understand what he was talking about. One thing that you could keep pure, one thing that you could keep untainted, and one thing that is pure and untainted is a watch on 40 yards. There ain't no way you can fuck that.

**Graves: I'm surprised you haven't written a book about boxing. Of course that's a subject that's been covered by a lot of other writers, and you've covered subjects almost nobody else has. I can't think of too many other karate novels for instance. You did a number on that one. But boxing ... I know Norman Mailer's written a lot about it, mostly nonfiction. Has it been a subject you've thought about?**

**Crews:** Yeah, I almost went to Zaire to cover that fight myself for *Playboy*. Mailer'd already got the job. They would've sent me if they hadn't already signed him. I don't know, man. The next two or three years are so lined out. See, I don't have any time for the next two or three years. By the time I get through with the novel I'm writing, by the time I get through the play I'm writing ...

**Graves: Have you ever made the talk show rounds to promote your books? The reason I ask is that I've never seen you on television.**

**Crews:** I don't like to talk about those things. I've been on national talk shows. They've all been an unmitigated horror. If you ain't seen me already, you'll never see me, 'cause I'll never do it again. You end up talking to people who have never read your book. Whose staff prepared some questions, and they can hardly read the questions, much less understand the answers you give. West German television, which has the biggest audience—bigger than the BBC—in Europe, came here and stayed with me two weeks and made a documentary. We went back to the Okefenokee Swamp and visited houses I had lived in, in Bacon County. We went to the place I work out over at my house, which is down by a creek in some woods. You see, my work has been translated into German and into French. *Car* did pretty well over in France. For the film we also went and saw my mom and my farm and the rest of it. I've done my share of those talk shows, although I wish I hadn't done any of them. The German thing was all right. I didn't mind that.

**Graves:** In your novels you use a method of enhancing your story that is something like editing techniques in movies. Like when a guy is falling off a cliff and the film cuts to another scene to enhance the emotional impact. How did you develop this technique?

**Crews:** It's one of the things I worked out on my own, by watching movies. One of the things was working with editors, and one of the things was talking to my betters. People who knew more about it. It was all a hit-and-miss sort of thing. The thing that you see, the thing that the public sees, is the finished product. They don't see all the fuck-ups you made. All the blind alleys you ran up.

**Graves:** Do you think your novels could catch on big with the American public someday the way Kurt Vonnegut's have?

**Crews:** Of course. I'll probably be dead. Maybe my heirs will be dead. I know how vain and full of myself that sounds, but I have every confidence that my books will endure.

**Graves:** Critics have said that you have one of the blackest senses of humor to be found in American literature. Do you think they are right?

**Crews:** They are probably right. Forty acres and a mule will give you not only a black sense of humor, but a black view of the world. Forty acres and a mule is a bad way to go. It's been a long time since I've been there, but I remember it *all* in an incredibly graphic sort of way.

**Graves: Do you find yourself sometimes enraged at the America of today? From reading *A Childhood* and your comments on the injustice of being poor in this country, I think you are.**

**Crews:** Dismissing *A Childhood*, the answer is yes. Anything that man has put his hand to is flawed. There is no perfect novel, no perfect short story, no perfect plays, no perfect poems, no perfect painting, no perfect photographs. Necessarily flawed. Appreciating and being able to identify the flaws of this country is every bit as important, it seems to me, as being able to appreciate and identify the strengths.

**Graves: In *A Childhood* you say that the world that was depicted by Sears and Roebuck in the catalogs they mailed to your family was a lie. You said that there has to be scars underneath the façade of those perfect-looking models. Do you feel this is true of life in general?**

**Crews:** Of course. *Of course*. It was then, and it is now and always has been and always will be. Insofar as we present our best face to one another. How many marriages have you known that the man and the woman would come into parties, they were smiling to one another? They were holding hands, they were arriving in the same car. They, as they say, "maintained appearances." And then one day you hear from a friend, "Did you know that Pete and Sally's gettin' a divorce?" And you think, "No, man! Wait a minute. I didn't know that. No, you gotta be wrong. Pete and Sally came to my house and they were all huggy-bear, kissy-mouth kind of bullshit thing." [*Lowers voice theatrically.*] But noooo. Underneath the worms were crawling. They're eating eyeballs.

The face we present to one another is an ideal face. I'm not immune to that. None of us are. We don't want other people to know that we have failed. Failed in marriage, failed in jobs, failed in money, failed with the wherewithal to look to the future, so that we take care of our children. So that we send them to college. You made X number of dollars and 10 years later you're broke, and you can't send your kid to school, and you can't take care of your wife or whatever it is. We all know that. It is our weak, misguided effort to be godlike. Everybody wants to be godlike. The family wants to be godlike. The government wants to be godlike ... Nixon, Lyndon Johnson, "Naw, we ain't bombing Cambodia." [*Lowers voice.*] "Huh-unh. We ain't doin' thay-yat." And of course, hell, we'uz bombing them motherfuckers out of existence. "So I appear to you as a man, but I really am a god." Nobody would be courageous or foolish enough to say that, but that's what all of us think. "I look like a man, but I am a god. I can see through to the other side. Come to me."

Of course there are the big hucksters and shysters, shucking and jiving. Great fortunes have been built on it. "You can't see on the other side of it, but I can. So you send me, each of you, 3,000 dollars and I'll take you down into Guyana there and give you all cyanide. And you will drink it because I'm me and you are you. And I'm different than you are." Well, no. Not really. Fucker thought he was dying of cancer. He wasn't dying of cancer. Had people run out of the shacks with chicken livers and chicken gizzards, and he told people they were cancers he had taken out of people. And on and on and on.

All very sad. All very tragic. And all very ugly enough to make a man almost murderously angry. But that's the nature of the world. I don't know about you, but the only world I know is the one I see.

# Natural Born Elvis: The Story of Bill Haney, The First Elvis Impersonator

*A hush fell over the audience as the lights dimmed. A low, rumbling bass blared from the public address system, followed by the first muted strains of "Also Sprach Zarathustra." The piece built to a blood-pounding climax, and before the kettle drums had been stilled the band onstage was well into "C.C. Rider." This was the ritual, and every person in the coliseum knew it.*

*Then, like magic, he was there, wearing a jumpsuit the color of a robin's egg with bell bottom flares out to here. The spangles and studs and rhinestones glittered under the spotlights like a disco ball, sending spears of light into every corner of the building.*

*There were restraining barriers; that was in the contract. But the fans, the true fans, would not be stopped. By anything. He looked down at the lip just beyond the footlights and there they were. The way they jumped and hollered and screamed and flopped reminded him of* **those big old ugly fish that waller in the water in the spillways of dams. Stage carp.**

*He threw a few moves on them. Karate chops and stuff. In response, they squealed and cried and like to have fainted. He smiled once and then sang a slow, tender song, "Are You Lonesome Tonight?," that jerked their little hearts right out of their chests.*

**Thankyouverymuch**, *he said into the microphone in that way that got them every time.*

*He took a red scarf from around his neck and wiped the sweat that poured off his face and exposed chest.* **Give 'em something** *to smell. He walked to the edge of the stage and dangled the scarf teasingly. He bent over to give it to one particularly excited fan when another one grabbed the thick gold chain around his neck and pulled for all she was worth. He tried to pull back, but by then another one had ahold of it, too. With two or three mighty jerks he was flipped right off the stage and onto his back without ever hitting the floor. The fans held him aloft and passed him over their heads like a coffin at an ayatollah's funeral. His legs were sticking straight up and wiggling, his white shoes dancing in the air.*

**I'm either gonna die or be the silliest-looking sonofabitch in history.**

Bill Haney never liked being called an Elvis impersonator. "I'm a lousy imitator," he says. "If you asked me to sound like anybody, I couldn't. I don't know how to change my voice. People automatically started comparing my voice to his. I never once tried to sound like Elvis. I tried to sound like Bill Haney."

It has been more than a decade since Haney, the world's first full-time Elvis impersonator, the man who little by little created what has become a permanent cultural iconography, hung up his jumpsuit and turned his back on the money, the crowds, the adulation, not to mention the competing fan clubs that stretched from Memphis to West Berlin. By the time he quit in 1982, there were an estimated 2,000 people doing the same thing Haney did for a living.

"There are too many bad Elvis acts out there stinking things up for the rest of us," he told a reporter at the time. There was a young Elvis, a fat Elvis, a black Elvis, a girl Elvis, a

Mexican Elvis, even a midget Elvis. The image of Elvis Presley on those stages was becoming increasingly sick and twisted and ugly, and the camp aspect of it—those people who thought the whole thing was some great white-trash joke—well, it all got to be too much for the boy from Blytheville, Arkansas, the one who started it all when he fell in love with Jerry Lee Lewis's red-hot piano.

Haney is now 55 years old—"13 years older than *he* was when he died," he says—and still carries himself with the athletic grace of his performing years. The lines around his eyes and the few telling signs of gray in his black hair are all that belie his youthful appearance. When he grins, which is often, Haney is still strikingly handsome, and one can guess what the effect of that smile must have been like in the early '70s when he was creating a new form of pop culture.

He is sitting in the break room of the Four Seasons Realty Company in West Memphis, Arkansas, a highly successful real estate enterprise he and his wife of 35 years, Gail, own. The office is decorated in nouveau West Memphis with tall cathedral windows, designer awnings, and peach-colored, floral-pattern furniture. The teal carpet is thick and cushiony, the matching walls bright and filled with sunshine. Bill is wearing a short-sleeved shirt with a bright red tropical print, khaki pants, and canvas deck shoes. He looks as if he has made afternoon plans to go sailing.

On first meeting him one is startled to discover that he doesn't look a thing like Elvis and, to the practiced ear, Haney's flat Arkansas drawl is nothing like Elvis's mumbling Memphis brogue. Yet the longer Bill Haney talks, the weirder it gets. Maybe it's the crooked grin, the careful coiffure, or the deadpan Southern wit. Or maybe it's some more mysterious osmosis taking place. Whatever the source, Haney is off the scale on the Elvis meter. At times, one finds it impossible not to simply sit and stare.

Bill was four years old when music moved center stage into his life. He heard his next-door neighbor in Blytheville pounding out a boogie-woogie on the piano and told his mother, "I want to do that." She saw to it that Bill got piano lessons and everyone was surprised at how quickly the boy became fluent, but before reaching his teens he had quit all formal musical training and was rocking on his own. Although eager for any opportunity to perform, Bill was too shy to sing, even though he had a strong, distinctive tenor voice. As long as he was behind his keyboard, though, everything was fine.

Shortly after Bill turned 15, his father announced to the family that they would be moving to Southern California. His father had been a policeman in Blytheville for over 25 years, but was willing to risk his family's future on the promise of a better job with a better salary. But Bill didn't take to California.

"As soon as school was out for the summer, I'd head back this a-way," he says. "I never liked California and was homesick. I've wondered a lot of times if things would've changed if I'd stayed back here to begin with and hadn't had anything to do with California. But parents have to change jobs sometimes ... back then everyone was goin' out there for the *gold*, the California gold. A lot more pay than you could make back here. I was there, but I hated it."

He was in high school when a swivel-hipped boy from back in Memphis took the music world by storm. "I wore my hair like Elvis. I always had. But at that time I thought Elvis was just a pretty boy for girls—you know, with 'Love Me Tender' and 'Teddy Bear' and all that, and those girls screamin'."

Bill was more interested in Chuck Berry and Little Richard and smooth piano players like Fats Domino. Then came the craziest, poundingest piano player the world had ever seen, a blond-haired demon who literally set his piano on fire: Jerry Lee Lewis, the Killer. Bill listened to all those singles on the Sun record label—"Great Balls of Fire," "Whole Lotta Shakin' Goin' On," "Breathless"—and was transformed into a flailing keyboard wild man. "Man, you oughta seen me," Bill says. "I wiped them pianos *out*. I was killin' pianos."

By the time he graduated from high school in Torrance, California in 1958, Bill had won several amateur talent contests with his piano act, including one on a television show, *Town Hall Party* in Los Angeles, that featured many of the nation's best country and western artists. He was invited back on the show to compete with other finalists and won the quarterfinals. He was invited again for the annual finals and won that one, too.

RCA Records came knocking.

"RCA got in contact with me after my win on *Town Hall Party* and wanted to groom me as an instrumentalist like Dave 'Baby' Cortez, who had a popular organ act going at the time. I wasn't singing at all then, but I didn't want to be just an instrumentalist. I wanted to have a band, so RCA told me to go ahead and get one.

"Well, I found a group of boys from Arkansas out there and we got up a band called the Flares and cut some singles for RCA. RCA got behind the records and sent us on a promotional tour to push the singles and we went across the country and were supposed to end the tour on *American Bandstand*. We started the tour and this old boy who was our singer, well, his daddy got sick and he had to leave the band. That left me as the only one in the band that knew the words to the songs. We were doing covers of Chuck Berry, Carl Perkins, Little Richard, and everyone else, and when I took over on vocals everybody was sayin', 'Hey man, you sound a lot like Elvis. Do you know any of his stuff?' Well, I hadn't learned any Elvis material, except for a few things that old boy, our singer, had done. So I started pickin' it up.

"At that time, if you were going to get a club to hire you, you had to play what the people were asking for so you could get up a crowd. Every time I'd go to play, people'd say, 'Do you know this song? Do you know that song by Elvis?' As they'd start naming them off, I'd go and learn them. And so people started to associate my voice with his. Even the songs that wasn't his came out *Elvisy*. It was easy for me; I didn't have to learn how to train my voice to be similar to his. I think it was because the colloquialisms we had, being from the South, were the same as far as the way we pronounced things and all. But then whenever I'd hear him sing something, it was just [he snaps his fingers] ... the song was just *natural* to me."

Although the singles the Flares cut for RCA didn't burn up the charts, Haney had tasted the musician's life and liked it. "After winning those contests out in California, I decided what

I wanted to do was either play baseball or play music. Man, I was heavy into baseball, but I decided to stick to music. Music just consumed me. You know, man, you see those pretty little girls and all and I says to myself, 'Forget baseball.'"

Still homesick for his native Arkansas, Haney moved back to Blytheville, recruited another band, and married a pretty hometown girl, Gail Slaughter. Throughout the late '50s and early '60s, he covered the Arkansas-Missouri Bootheel circuit, playing many of the roadhouse honky-tonks that Elvis had played when he was still called the Hillbilly Cat and recorded for Sam Phillips's Sun record label. The tough clubs and joints that Jerry Lee Lewis and Carl Perkins toured became Haney's stomping grounds—clubs like the Rebel Inn in Osceola, the B&B Club in Gobler, the Zanza Club in Haiti, Top Hat in Kennett, Twin Gables in Blytheville.

People kept requesting Elvis songs and Haney began to develop a core of fans who came just to hear him do Elvis. Even though he sat behind a piano, didn't particularly look like Elvis, and sang in a much lower key, people told him over and over again how much he reminded them of Elvis.

Unlike many musicians, Bill Haney was a savvy businessman. With a wife and two young daughters to support, he knew his success depended on his ability to deliver onstage and knew if he could pull in a packed house, his bookings would multiply, and he could demand more money. And Elvis had never let him down.

Although Haney had played throughout the South, he had purposely avoided Memphis. "I didn't move into the Memphis market because I was hesitant about going where that Elvis monster was. I didn't know how I'd be accepted over there based on the kind of stuff I was doin'. Well, I wound up playing on *Dance Party* a couple of times, which was a local music show on WHBQ television station in Memphis that was hosted by Wink Martindale. Anita Wood, who was Elvis's girlfriend at the time, was on the show that day, and I didn't know who she was. She walks up to me and says, 'You know, when you're on TV, you remind me a lot of a good friend of mine.' I says, 'Oh really?' I thought she was just some gal who was goin' to Memphis State University and happened to be on there as an extra that day. She said, 'Yeah, and I'd like to introduce you to him, but he's out of the country right now.' I says. 'Well, who is it?,' 'cause I was still in the dark. She says, 'Elvis Presley,' and I says, 'Oh yeah, man. I'd love to meet him.' But they busted up and that was that."

Around this time, Haney began to have doubts about his career as an entertainer. He'd had more fun than any man was entitled to and had left his mark in the small towns that dotted Memphis's tri-state expanse, but he wanted to be a devoted father and husband. Shortly after the Beatles had nudged Elvis off the charts, Haney decided to leave the business. He obtained a real estate license and began to concentrate on selling homes and lots around Hardy, Arkansas. It was something he liked, was good at, and it provided a solid, steady income. But there was still that call of the wild.

"I played for all the parties the real estate company I worked for would put on. And I played and practiced at home, keeping up with all the new stuff. When we had sold off most of the residential lots in Hardy, I told my wife I was going back into music. I missed it. I wanted to move the family back to Blytheville, and one day when I was visiting there I went out to the Ramada Inn and they had someone in the bar playing your ordinary, basic piano music. There were a few people there who knew me, and they asked if I'd get up and play something. I let 'em talk me into it, and so I got up and played and sang a few songs.

"The people just ... God ... they was goin' wild. They was coming in from the lobby and all over the hotel to watch me. Even the help was comin' out from everywhere. I knew I was onto something."

Bill Haney was by no means the first person to imitate Elvis Presley. Undoubtedly, there were Elvis imitators performing in living rooms all over Memphis the same night disc jockey Dewey Phillips premiered "That's All Right" on his radio show. Even before Elvis's historic appearances on *The Ed Sullivan Show*, several comedians had incorporated an Elvis bit into their routines, along with impersonations of Dean Martin, John Wayne, Kirk Douglas, and whoever else would get a laugh.

As early as the mid-'50s a British singer, Terry Dene, had a short-lived Elvis-inspired act that toured England. According to Elvis intimate George Klein, there were one or two other performers who did an Elvis song or two as part of their routine. But these artists performed much more comically and tongue-in-cheek than with the studied seriousness we associate with modern-day Elvis impersonators.

Ral Donner was one of the first successful Elvis soundalikes on record and was followed by Terry Stafford, who had a huge hit with "Suspicion" and was never heard from again.

Hollywood, in its own way, got in on the act with bland Elvis clones like Fabian, Tommy Sands, Frankie Avalon, and Ed "Kookie" Byrnes.

The great leap of faith had not yet happened; no one had been asked to *believe*, to pretend for an hour or two that the person on stage was not some talented mimic from Blytheville, Arkansas, but the real deal—the King himself in the flesh. This leap is what separated mere imitators from impersonators.

By 1968 Elvis Presley's career was in serious decline. After his stint in the Army, the hits began to dry up. When Elvis gave up live performing for Hollywood B-movies and lackluster soundtrack albums, the Beatles and all the other Brits rendered him passé. Between 1962 and 1969, Elvis Presley, the King of Rock & Roll, didn't have a single Number One hit. He hadn't appeared on TV since he'd teamed with Frank Sinatra in 1960 after being discharged from the Army, and hadn't performed before a live audience in nearly a decade. The movies were getting worse *practically frame by frame*; even the die-hard fans were beginning to wonder what had happened to Elvis.

Finally, in 1968, Elvis stood up to Colonel Tom Parker, his smothering manager. There would be no more dumb movies, and he would start performing again. He was also determined to make some more decent records. Elvis must have been stung when he met the Beatles in 1965 and they asked, "Why don't you go back to your old style of record?" He wanted to prove to the world he was still the King and filmed a television special, now known as the '68 *Comeback Special*, that fully restored him to his throne. Clad in skintight black leather, Elvis was all raw animal power. The world watched and the world responded. Elvis was back.

In 1971, an Elvis fan and singer named Dave Carlson from Oak Forest, Illinois discovered the same thing Bill Haney had a few years earlier: Elvis fans, the true-blue fans who would be called Elvi in years to come, were starved for their idol. Carlson, like Haney, had started in bands singing a few Elvis songs. The Elvis fans wanted more and told him he sounded just like Elvis. Carlson soon found he could draw a consistently bigger crowd by playing to the Elvis contingent.

"You've got to remember," Carlson says today, "that for years in the '60s Elvis was unavailable. It was like he was in hiding, a recluse. Until 1969, he didn't perform live and nobody had seen him. Even when he started touring again, if you were lucky he came to your city once. And in those big auditoriums and arenas who could feel close to him? He was underexposed to the public and had been for years.

"You've got to understand one thing about the real Elvis fans: they're like drug addicts. They can't get over Elvis or ever get enough of Elvis. These people were having severe withdrawal symptoms, and guys like me and Bill Haney, and one or two others who were out there before Elvis died—Johnny Harra and Elvis Wade—were filling that void, that emptiness. If you're a heroin addict and you can't get any heroin, morphine is a good substitute. Well, we were like that—the second best thing. Sometimes the second best thing can satisfy for a moment."

Haney moved back to Blytheville and began performing regularly at the Ramada Inn there. Rather than performing Elvis oldies, he began to concentrate on the newer material, "Suspicious Minds," "C.C. Rider," "An American Trilogy," and "Polk Salad Annie," and tried to keep the song list as current as possible. The response was overwhelming. The people, especially the women, went crazy.

"I played at that Ramada Inn for about a year, and business was better than they had ever had. The manager got sent down to manage the Levee Lounge in Memphis at the Ramada Inn on Lamar Avenue. It was new at the time, and they were bringing in some big outfits, some big-name bands. He wanted me to come down there and play, but I was intimidated by it … I was playing with a little ol' four-piece group and still singing from behind the piano. I went down there nervous as hell, you know. I never had worked Memphis. But the response was good, real good, so he fixed me up for another couple of weeks.

"We started off and people was acceptin' it and I got a little more comfortable. I decided to add a few things to the group. So I added a light man, upgraded the equipment, hired me another keyboard player who played the strings stuff and the Hammond B-3 organ—I was still playing the piano—then we go along and I started wearing different stuff. Stuff that more closely resembled what *he* was wearing. I thought, 'Well, if I'm going to do this Elvis thing, I may as well give the flavor of it. What the hell, I'm not going to copy him.' Then I started having stuff made up for me, you know, jumpsuit-style and all. I started wearing it and people really liked it, it got a response. And I thought, 'Well, I can make it even better than that.' And I did some more and the response was even better.

"I seen that my Elvis act was really going over good even in his hometown, and I said to myself, 'Hey man, it's showtime.' But it wasn't until 1974 that I was doing a stand-up Elvis routine. I felt lost without that piano. Piano was a part of me and still is. But promoters and everybody kept telling me that I could make a lot more money if I could get out from behind the piano and do a stand-up.

"I said, 'Man, I can't do that.' I was thinkin', 'What am I gonna do with myself out there?'

"Charlie Hodge, who was one of Elvis's Memphis Mafia boys, used to come to the show a lot. He walked up and says, 'Man, you get your butt up off that piano and give those people something to see.' I said, 'Man, there *ain't* nothin' to see.' Hell, I'm proud of the piano work that I do and I didn't want to leave that. Charlie finally says, 'You either stand up out there or I'm goin' to embarrass the hell out of you.' So I got up and I was nervous, man ... that's probably the second hardest thing I've ever done in my life. The first was ever singin' in front of people in the first place.

"Well, I got up there and as I went along I decided I'd see if I had enough balls to keep on with it. It's hard to do for someone like me who's a little bit reserved. Now even when I went stand-up, I never studied Elvis, so even now I don't know exactly what all he did. But I sure didn't want to *copy* nothin'. I'da felt like a idiot doin' that. So whatever I did, it was something that felt comfortable to me. If it was somethin' that would turn on the gals some way or other, if it was somethin' that would get their attention, I'd say 'Hey, I think I'll do that again.' So you learn as you go along. I was learnin' more about this and that, and then I started getting braver and not letting it bother me. Like doing karate moves and all when I'd never took karate. I just punched with the beat. The thing is, it seemed to work because what I did was me and it was natural and wasn't like saying, 'Okay, he used two fingers to do this and he put his foot down here, and he …' You know, I didn't want to get into that at all. I would've been too embarrassed to do that. I have to do it *my way*."

When Haney got away from the piano and stood by himself in the spotlight, the effect was complete. The jumpsuits, the belts, the spangles, the shades, the red scarves, and the note-perfect song arrangements made Haney's act much more than a clever illusion—they made it *reality*.

The crowds had always been good, but they soon became unbelievable: standing room only every night, reservations weeks in advance, long queues. Haney was pulling down thousands of dollars a week and word got out that seeing Bill Haney perform was as good as seeing Elvis himself, maybe even better. Haney, after all, would nod toward your table and dedicate a special request, save a scarf just for you, speak to you sweetly during a break, maybe even give you a hug and a kiss and thank you from the bottom of his heart for coming out to see him.

Elvis fans weren't the only ones curious about this guy who looked and sang just like Elvis. Bill Burk, a columnist and music writer for the *Memphis Press-Scimitar* who had covered the Elvis beat for a number of years and is now the editor and publisher of *Elvis World* magazine, heard about Haney's unusual act and went to the Levee Lounge to check out the rumors. Like so many others, Burk was astounded by what he witnessed: "The crowd response to Haney was unreal. The girls would scream and crowd the stage and grab for the scarves.

"Bill's timing could not have been better for what he was doing. Elvis had been away from the public spotlight for a long time and when he made his comeback in 1968—it ignited the whole Elvis thing all over again. Plus, Haney was good. I've seen literally hundreds of Elvis impersonators over the years and only a handful have been worth a durn. Haney was about the best I ever heard."

Tourists who came to Memphis to see Graceland and maybe catch a glimpse of Elvis found out about Bill Haney and went home telling their friends about this amazing guy who imitated Elvis. Fan clubs began to form including a hardcore group of locals who dubbed themselves Haney's Honeys and wore special T-shirts to all his performances. A rival group called Haney's Heinies banded together and they engaged in a friendly, but earnest, competition with the Honeys.

The Elvis Presley fan clubs also heard about the Elvis wannabe and were none too pleased about some copycat who thought he wanted to be the King. Before one of his shows at the Levee Lounge, Haney was approached by a middle-aged woman who informed him she was the president of one of Elvis's largest fan clubs.

"I just want to know who the hell you think you are?"

"Just Bill Haney, ma'am," he answered.

"I want you to know one thing," she went on. "There is only one Elvis and there ain't never going to be another. Who are you? You don't look like him, there ain't nobody who sounds like him—"

"I hope you're not offended lady," Haney politely interrupted. "I'm just doing a show based off his. That's all."

After the show, the club president approached him again, this time with tears in her eyes. "I want you to know something. I really enjoyed that. You are for real and I'm a Bill Haney fan now. *Believe me*."

The hubbub over Haney didn't escape the attention of the Memphis morning DJ Rick Dees, who is now one of the nation's best-known radio personalities. Dees had been poking good-natured fun at Elvis for a number of years with a series of hilarious imitations, including one about Elvis eating too many jelly doughnuts. Dees called Haney on the air to rib him about taking over Elvis's job and concocted an imaginary rivalry between the two, claiming Haney wanted to change the name of Elvis Presley Boulevard to Bill Haney Avenue. Dees staged a sing-out on the show between Haney and Elvis, and did both voices himself. The publicity brought even bigger crowds willing to pay more money to get in, including several of the secretaries who worked at Graceland, and practically all of Elvis's Memphis Mafia.

The commotion didn't go unnoticed at Graceland. Every time one of Elvis's songs would come on the radio out at Graceland, one of the Memphis Mafia would quip, "Hey man, there's that cat who sounds just like Bill Haney." And they would all laugh.

One weeknight after Haney's show, the Levee Lounge manager came up to him and asked, "Do you know who was here just a while ago?"

Haney shook his head no.

"Elvis."

"I looked at that manager and says, 'Man, you're kidding me.'"

"He says, 'Naw, man.'"

"And I says, *Holy shit*."

"And the manager says, 'Charlie Hodge is still here and he wants to talk to you. Elvis was sittin' right back there in that booth. I went back and let them in through the kitchen 'cause they called before they came and told me what they wanted. They didn't want any attention, they wanted lights out, and they wanted back in a dark corner somewhere.'

"And that's what they did. They turned the lights out back in the booth—several booths, actually—and he came in with a cowboy hat on, sat in the back with the lights all out. Nobody even knew he was there and there was people all around him. It's probably a good thing I didn't know about him being there. I probably would've got all tongue-tied on the stage.

"Well, the manager brings Charlie Hodge around and Charlie says, 'Hey man, where you want me to pick you up?'"

"I says, 'What you mean?'"

"And he says, 'You do want to meet Elvis, don't you?'"

"I says, '*Oh, hell yeah*.'"

"And Charlie says, 'Elvis told me to stay and bring you out to the house for a while.'"

"So we started over there to Graceland and I thought

that was great, but the impact didn't hit me until those gates opened up and we started up the drive and I thought, *'Holy shit! I'm really gonna meet this guy!'* You know, hundreds and hundreds, millions, of people would like to meet him, and here *I* am going in to meet him.

"I went in the house, and Elvis was upstairs and me and Charlie just messed around in the Jungle Room, Charlie joking around and stuff. Finally, Charlie says, 'Hey man, c'mere, c'mere, Elvis is coming down the stairs.'

"Well, Charlie introduced me to him and Elvis stuck out his left hand and said, 'Excuse my right hand, man, I've got a burn.' I couldn't help but notice that his left hand was just full of diamonds. Both his hands were *unusually puffy*. Soft, puffy. When I seen him come down the stairs it was like there was some damn aura around the guy. I mean he was *different*. More different than anybody I've ever met. I've never met anybody who projected that type of electricity. It was … *different*. I've met a lot of stars in my lifetime … Jerry Lee Lewis, Roy Orbison, Johnny Cash, Ricky Nelson … and I never met anything like Presley. And never will.

"When I was out there with him he says to me, 'Hey man, come on outside. I wanta show you my motherfucking cars.' We went outside and there was a brand new Lincoln Mark IV; he had just given away five brand new Marks to people. He looks at me and says, 'Ain't this one a motherfucker man?' And I said, 'Yeah man, that is *nice*.' He made me feel pretty easy. We sat around in the house for a long time just talkin', jokin', and playin' with the dogs. Charlie was cuttin' up and asks him, 'Elvis what do you think about ol' Haney?' Elvis looks at me and laughs and says, 'I like his *style.*'

"I went out to Graceland many more times after that, not to see him, but to visit all his people who I had become good friends with. That was the only time I went out there just to see Elvis. After that, my schedule of concerts and his schedule of concerts often was in conflict with each other, and I didn't get to see too much of him. Plus, he really wasn't in that good of health after that. We waved and said hi to each other and that was about it. You could really see that he was changing. You could tell he was getting way, way overweight and didn't seem to be like he was. He stayed in his room nearly all the time; you just didn't see Elvis that much."

After meeting Elvis, Haney would frequently get calls from Graceland. "We've got a bunch of stuff Elvis doesn't want and we're going to bring it out to you," they would tell him. Haney was given teddy bears and other stuffed animals, sweaters, and even one of Elvis's custom-made jumpsuits that wasn't the color he had ordered. "It was brown," Haney says, "and he didn't like to wear browns. So they re-did Elvis another one in black with silver trimming."

On August 16, 1977, Haney was booked to play Hot Springs, Arkansas and was relaxing in his motel room when one of his band members came into the room with a pained look on his face. "Did you hear about Elvis?"

When he was told that Elvis had died, Haney slumped in his bed and held his head in his hands. He felt as if he had lost a member of his family, perhaps even some part of himself. He wanted to cancel that night's show, but was under a tight contract; the show had to go on. He went onstage, but the crowd was unusually quiet and reserved. There was no screaming, no fainting, none of the usual frenzy. Instead, many of the women cried softly. "When I did some of his songs that really hit home," Haney says, "well, all I can say is it was real emotional. For me, too."

Elvis's death had both a positive and negative effect on Haney's career. He was soon out of the clubs and lounges and playing large arenas and coliseums. Only days after Elvis was laid to rest, Haney nearly sold out the Pine Bluff Coliseum in Arkansas, and the crowd reacted as if he were the King resurrected from the grave. "We took in over 32,000 dollars that night on the gate. Conway Twitty and Loretta Lynn only did 28,000, so that gives you some idea of what kind of impact his death had."

From there, Haney got an exclusive contract to play the Silver Bird in Las Vegas. The management there gave him a suite, a hairdresser, a makeup artist, and a wardrobe assistant. He played the Cow Palace in San Francisco and the Los Angeles Sports Arena. He was featured numerous times on television news programs. The money was better than Haney had ever imagined. The road, however, was beginning to take its toll. He was tired, burnt out, and lonely for his family. His wife had begged him for years to get off the road and join her in the real estate business again.

Before Elvis had died, there were only a handful of impersonators, all of whom, it would seem, had followed in Haney's footsteps. Now there were hundreds and they were turning the whole thing into a sour joke.

"I knew when he died others would be coming out of the

woodwork," Haney says. "I always said I wouldn't become part of some circus. There were so many cheap acts—I mean, *cheap*—some guy wearin' a few dollars worth of bad clothes, didn't look like him, didn't sound like him except in the shower, got some musicians together and decided he wanted to do a show. That hurt the business, I couldn't watch those guys. They made me want to throw up."

The fans had changed also. After Elvis died the hard-core fans seemed to become more aggressive, almost militant. "They were people who idolized Elvis, and then Elvis was gone. Their second choice was me. They were great fans because they supported me everywhere I went. Without them, I never would have gone anywhere. They made things more exciting, they screamed and carried on and gave me a little taste of what Elvis would have felt like. But I've said many times that I never understood the people who would go crazy. I've seen women bite each other, get in fistfights, knock cops all around. At times, we would just be mobbed by fans and they would grab at you, pulling and tearing at your clothes. I would think, 'Man, these are some expensive friggin' suits to be tearin' up.' But they would go for anything, necklaces, belts, anything. There were quite a few who would climb up on stage and grab ahold of you and not turn loose. We would have to pry them off.

"I was hit one night by three girls all at the same time. These girls, I swear to God, looked like Green Bay Packers. They all hit me at the same time and knocked me about 10 yards back, flat on my ass. I just laid back on my ass and sang the rest of the song looking up at the ceiling."

When asked how the fan worship affected his wife and their relationship, he sighs and answers, "Trouble, man. Lots of dark clouds. Lots of things to overcome, lots of growing up to do, lots of questions to answer, all kinds of shit. Many times I've asked myself if it was all worth it. All the late-night phone calls. I couldn't afford to have an unlisted number because I was doing my own bookings most of the time. I finally got to where I couldn't handle the calls anymore, though. Fans might call at any and all hours of the night; they might find out where you live and come to sit around for a while? I understand that part of it, I really do. They just didn't realize how inconvenient it could be. Imagine you've got a gal callin' you up at all hours, sayin' how much she loves you and all, and you've got a wife who's mad as hell layin' in bed right next to you. And you're trying to talk and be polite to some fan. It was a lot to go through.

"The girls coming up on stage, all the kissing, the worship aspect of it ... it was pretty heavy, man, plus the fact there was some awful pretty girls around sometimes. To sum it up for you, if my wife didn't go along to the shows, we got along a lot better."

Elvis impersonator Dave Carlson, who continues to perform after 25 years of doing Elvis, is even more blunt about the problems associated with fan worship:

"At times it becomes a big monkey on your back. Some of those fans literally want a piece of you. Imagine what it's like to be idolized by overweight, ugly, blue-haired old ladies who want to fantasize about you as Elvis. I feel sorry for those people—that's all they have. But they get jealous of one another and they all think they're your number-one fan. If you forget to dedicate a song to them or speak to them at their table, they can turn on you and it can get very ugly. Some of the worse-off ones will claim to be having your baby and everything else. Imagine how that kind of thing goes over with your family.

"I've had kids who've grown up and come up to me and tell me their lives were ruined and they got into drugs and trouble because their mothers were in love with me and spent all their time at my concerts or in some lounge watching me. That's so sad.

"Now I only play private gigs, conventions, and so on. I make good money and don't have to deal with girls getting their arms broken stampeding the stage, or choking each other with the scarves I've given them. I'm a novelty act to the crowds I play now, and some of them enjoy it as a joke, or for laughs. But at least I don't have to put up with that frenzied kind of adulation anymore."

In 1982, Haney quit the road and put the jumpsuits in the attic. He has played on rare occasions, including a gig at the National Homebuilders Convention where he shared the stage with Frankie Valli and the Commodores. He has toned down the Elvis and gotten back behind the piano. When he performs now, he plays a lot of songs Elvis never recorded. He also has gone back to wearing ordinary stage clothes. People still come out to see Elvis, but aren't that disappointed when all they get is Bill Haney. He can still do a mean Jerry Lee Lewis.

"I'm recording a gospel album right now," Haney says. "I'm trying to develop something that nobody can identify

Elvis-wise. I don't want to sound like Elvis. If it sounds anything like Elvis, I won't do it. Seeing as how my voice was always connected to Elvis, I've started singing a little bit different ... softer, easier. I've always been in a lower key-range than Elvis. Always. How someone could identify me singing a song in C that he would sing in E or F in a high voice, I don't know. But they did. It's weird.

# The Cajun Hank Williams: D.L. Menard

DESPITE HIS STATUS AS a musical legend among the people of the Cajun heartland, I had been told D.L. Menard lived a modest life in a country home. Still, when I pulled up to the address I had been given, I was positive I had made a wrong turn somewhere. The house was built of mismatched materials, some brick, some concrete, some wood, some of what looked like tar paper—a Heinz 57 of a house that leaned together precariously and in no way suggested the home of a Cajun superstar, a man who had performed before presidents and queens.

I had followed D.L.'s directions, driving from Lafayette, Louisiana to Erath (pop. 2,250). This backwater town is located smack in the middle of the triangular geographical area called Acadiana that extends for roughly 300 miles along the Gulf Coast to a point in Avoyelles Parish far north of New Orleans. But I thought I must have missed a turn-off, and had just put my car in reverse when a lanky, grizzled man in a navy blue mechanic's uniform, who looked to be in his mid-to-late 50s, came out the front door grinning and motioned me back into the driveway. He had two or three days' growth of beard, and his clothes were covered in machine oil and scatterings of sawdust. His wrist was wrapped in cotton gauze. The bandage was smudged nearly black and was partially unraveled. But as soon as I heard the voice, I knew I was in the right place.

According to many of those who lived through it, Cajun music came close to dying out as a result of World War II. During the military buildup prior to America's involvement in the war, hundreds of Cajuns were hired to work in the shipyards and oil fields along the Texas coast. It was during this period that many Cajuns first became acutely aware of how they stood out from the rest of America; how anyone who didn't fit into the standard American blueprint was automatically suspect. As automobiles, paved roads, telephones, motion pictures, and radio opened Acadiana to a broader American culture, many Cajuns became ashamed of their heritage.

In many Cajun parishes, it was forbidden for teachers or students to speak French on school grounds on threat of dismissal for teachers and paddling for students. To outsiders who didn't understand their ways, Cajuns seemed clannish—suspicious at worst, and eccentric at best. Their music was deemed—correctly—uncommercial, with little hope of crossover appeal. By this time, Cajuns themselves were reluctant to buy their own records. And though even the poorest Cajuns who lived on the remotest bayous owned battery-operated radios, it was seldom that a Cajun French song of any kind was aired.

At the dance halls and house parties and *fais do-dos* where Cajun music had once flourished and musicians had passed their knowledge and talents from father to son and mother to daughter, country-and-western music was what audiences clamored to hear. Even the jukeboxes in the region, which had once stocked 78s by local Cajun favorites, had given way to the country-and-western hits. While working in the Texas oil fields and shipyards, a number of Cajun men fell under the spell of country swing as played by Bob Wills and His Texas Playboys and other bands. When they came back home after the war, these men brought the sound and new instrumentation with them.

As a teenaged cane cutter for the Erath Sugar Company (like his father and his grandfather), Doris Leon "D.L." Menard heard Cajun music on his grandmother's windup Victrola and, on rare occasions, on his daddy's battery-powered wooden radio. But it wasn't until D.L. turned 16 and went to a party at his Uncle Paul Menard's house that he saw his first live Cajun band. "Oh man, that was the most exciting thing I had ever seen," D.L. says today. "I couldn't believe my eyes and ears that they were playing Cajun music and singing *in French!* I listened to those guitar players in that band, and I said to myself right there, 'Man, I want to do that.'"

So he sent off to Montgomery Ward for their cheapest guitar, which was 11 dollars, postage paid. "It had no name brand printed anywhere on it," he laughs. "It was a nameless guitar."

D.L. learned to play choke rhythm, a percussionistic style of strumming with the guitar often tuned to an open chord. Six months later, he had learned enough to play his first dance job.

After performing in front of an audience, D.L. felt his guitar wasn't good enough. He sold it and sent off for a $24.95 model from Sears Roebuck. He couldn't afford their top-line guitar, which cost 45 dollars. When he went to the post office to pick up the new guitar and opened the case to take a look at it, he saw that Sears Roebuck had mistakenly sent the more expensive model instead of the one he'd ordered.

"When I opened that case and seen that it was that 45-dollar guitar I closed it quick; I was afraid that man at the post office would make me send it back. So I hurry up and I high-tailed it back home, Jack. In those days it cost too much money to send a package back. And man, I wanted to keep that guitar."

In addition to playing the guitar, D.L. had become a confident singer. But instead of being influenced by Cajun vocalists, he patterned himself on Ernest Tubb, Lefty Frizzell, and his idol, Hank Williams. His voice was a comfortable fit between the high twang of Hank Williams and the weary flatness of Ernest Tubb. After several months of performing with various area bands, D.L. was invited to join the veteran Louisiana Aces, a successful unit headed by accordion player Elias Badeaux that had long been a favorite on the Cajun circuit. In addition to playing choke rhythm, D.L. was hired to sing all the English songs. The Louisiana Aces, like other popular Cajun performers, such as Rusty and Doug Kershaw and Jimmy Newman, were incorporating country-and-western into their repertoires. But for the next several years the other band members in the Aces covered the traditional Cajun French material.

"A Cajun band that couldn't play country-and-western some, they weren't working, partner," says D.L. "The first thing they'd ask when you'd go to a dance hall or club and ask for a job was if you could play country-and-western music. If you couldn't play country music, they couldn't use you. So, about half of the dances was Cajun and half country. There was still a demand for Cajun French, but it had almost died out."

D.L. also had changed day jobs. He worked six days a week at the Phillips 66 service station in Erath and often played five or six gigs a week as well. He rode a bicycle to work every morning, even after he married Lou Ella Abshire in 1952 and began raising a family. It wasn't uncommon for him to be out until two o'clock in the morning playing a job, only to have to get up again at six to put in a full day at the service station.

One afternoon in 1961, while he was still working full-time at the Phillips station, D.L. kept hearing the old Hank Williams tune "Honky Tonk Blues" in his brain. He began to experiment with the melody and took a notion to jot down a few words to sing along with it. As D.L. related the story to Ann Savoy:

"If I could've sat down and wrote the song right then and there, the time I put in it, I didn't put more than a half hour, I had my little pad in my pocket; I'd write a few words and then there's a car that would come; I'd have to go pump gas or grease a car, service a car ... It would stop me ... When I had a little time I kept on writing the words."

What he came up with was a song he called "La Porte D'en Arriere," or "The Back Door." Laced with Cajun irony, "The Back Door" tells the story of a young Cajun and his gal who go to a dance and have so much fun that they decide to visit *all* the honky tonks. They stay out so late that when they arrive at their homes the next morning, rather than risk punishment by going through the front, they sneak in through the back door. The young Cajun isn't quite through with his merrymaking, however. That afternoon he goes back into town, gets plenty drunk, and when he returns home finds strange company at the house. Because he doesn't recognize the company and because he is drunk, he again goes in through the back door. Come Friday afternoon, the young man goes back into town, gets into a fight, and finds himself in trouble with the law. The police haul him off to jail, and he enters it through, of course, the back door.

"I played that song for my family," says D.L., "just for fun, you know, and every time I got my guitar out, the kids was after me to play that 'Back Door.' I decided to try and make a record out of it so my kids would have a souvenir of the song. It cost me 175 dollars to make the record with the band and get it pressed up. Man, I had no idea at all that song would become a hit. I said, 'If I only would make my money back ....'"

The song, recorded at Floyd Soileau's tiny recording studio in nearby Ville Platte with the Louisiana Aces, opens with the accordion, drums, and D.L.'s choke rhythm guitar all diving onto the beat, followed by a simple single-note 1-2-3, 1-2-3 melody picked on the steel guitar. Steel guitar, even today, is typically thought of as the instrument that gave the "Nashville Sound" its customary whine, which led to the term *crying-in-your-beer* music, and to a lot of jokes and parodies of country-and-western music. The steel guitar, however, is capable of an astonishing array of sounds, and the Louisiana Aces most certainly weren't going to play crying-in-your-beer music.

Unlike zydeco music, which is more directly influenced by the backbeat percussion of rhythm and blues, Cajun music primarily accentuates the front beat. For many years some people differentiated black music from white music simply by where the beat fell in the song. Front beat records—"white people's music"—were considered by hipsters to be far less funky and danceable than the overtly sexual backbeat of black R&B. Cajuns, however, play some of the hardest-driving front beat music ever recorded. Cajun music by its very nature is dance music, and the Cajun two-step and waltz demand very precise rhythm patterns. D.L. and his backing band upped the ante significantly on "The Back Door" when they added the locomotive pull of their combined percussion. On top of the breakneck pacing, a young D.L. begins a tongue-tripping vocal that falls in right behind the beat and occasionally slides slightly off-key on purpose for effect. Menard's voice was higher in 1961 than what is heard on the vocals he recorded for Rounder Records in the '80s and '90s, and it didn't then have quite the sadness that was so reminiscent of Ernest Tubb. Instead, his voice was less polished, rawer, and more sexually precocious than Hank Williams. Menard particularly had fun when phrasing the irresistible chorus of the song, "*J'ai passé dedans la porte en arriére*," dragging out the last word "*arri-uuuuuhhhhhhh*," as long as he possibly could.

"Back then you made records mainly to help you get jobs playing in the clubs and dances—to boost our pay, you know, and make ourselves a drawing card," D.L. explained. "On Fridays and Sundays we made six dollars a man playing Saturday night was the big night when we made the big money—we'd make eight dollars a man. Hot dog! The first night that we played the Jolly Roger Club after we had put out that song, man, we could hear that 'Back Door' playing on the jukebox in there. Hot damn, that was a good feeling, man! Oh Lord, to hear yourself on the jukebox after all these years! I was walking in that club with my chest sticking out, don't you know. Hot dog!

"The owner of that club said, 'Y'all hear that record of yours that's playing on that jukebox? When I opened this club at seven o'clock this morning to come clean this place here, there was some people that walked in and put on that record, and it has not stopped since.' He said, 'I cannot hear it no more!'

"Well, that night I had to sing that song seven times. I'd finish singing it, and a new group of people would come in and say, Y'all play that 'Back Door.' So I'd have to sing it again. It was that way every time we would play, I'd have to sing it five or six times. Man, I got to where I hated that song so darn much I could spit on it, because I couldn't sing nothing else. I'd want to sing something else, and the people wouldn't let me. They'd want that 'Back Door.' Every night. All the time. It hit the people just right."

The single took off in the region and was requested so often on the local radio stations that it was just about placed on virtual permanent rotation—an honor awarded few Cajun artists at the time and practically unheard of for a song sung completely in Cajun French.

On the success of "The Back Door," D.L. wrote and recorded several other Cajun French hits, such as "Valse de

Jolly Rogers" and "Rebecca Ann." Life for D.L. Menard was good. He had his steady job at the Phillips 66 station, a loving family of six boys and one girl, and a full schedule of bookings at increasingly better wages. And he had written a song that some people were calling the Cajun national anthem.

Dick Spottswood, an organizer for the National Folk Festival at Wolf Trap in Vienna, Virginia traveled in 1973 to many of the small towns in Cajun country scouting new talent for the folk festival. As D.L. tells the story: "Dick Spottswood went to visit Marc Savoy in Eunice, who owns Savoy's Music Center, and he asked who in hell was that playing on that new record he kept hearing, 'The Back Door'? Well, Marc laughed and said, 'That ain't no new record, partner. That's 12 years that record's been playing.' Dick Spottswood said, 'Oh no, it's got to be a brand-new record because it plays constantly, oh yeah! Who in the hell is singing that song?'

"A few weeks later I get a call on the phone. It was this fellow Dick Spottswood from Washington. And I told him, 'Oh, I know where that is. Down south of Opelousas.' He laughed out loud and told me, 'I know where that place is too, but I'm calling from the District of Columbia.'

"I had never had a phone call from that far away before. I thought to myself, What in hell I done now? He said, 'We'd like y'all to come play music for us over here.' I said, 'Go to Washington, D.C., to play music? Not no, but *hell no*. That's too far for us to go just to play music.' I knew nothing whatsoever about a folk festival. I had never heard about that. He was a good talker, this Dick Spottswood, you know. He stayed on that phone there just about an hour with me. My arm was gettin' numb, man, 'cause it was gettin' tired. He said, 'Look, we pay all expenses. It don't cost y'all nothing. We pay you a fee on top of that. Y'all can drive, y'all can take the bus, y'all can take the train, but the best way for y'all to get here is to fly.' When he mentioned that—fly—I had always said I'd never fly, because, you know, those things falls too much—I said, 'I'm not gonna decide that. I'm gonna talk to the guys. Whatever they decide, well, that'll be it.'

"Well, we decided to go, and we decided we would fly. The captain didn't know who was on board that plane the first time, but I think that son of a gun flew the way he did on purpose. I would have swore he knew we were on board and it was our first time. We had to go to New Orleans first, but he took off toward Lake Charles and he banked that plane 90 degrees down and I put my hand down. To me, I was gonna fall out. And that window I was looking out, well it was dirty on the outside and I wanted to clean it.

"We went up there to Wolf Trap and, man sakes alive, we made a hit you would not believe. There were people there as far as your eye could see. About 6,000. It was an open door theater. Mother Maybelle Carter and the Carter Family was there. Oh man, I enjoyed the hell out of them! When we got on that stage, well Lord Jesus Christ, we had a standing ovation. I can't even begin to explain to you how we felt up there. How good it was, man! I was scared half to death, you know, at first, because I had to do all the talkin'. After that they couldn't shut me up. I talked in English, but I sang all in Cajun French.

"It was shortly after that when that fella Bob Norman

wrote us up in *Sing Out!* magazine and called me the Cajun Hank Williams."

Only weeks later, the band was invited to play another folk festival in El Paso. Some of the record executives at Rounder Records in Cambridge, Massachusetts heard Menard there and signed him and the band to a contract that eventually netted several outstanding albums. They were invited again the next year to Wolf Trap and were contacted soon thereafter by officials from the State Department. D.L. and the Louisiana Aces had been selected for a State Department tour of Central and South America, and later of Europe and Asia.

I was able to extend my stay in Acadiana when D.L. was unexpectedly booked to play at Vermilionville, a tourist attraction operated by a local nonprofit organization, which features a recreation of an authentic Cajun village. Located in Lafayette, Louisiana, Vermilionville boasts a large, barnlike auditorium for dances and entertainment by the area's popular Cajun and zydeco artists. By the time D.L. was ready to perform on Sunday afternoon, I had spent time at the Liberty Theater in Eunice watching the Cajun equivalent of the Grand Ole Opry, toyed with one of the diatonic accordions sold at Floyd's Record Store in Ville Platte, sampled fried garfish at a roadside stand near Opelousas, drank a few Dixie beers to wash down a bagful of hot pork cracklins, and heard several outstanding bands, such as Steve Riley and the Mamou Playboys, play "The Back Door."

When I arrived at Vermilionville, D.L. and his band were already onstage playing. The crowd was surprisingly small, about 50 people, and because the auditorium seemed so big in comparison, there wasn't the degree of intimacy I had hoped for. It had been a last-minute booking, and most of the audience was comprised of tourists—non-Cajuns who tapped their feet instead of strutting their stuff on the dance floor.

D.L. was joined onstage by a very young drummer and a middle-aged fiddle player who played his instrument Doug Kershaw-style, with the base cradled in his armpit instead of under his chin. D.L. was also joined by one of Cajun music's hottest young stars, Horace Trahan, on accordion. Trahan, a tall, strikingly handsome fixture on the bandstand, was one of Menard's favorite partners. "Ain't many got that," D.L. told me, "that real Cajun sound. When he sings, it's just there; ain't no trying to it."

Trahan added an intense moodiness to the band, a kind of James Dean cool that was unmistakable. He sat on a chair pumping the small accordion with great facility, his cowboy hat hanging low over his eyes, giving him an air of menace and mystery. D.L., by contrast, who was now clean-shaven and sporting powder blue cowboy slacks, had his cowboy hat tilted way back on his head, giving him a slightly comical appearance, which he used to great effect when bantering with the crowd. A contingent of fans from Thibodeaux had come to see D.L., and he frequently spoke directly to them in Cajun French, drawing great laughs from the Thibodeaux group and lots of head-scratching from the tourists.

At one point, D.L. said to the whole crowd, "These folks here, they come up from Thibodeaux to see me. They some good folks. They remind me of myself." There were numerous requests for "The Back Door." Menard always obliged and always closed his eyes when he sang.

A couple sitting nearby had noticed D.L. wave at me when I came in and were curious why I was taking notes and shooting photographs. I explained that I was a writer working on a story about D.L. Menard. "That guy up on stage?" the friendly husband asked. "Heck, I just thought they were the Beverly Hillbillies or something. I didn't know he was supposed to be good."

D.L. had suggested that since I was staying overnight in Lafayette, I should go hear one of his favorite bands, Jambalaya, at a restaurant and club called Randol's. Expecting a juke joint along the lines of Fred's Lounge back in Mamou, I was surprised that Randol's was an upscale restaurant geared somewhat for tourists, but with a bandstand, large dance floor, and state-of-the-art sound system.

Although it was easy to spot the tourists on the dance floor—they were the ones who couldn't dance—it was obvious that the locals were the driving force behind the restaurant. The women, in particular, were gaily attired, and many of them wore skirts and dancing shoes. On some high-energy songs, the dance floor was a colorful blur of whirling motion, the dancers dervishes of ever-accelerating speed.

On some of the slow waltz numbers, I watched as grandmothers taught their young grandsons how to dance in time to the music. There was none of the boot-scootin' common to country-and-western bars. The steps were precise, graceful, and, if one read the expressions on the dancers' faces correctly, fun. Fathers danced with daughters, mothers with sons, gray-haired men held young Cajun princesses respectfully in their arms, all of them smiling and laughing and feeling the music.

I was having such a good time at Randol's watching these people celebrating and dancing without shame or self-consciousness that I almost got angry when they invited a little boy, no more than five years old, to the bandstand to sing a song. He goofed the opening, and they patiently cued him again. The little boy started tentatively then quickly got the hang of it, singing fluently in Cajun French. It wasn't until the end of the first verse that I noticed the refrain "*J'ai passé dedans la porte en arriére.*"

He was singing "The Back Door."

# In The Midnight Aisle: The Story of The Blackwood Brothers Quartet

# Prologue

THERE IS LITTLE ARGUMENT among serious Elvis scholars on at least one issue: Elvis's favorite music, the music he most closely followed, enjoyed, studied, and imitated was Southern gospel music. Ironically, it is the aspect of the King least explored by these same scholars. The reasons for this discrepancy are manyfold and have as much to do with one's raising as anything. Few of the major Elvis writers grew up with Southern religion or were marinated in its music forms. Those who have tried to backtrack to the golden age of Southern gospel music, roughly from 1945 after the Second World War until about 1965 after the Beatles' invasion of America, have all-too-frequently found themselves mired in the *now* of the Christian Right and some of the highly visible fringe elements of fundamentalism as embodied by Pat Robertson, Jimmy Swaggart, and Jim and Tammy Bakker. Which is to say, times have changed.

But Elvis's love of the music never did. Graceland sources have told me that the final album played on Elvis's stereo was by J.D. Sumner and the Stamps Quartet. I have it on good authority that the album still rests on that turntable.

Scholars and critics debate which Southern gospel group

was Elvis's favorite. Some say it was The Blackwood Brothers—after all, Elvis wanted more than anything to be a member of that august group in his early years—and some say it was The Statesmen Quartet. On close listen it would appear, arguably, that Elvis leaned more closely to the Blackwoods than the Statesmen in his own gospel output. And the Blackwoods were certifiably Gladys Presley's favorite group and led the singing at her funeral, which should end the argument once and for all.

I was raised in Memphis and steeped in the sounds of The Blackwoods and countless other gospel groups. Indeed, it was the only type of music my parents truly loved. In this short book, I turn my attentions to The Blackwoods, inarguably the most influential gospel group in the history of the form.

# Chapter One – Ring of Fire

WHEN I WAS A child my parents owned three long-play record albums that my brother and I played over and over on a tiny table-top record player. One of the LPs, a Lawrence Welk album titled *Scarlett O'Hara*, curiously had a paint-peeling version of the surf guitar instrumental "Pipeline." Then there was the *Hawaiian Favorites* LP, much handled, seldom played, that featured a cover photo of the most exotically beautiful lei-clad Hawaiian dancer my young eyes had ever seen. Last, there was a live in concert album by my parents' favorite singing group, The Blackwood Brothers Quartet, not coincidentally one of the young Elvis Presley's favorite singing groups too.

I was already familiar with much of the material on this album because I was awakened every Sunday morning of my early life with the sounds of our fellow Memphians, the Blackwoods, harmonizing from the family television set. When the Blackwoods came on, that meant it was time to get up and get ready for church. One song on that album, *The Blackwoods in Concert*, particularly caught my fancy. The song was "The Devil Can't Harm a Praying Man," a reworking of a black gospel tune by the Dixie Hummingbirds. My misinterpretation of the lyrics of the song gave me a measure of spiritual solace as a child. I heard the lyrics "Early in the morning, early in the evening, late, way over in the midnight hour" as "over in the midnight aisle." In my innocence I thought of the midnight aisle as a poetic last place of refuge, where a sinner might still find comfort with God when all other church doors were closed.

Like millions of other young Americans, I began to beg my parents for new record albums by the Beatles when that group took the world, and Memphis, by storm and thunderclap in 1964. It would be many years before I would dust off that old Blackwood Brothers album, play the song, "The Devil Can't Harm a Praying Man," and discover that the lyrics in my head were wrong, yet so very right.

In June 1954, one month before I was born, the Blackwood Brothers Quartet was without question the number one gospel group in the world. After years of battling the grind of the road, which included hundreds of car breakdowns, blizzards, floods, last-minute cancellations, and mile upon mile of torturous, cramped seating, the Blackwood Brothers were signed to a major record label, some would say *the* major record label, RCA Victor, and selling out auditoriums from east coast to west. The memories of catching a few sad moments of sleep in back seats with their feet propped on stacks of their record albums and songbooks were beginning to fade. They now took to the skies to meet their concert obligations and had just purchased their third aircraft, a massive twin-engine Beechcraft 618 that could seat up to 10 passengers. One member of the group, R.W. Blackwood, had earned his wings and piloted the group to its virtually endless succession of engagements.

Business for the group was good, so good in fact that two of the brothers from the original Blackwood Brothers Quartet, Roy and Doyle Blackwood, had retired from singing entirely and were managing the group's exploding booking and business affairs, which included a recent merger with the Stamps Music Company, one of the oldest and most venerable names in Southern gospel music. The original Blackwoods group was comprised of brothers Roy, Doyle, and James Blackwood, along with Roy's son, R.W. Blackwood. James and R.W., who were born only two years apart, had grown up together more as brothers than as uncle and nephew. Although no recordings exist of the original line-up, legend has it that they sang some of the most beautiful close harmony ever to grace a gospel stage. With Roy and Doyle committed to the Blackwoods' various business enterprises, two new members had been added to the group, Bill Shaw of the All American Quartet, who possessed a soaring high tenor voice, and a tall, lanky bassist with a velvety *basso profundo* voice, Bill Lyles.

One of the factors in the Blackwoods' unprecedented ascendance as a Southern gospel group that is seldom mentioned—for obvious reasons—was their undeniable sex appeal. In addition to their unquestionable singing talent, the Blackwoods were simply better looking than practically all of their competition. Southern gospel music, even then, was equated with old men from a bygone, backwoods era. James and R.W. Blackwood, in particular, cut dapper figures in their day. Surviving film footage of this version of the Blackwoods shows a youthful, kinetic, slyly humorous, and impeccably-tailored group of men with dazzling white Hollywood smiles. Undoubtedly the hand fans of many Southern matrons were set a-flutter when the Blackwoods stepped into the floodlights.

Their charismatic stage presence helped land them a spot that June of 1954 on *Arthur Godfrey's Talent Scouts*, a prime-time talent competition on CBS in which, like *American Idol* today, the audience determined the winner with their votes. The Blackwood Brothers were the first Southern gospel group to break onto national television. Their appearance was not without risk to their reputation. After all, they could lose. The urbane New York audience could reject the Blackwoods' Southern-fried charm or their seemingly outdated quartet style of gospel singing.

Such was not the case, however. Performing their new RCA single, "The Man Upstairs," the Blackwood Brothers Quartet wowed the nation, easily winning the *Talent Scouts* competition, which in turn earned them a week's worth of appearances on Arthur Godfrey's daily morning television show that was simulcast on CBS radio. The exposure gave Southern gospel music a quantum goosing. Once considered a music strictly for regional low-church tastes, the Blackwood Brothers proved that gospel music could cross over to a mass audience.

The rest of that month the Blackwood Brothers sold out every one of their scheduled appearances. Their last booking of the month, on June 30th, was at the annual Chilton County Peach Festival in Clanton, Alabama, where thousands of festivalgoers were expected. As was usual, R.W. Blackwood piloted the big twin-engine Beechcraft with bassist Bill Lyles serving as navigator and co-pilot in the seat next to him. They landed, were welcomed by hundreds of fans, performed at a noonday luncheon for the local Lions Club, and spent the afternoon mingling with fans and signing autographs.

The Blackwoods also were to perform that night in one of the airplane hangars, sharing the bill with the popular Statesmen Quartet from Atlanta, another preeminent gospel group that had been signed to RCA. After the concert the group planned to fly back to their home base in Memphis. R.W. was fretful; he told the other members that he was concerned about the short landing strip in Clanton. He decided to practice a few take-offs in the Beechcraft before dark just to be sure—he wanted to get a feel for the runway. R.W. knew the runway would not be lighted at night. On several occasions prior to their date in Clanton, the Blackwoods had asked fans to pull their cars up on opposite sides of an air strip and turn on their headlights to provide them with makeshift runway lights. The feeling this day was that the short landing strip might necessitate another plea to their fans.

James Blackwood, at 82 (at the time of this writing), is today the sole surviving member of the original Blackwood Brothers Quartet. He takes a deep breath in his East Memphis home as he finishes the story, a story he has had to tell many times:

"R.W., Bill Lyles, and the young man who was with them [18-year-old Johnny Ogburn, a fan, who was the son of the founder of the Peach Festival], they went up in the Beechcraft and were flying around. I noticed that the wind had shifted.

When they came in for a landing, the wind had shifted so that R.W. had to approach the field from the opposite end of where we had landed earlier that day. Well, at this approach there was a hill at the beginning of the runway. With the runway already being short, he was trying to get on the runway as quickly as he could, but in clearing the hill and to lose altitude he was picking up air speed. So by the time he was anywhere near the ground he was going too fast to land.

"I saw his problem, of course. I was standing there watching, as were several hundred people by then, including our other tenor Bill Shaw, our piano player Jackie Marshall, and Jake Hess of the Statesmen. R.W. didn't even touch down, he just pushed the throttle, lifted the gear, and flew off to try the approach again. On his second approach I saw again that he was having the same problem. He was about a fourth of the way up the runway and he gave the plane a little drop, which he had done before. Sometimes the wheels stick to the ground and sometimes the plane bounces too bad and you have to go back up. Well, it bounced too bad. So he just lifted his gear and pushed his throttle and this time the plane went nose up in a vertical climb. It went straight up several hundred feet until it stalled out and then it came straight down, nose first. I've since talked to several pilots who have flown that type of aircraft and they seem to think that R.W., on that second trip, forgot to retrim his tabs from landing to take-off. When he gave it full throttle it shot the plane straight up.

"Well, the plane crashed and then exploded, flames everywhere. I started running toward the plane—the cabin door was open. I started there first, and then I heard Jackie

Marshall, who was around front yelling 'Here they are!' Well, I didn't know if they had been thrown free of the plane or what ... I was in a state of shock and didn't know what ... I ran around front and the Plexiglas cover to the cockpit had been shattered and I could see R.W. through the flames. He was slumped over. They later told me that both R.W. and Bill had died on impact with their necks broken before the flames got to them.

"But I started in through the flames, not knowing what I was doing. Somebody grabbed me from behind and held me, wouldn't turn me loose and carried me off the field. Years later in The Masters V group, I was singing with Jake Hess and he said, 'Do you know who kept you from going in that plane that night?' And I said, 'No, I really don't.' He said, 'It was me. You fought me so bad I just had to manhandle you and hold you. My shins were black and blue for a month where you had kicked me trying to get a-loose.'

"Jake saved my life really. If I had gone in there I would have been killed instantly. That night when the Statesmen put me in their car and drove me back to Memphis, I told them, 'I'll never sing another note. I'm through.' We had just won on the Godfrey show, had a record on RCA that was one of RCA's top ten sellers that summer, the song 'The Man Upstairs' that we had sung on the Godfrey show. We reached the highest peak we had ever reached in our career—first gospel group that had ever been on nationwide television. After that show every place we played was packed. When they introduced us, we would get a standing ovation when we came on the stage before we had even sung a note, just because we had done something for gospel music nobody else had ever done.

"Then I saw it all go up in flames ..."

# Chapter Two – Alpha and Omega

THE PLANE CRASH THAT June in 1954 was the alpha and the omega of the Blackwood Brothers Quartet, the beginning and the end. It was the beginning of a new Blackwood Brothers Quartet, a quartet that would become the very definition of Southern gospel music, a group that would tour over 35 countries including the Soviet Union during the chill of Cold War, perform for presidents, kings, and the King of Rock and Roll, star on their own syndicated television show, and sell records by the hundreds of thousands. A group with an almost Biblical ring of fire as the touchstone of its legend and its tragedy.

It was the end of the tight-knit family group that grew up singing together on a sharecropper's farm in Ackerman, Mississippi. A group with the kind of achingly sweet close harmony that comes only from the investment of years of family singing. The roots of the Blackwood sound can be found in the music of the Baptist churches they initially attended, where the family sang the traditional hymns and sacred music favored in the more austere and holy setting of the Sunday congregation.

In the rural South during the first decades of the 20th century, evangelical Pentecostal revival meetings swept through the small communities and towns, offering a more ecstatic version of Christianity accompanied by music that as often as not had a beat. Poor white Southerners, such as the Blackwood family, found this brand of religious music entertaining and joyous, if nothing else, and were too busy enjoying it, especially if it were a Friday or Saturday night, to note the similarities between this "gospel" music and the barrelhouse piano styles employed at the swankier houses of ill repute on Beale Street in Memphis. These white Southerners also didn't bother to note that this music took more than a page or two from the Negro churches across town. This curious cultural cross-pollination took no stranger twist than when juke joint entertainer Georgia Tom, famed for his risque blues recordings such as "It's Tight Like That," received the Calling and became even more famous as Reverend Thomas A. Dorsey, the Father of Gospel Music, who penned such classic religious songs as "Peace in the Valley," a song gospel fan Elvis Presley would insist on singing for his mother on *The Ed Sullivan Show*. Reverend Dorsey, in fact, is the man credited with creating the term "gospel music."

The traveling evangelists in the '20s and '30s who crisscrossed the Deep South, often with musical guest artists in tow, provided a sort of sanctified vaudeville show to hundreds of backwoods families who would hitch up their horses or mules and drive their wagons over miles of dirt roads to attend. Although many of these meetings took place in tents—hence the familiar term "tent revival"—a great many more were in "brush arbors." The late Doyle Blackwood provided the following description of a brush arbor in the book *Above All*, a 1965 biography of the Blackwood Brothers:

"By the time the evangelist who was holding the revival had arrived, everyone in the countryside would already be well aware of the details of the meeting. Men of the community would pitch in as volunteers to help prepare the arbor.

"An area in the woods, sometimes quite remote, would be cleared. Then long poles would be nailed horizontally from tree to tree around the cleared space, at a height of about seven feet from the ground, thus forming a frame, or perimeter, to support the roof to come. Other poles would then be laid at intervals across the perimeter and branches, bushes, and brush of all kinds would be laid on top of these as protection from sun or rain. When it was finished the arbor would cover a surprising amount of space, and I've seen some that would hold audiences of several hundred people."

It was at these brush arbor meetings that the Blackwoods first encountered the kind of atomic-powered, Holy Ghost-filled vocal groups that would forge what would come to be known as the quartet style of gospel singing. There were numerous other influences on this style of music, however. The high tenor, lead tenor, baritone, and bass structure of such groups was straight out of the barbershop quartets and songs such as "Sweet Adeline." The spread of battery-operated radios through the rural South also brought The Grand Ole Opry and artists such as the Carter Family, Jimmie Rodgers, and the Delmore Brothers to this audience.

There were other influences on the Blackwoods that

would be evident in their recorded output, seemingly odd ones, such as the Sons of the Pioneers, the Chuck Wagon Gang, Gene Autry, Roy Rogers, Bob Wills and His Texas Playboys, crooners such as Bing Crosby and Frank Sinatra, pop harmony groups such as the Mills Brothers and the Ink Spots, and even the pre- and post-War vogues for Hawaiian music. Last, but certainly not least, was the obvious influence of black gospel groups such as the Golden Gate Quartet, the Pilgrim Travelers, the Dixie Hummingbirds, and the Soul Stirrers.

The foundation of the Blackwood Brothers Quartet began in the mid-1920s when Doyle Blackwood, then in his teens, and his younger brother James, who was seven, began singing duets together and became proficient enough that they soon were in demand at local churches, schools, and civic functions. Doyle was ambitious enough to take singing lessons, which he in turn passed on to his brother James. Their older brother Roy, by this time, had become a minister in the Church of God, a Pentecostal denomination, and was called to pastor several churches in several Southern states. In 1934 Roy moved his family back to Ackerman, Mississippi when his wife was expecting their second child. That year they would become parents of another boy, Cecil, who would replace his older brother R.W. some 20 years later after the ill-fated plane crash in 1954.

With Roy and R.W. back home, Doyle and James enlisted them into performing as a quartet. Roy had an automobile—a 1929 Chevrolet—and through his ministry he had made several contacts that provided them with bookings. This was during the middle of the Great Depression when money for entertainment of any kind, particularly in the poverty belt of North Mississippi, was practically non-existent. Nonetheless, the Blackwood Brothers Quartet earned just enough to soldier on, sometimes dining for days on nickel hamburgers. Their first break came a couple of years later when they auditioned for a nearby radio station in Kosciusko, Mississippi. The small, unaffiliated station was starved for talent and eagerly accepted the Blackwoods as part of their programming—all without payment, of course. The Blackwoods soon found that mass media had its benefits, however, when their bookings increased and they were able to ratchet up their fees.

In 1938 the group auditioned for WJDX radio station in Jackson, Mississippi, the largest market in the state. The station hired the Blackwoods for a daily broadcast which proved lucrative enough that the group members and their families—all the group members were married by this time—were able to move to Jackson and make it their home base. The Blackwood Brothers Quartet now were seasoned pros who had honed their act until they were, as music writer Peter Guralnick described them, "the most progressive and businesslike of all gospel groups." Doyle Blackwood served as the master of ceremonies for the group, and because of his deep, resonant announcer's voice and his short stature was dubbed the Mighty Mite of the Mike. The group had rigged a public address system in their car with large loudspeakers mounted on the roof *a la* the Blues Brothers. Doyle and James took turns hawking their concerts as they drove through the towns and cities where they were booked. Every little bit helped.

In rapid succession the Blackwoods were hired away to Shreveport, Louisiana then to Shenandoah, Iowa after forming a partnership with V.O. Stamps, who was then the most powerful and respected name in gospel music promotion. The Stamps organization arranged the bookings for numerous gospel acts and assigned them to specific territories to maximize their draw and optimize their radio audience.

The Midwest proved to be a highly profitable market for Southern gospel groups, and the Blackwoods' radio program on KMA in Shenandoah, Iowa reached a huge and accepting audience. The Blackwoods, all sons of the South and its mild climate, initially found the Midwest a strange and forbidding territory:

"We had just moved to Iowa, this was in 1940 on Armistice Day, and we had gone over into Northeast Missouri for a concert," remembers James Blackwood. "On the way back, crossing over into the southern part of Iowa, we ran into a blizzard. We, of course, were from the South and had never run into a blizzard before. The car used a lot more gas facing into the blizzard than we had figured on, and about one-thirty in the morning we ran out of gas out in the middle of nowhere. Doyle walked to a farm house we spotted and knocked and knocked then started calling out. Finally the farmer stuck his head out the window and said, 'Just a minute Doyle. I'll be right down.' It turned out the farmer's wife heard Doyle hollerin' out and woke up her husband and said, 'That's Doyle Blackwood down there. I recognize his voice from the radio.'"

Their tenure in the Midwest proved short-lived as war

intervened. One by one the Blackwoods were hired away into the defense industry, relocating to California during most of the War years to work in aircraft factories. The intimate knowledge of airplanes that they gained during this time, ironically, would later lead to their interest in air travel for their group. R.W. Blackwood was drafted into the army and fought in the Pacific theater during the War.

After R.W. was discharged from the service in December, 1945, the Blackwood Brothers Quartet reunited and resumed their daily radio programs on KMA in Shenandoah, Iowa. Doyle Blackwood, the Mighty Mite of the Mike, left the group for a radio announcer position in Chattanooga, Tennessee. The group would undergo several personnel changes in the next few years until settling in to the line-up of Bill Shaw, James Blackwood, R.W. Blackwood, Bill Lyles, and pianist Jackie Marshall, a line-up they would keep until that June of 1954.

The relative prosperity of the post-War years saw a boom in Southern gospel music. The advent of radio transcriptions, which allowed the group to pre-record their radio shows, gave the Blackwoods the freedom of not always having to perform live in the studio, thus expanding exponentially their radio market. The new medium of television also greatly increased their audience, and their telegenic appeal put them into contact with high-profile evangelists such as the Reverend Billy Graham, who in coming years would have them perform at his crusades. In 1950 the Blackwoods were hired by high-wattage station WMPS in Memphis to do daily live broadcasts, and they moved their families, mail-order business, offices, and effects to music-rich Memphis, making it their home base from that point on. The Blackwoods had recorded several 78 rpm singles on their own record label, which they flacked at their concerts and on their radio broadcasts. In 1951 RCA, taking note of the rising popularity of Southern gospel music, signed the Blackwood Brothers Quartet, making them the first gospel group to be marketed nationally by a major record label. By 1954 no other gospel group had come close to the success of the Blackwood Brothers. To other gospel performers, some of whom were outspokenly jealous, it seemed the Blackwoods could do no wrong.

# Chapter Three – Aftermath

"A LOT OF PEOPLE remember where they were and what they were doing when they heard the news about the crash in 1954, just like when JFK was shot," says James Blackwood. "Just yesterday I was at the grocery store and the armed guard who works there, he recognized me. He told me where he was and what he was doing when the news came over the radio. I get that a lot."

As James Blackwood wrestled with the unanswerable question of why?, gospel fans were thunderstruck by news of the plane crash. One such fan was a young Memphian named Elvis Presley, who was so overcome with grief when he heard about the crash that, according to James Blackwood, he went to a nearby park with his girlfriend, Dixie Locke, and cried for 30 minutes. The story of the crash was picked up by the national wire services and was reported on all the national television and radio networks. Barely two weeks after the Blackwoods' triumph on *Arthur Godfrey's Talent Scouts*, Godfrey offered his condolences to the group and their families on his television show.

For the first time, Ellis Auditorium in downtown Memphis,

the scene of innumerable All Nite Sings headlined by the Blackwoods, would be used for the double closed-casket funeral of R.W. Blackwood and Bill Lyles. An overflow capacity of 5,000 mourners attended the funeral service, reportedly the biggest funeral event in Memphis history. Tennessee Governor Frank Clement spoke as did several prominent local clergy. The Statesmen and several other gospel artists provided the music. Presley, who would start a music revolution within days when he would record "That's All Right" at a small Memphis recording studio, was in attendance and was profoundly moved by the collective outpouring of grief. *The Memphis Press-Scimitar* newspaper reported that "A number of negroes called the Auditorium asking if they could attend the funeral, and the galleries were reserved for negroes ..." An estimated 200 sprays of flowers were delivered to the auditorium. Southern gospel music would never get over the tragedy.

# Chapter Four – Daddy (Sumner) Sang Bass

WITHIN DAYS OF THE biggest funeral in the history of Memphis, Tennessee, R.W. Blackwood's younger brother, Cecil, received a phone call.

"I was just 19 years old," Cecil recalled to Bill Gaither about being asked to join The Blackwoods. "I had nervous problems for a long time, a lot of fear. Everybody thought, well, he's so timid and bashful—it wasn't so much that. I felt so inadequate to take my brother's place, who was one of the superstars of gospel music. To overcome that fear I would pretend I was him on stage and try to sing like him and try to imitate him."

J.D. Sumner, singer for the Sunshine Boys who was dubbed "the world's lowest bass" and had been one of the most vocal rivals of the Blackwoods, also was asked to join the new Blackwood Brothers Quartet. Sumner not only had one of the greatest bass voices ever recorded, but brought a wealth of song-writing talent to the group. His bass lines, unlike some bassists who provided little more than foghorn antics, were exquisitely musical, providing a thrilling and melodic counterpoint to the twin tenors of the equally astounding Bill Shaw and James Blackwood. It took time for the relatively inexperienced Cecil Blackwood to come out from under the shadow of his brother R.W., but he nonetheless provided a solid baritone anchor to the pyrotechnics of the other three vocalists.

The Blackwoods had always been masters at working a crowd, using their big, squarish RCA microphones as props for knee-drops, pushing a note higher as they leaned the mike forward, sinking a note lower while slanting the mike stand backwards, backing away from the mikes to fade out a song, or rushing the mikes to drive home a phrase. They never lost sight of the fact that their audiences came to be entertained as much as blessed by the music, even though James Blackwood in particular took the ministry aspect of their concerts dead seriously. The Blackwoods knew that a sizable number of their audience would not darken the door of a church—they simply loved the music and accepted the shared joy, if not the totality, of the message.

Going to a gospel sing in the '50s was, above all, fun, but the harsh memory of the Blackwoods' recent tragedy could have easily derailed the jubilation and emotional high of their performances. The addition of J.D. Sumner during this crucial period was doubly fortuitous for the Blackwoods. Sumner brought not only a more rhythmic sensibility to their sound, as well as his jaw-dropping vocal virtuosity, but added much-needed comic relief to their show. The 6-foot-6-inch Sumner towered above the other three Blackwoods and looked not unlike a mischievous Boris Karloff. His gravelly voice and deadpan delivery, not to mention his often hilarious between-song ad-libs, instantly made him an audience favorite.

One such Sumner moment, recorded for posterity, occurred during his showcase song, "He Means All the World to Me." After singing several verses of the song, the other vocalists stop, leaving Sumner to slowly articulate the words "just inside the pearly city," plunging the last note of "city" lower and lower, past the cellar and into the well, until he can't possibly take the note any lower. At this pregnant moment, Sumner dramatically pauses, then picks up the note and unbelievably slides it down another notch. During the recording of their album *The Blackwood Brothers on Stage*, just as Sumner gets to the magic moment and pauses for effect, a baby screams out during the silence, the tape recorders easily picking up the cry. Sumner, his voice lower than low, says, "Bless his heart," picks the note right back up and dives even deeper. Needless to say, it brought the house down.

"People always called that album, not by its name, which was *The Blackwood Brothers on Stage*, but 'That album where the baby cries,'" adds James Blackwood. "Several years later when we were singing out in California a man came up to us after our concert and said, 'I'm the baby that cried that night on that record.'"

With the horror of the plane crash indelible in the minds of the surviving Blackwoods, they opted once again for travel via automobile, which proved to be just as slow, cumbersome, and exhausting as they remembered it. J.D. Sumner came up with the fanciful idea of purchasing a bus and outfitting it with rooms and sleeping quarters—a motel and office on wheels. At the time, this was unheard of, considered far too costly and impractical. The group still felt the idea had merit and purchased a 1947 Arrowcoach bus and had it extensively customized. Except for the expected breakdowns, the bus proved an almost ideal solution, and this innovative mode of travel for a group of performers swept through not only the gospel community, but the entire American entertainment industry.

In 1956 Arthur Godfrey asked the Blackwoods to appear again on his *Talent Scouts* program. As before, they would be competing against other talent, and there was the added concern that the new version of the Blackwood Brothers Quartet would be compared, perhaps unfavorably, with the earlier version of the group. Once again, the fears were unfounded. The audience enthusiastically endorsed the Blackwoods for a second time.

Over the next 10 years the Blackwood Brothers would take Southern gospel music to heights few in the community would have dreamed possible. They performed on *The Today Show*, appeared on Tennessee Ernie Ford's daytime show wearing snow parkas after arriving late from a concert in Alaska, sang at the funeral of Elvis Presley's mother, bought out the Stamps Music Company, became a distributor for RCA Records (a perk no other RCA artists were ever allowed), ran a successful gospel music record store in Memphis as well as a thriving mail-order business, sponsored and promoted other off-shoot groups such as the Junior Blackwoods, became traveling ambassadors of Southern gospel music throughout the world, and recorded and released dozens more albums.

The unprecedented success and celebrity of Elvis Presley and the popularity of the gospel albums he recorded for RCA, for which he received his only Grammys, brought thousands of new fans to a music form that had been, even at its peak, a niche market. The Blackwood Brothers became familiar faces to millions of Americans on their syndicated Sunday morning television show. Although pressured many times, the Blackwood Brothers steadfastly refused to cross over into popular music, as the Statler Brothers and Oak Ridge Boys, which had once been gospel-only groups, had done.

# Chapter Five – Gospel Music Into Praise Music

JAMES BLACKWOOD, NOW ENTERING his 66th year as a singer of gospel music, is today the unquestioned patriarch of Christian music. His press release states that he officially retired from the Blackwood Brothers Quartet in 1981. But the hardest working man in Southern gospel music hasn't had much time to rest on the laurels of his nine Grammy wins and 30 Grammy nominations, his seven Dove Awards, his Lifetime Achievement Award from the Gospel Music Hall of Fame, and his endless other awards, citations, and honors. After "retiring," he formed the Masters V group with J.D. Sumner and Jake Hess and Hovie Lister of the Statesmen Quartet. Those recordings netted him yet another Grammy. In recent years he has performed at a Johnny Cash tribute concert singing a song written by Cash specifically for the Blackwoods, appeared on the 700 Club, PTL, and TBN, and he has recorded bluegrass-oriented gospel albums with the Light Crust Doughboys. He has plans to record an album with the Jordanaires, the gospel group that backed Elvis on many of his early recordings. His brothers Roy and Doyle both died in the early 1970s, and his good friend and fellow bandmate J.D. Sumner, once a bitter rival who half-seriously threatened to "whip" him, died only three years ago. Sumner had left the Blackwoods in 1965 to manage and lead the Stamps Quartet, which was owned by the Blackwoods. Sumner and the Stamps Quartet later toured extensively with Elvis. When Elvis died, the album last played on Elvis's stereo at Graceland was by the Stamps Quartet. According to my sources, it remains on the stereo turntable today at Graceland, right where Elvis left it.

After Sumner left the group in 1965, the Blackwood Brothers Quartet went through a confounding array of permutations, yet they consistently remained the number one draw on the gospel circuit. After RCA cleaned house of its gospel stable in the early '70s due to diminishing interest, only the Blackwoods remained on the label—their savvy marketing and promotions kept enough product moving to keep RCA happy.

The Blackwood Brothers Quartet is still performing and still on the road more than 200 days each year, traveling in a customized bus seen often in and around Memphis. Cecil Blackwood, who took over for his older brother R.W. after the plane crash in 1954, is the only recognizable figure from the heyday of the quartet in the '50s and '60s. The music and the message have both changed.

"There is a great deal of controversy over the state of contemporary gospel music," says music writer and historian Charles K. Wolfe, one of the few experts on Southern gospel music. "Groups such as the Blackwood Brothers and the

Statesmen were highly professional entertainers who basically professionalized what had been a totally unprofessional form of music. It was music that was sung from a pulpit or on sawdust floors at a tent revival. Early on there was controversy over whether there should be an altar call at the end of gospel concerts and All Nite Sings. Many people thought that the whole purpose of gospel music should be to bring people to their version of Christianity. But to their credit nearly all the gospel groups, including the Blackwoods, resisted this idea. They saw themselves as entertainers, entertainers of a certain type with a certain message, but nonetheless entertainers."

As the music world changed at a dizzying pace in the late '60s and early '70s, so did the gospel world. The quartet style of singing with only a piano as accompaniment changed to a more combo approach with guitar, bass, and drums in addition to numerous keyboards. Polyester and men's hairspray seemed custom-made for gospel singers, and as gospel became less and less hip the message became more and more strident. Gospel concerts in the late '70s and early '80s were shockingly angry and politicized. It was near impossible to get through an All Nite Sing without rants on abortion, prayer in school, and a host of concerns now closely associated with the religious right. It was as if the Christian soldiers had received their marching orders. There were not a lot of smiling faces in the crowd.

"I think the change started in the '60s with the so-called 'praise' music out in California," explains Charles Wolfe. "Praise music was music that served as a vehicle for praise, conversion, and proselytizing. These were songs performed as church. Bill Gaither, who is familiar now on the TNN cable network with his *Homecoming* specials on gospel music, was the one who really got this going, and his influence started the movement that reinvolved the church. In my opinion Gaither's original impetus was to bring more music to his song and music publishing businesses. I think he was smart enough to see that there was a deep schism between the old and new styles of gospel music, and I think he hopes to heal it with his *Homecoming* programs.

"I once heard Hovie Lister of the Statesmen several years ago go on a tear about praise music, calling it the 'devil's music.' Well, they've all embraced it now and you'll see all of them on Gaither's shows. Gaither gave them a new visibility and rescued the old style of gospel from obscurity. But at a price."

James Blackwood is a man fond of quoting numbers. He takes well-justified pride in the many accomplishments of the Blackwood Brothers and can instantly give facts and figures related to sales, awards, and who played what when. He sincerely insists that the market for gospel music today is bigger than it ever has been, and when one sees him front and center in the Gaither *Homecoming* videos, commanding the love and respect of those surrounding him, it is hard to question his figures. But at the same time one can't help but wonder if gospel artists are more and more singing to the choir these days.

J.D. Sumner in 1993 gave his candid opinion on the matter to Australian interviewer Delviz: "Some people do not live what they sing about, or what they talk about, but I'd say that 90 percent of your Southern gospel [artists] are Christian people and live what they sing. Now, moreso than ever ...

What made it change was when they started preachin.' Unless you get on the stage and preach, they do not maybe keep their eye on you. But when you get up there and start tellin' them how to live, then you should be livin' it yourself. So the more that is done in Southern gospel, and I hope that you can understand what I'm tryin' to say, it's almost ruined our business, you know it's just absolutely ruined it. Because there's a lot of people that will not go out and hear preaching and crying and testifying. They want what the Stamps Quartet do, they want entertainment."

In the past listeners weren't required to believe. They were, however, offered some of the most seductive visions of afterlife ever put on record. The Blackwood Brothers' benchmark song, "The Old Country Church," presents a version of heaven as an All Nite Sing with long-deceased loved ones. Their Hawaiian-themed "Paradise Island" is about heaven as a tropical paradise where "songbirds fill the air with mel-o-dy."

When he talked about the plane crash that happened in 1954, exactly one week before I was born, I heard a catch in James Blackwood's voice and saw his eyes fill with tears. This wasn't just a story he had recited dozens of times to interviewers. It was real and the hurt was very much alive, never mind that it happened nearly 50 years ago. James Blackwood is such an unfailingly kind and sincere man—an inspiration, if truth be told, even to a sharp-penned critic such as myself—that I couldn't bring myself to press him on how he could reconcile his notion of a loving God with those flames of death. In Gaither's recently released *Homecoming* special on the Blackwoods, James Blackwood gave his definitive answer to this question:

"After the plane crash, I'm sure I was in a state of shock for some time. I had nightmares about it. I would dream that the quartet as it was after the plane crash was singing and that Bill and R.W. would walk into the back of the auditorium during the concert and that somehow they didn't really get killed in that plane, that they had been somewhere and had recovered and come back. I would wake up crying.

"I prayed about it and asked the Lord to give me peace about it. My dad had died in '51. He and R.W. were very close. R.W. was more like his son than a grandson. One night I had a dream and I viewed the scene of R.W. getting into heaven, and that Poppa was standing there to welcome him. And they each put their arms around each other and hugged each other. I never had a bad dream about that anymore. The Lord gave me peace."

James Blackwood has had several strokes since he left the Blackwoods in 1981 and has had yet another since I began these writings. At his advanced age he probably hears the words to those heaven-laced songs in his mind more and more. There is no question however that he has found his own midnight aisle.

**Author's note:** James Blackwood died of complications related to a series of strokes on February 3, 2002. Cecil Blackwood preceded him in death November 13, 2000. As of this writing the only surviving member of the early incarnation of the Blackwood Brothers Quartet is tenor Bill Shaw.

# Afterword

THE WORDS SOUTHERN GOSPEL music really are a euphemism for white gospel music. Black gospel music is considered almost a wholly separate form, both by the different audiences for white and black gospel music, and by most music writers. In the many books documenting black gospel music and some of the stars who emerged from it, such as Sam Cooke, you will be hard-pressed to find any mention of white gospel groups or performers. It is as if there were some sort of unspoken *de facto* musical erasure. Even worse is the conceit that the musical influences flowed only one way—from the more "authentic" black gospel music to the more staid and conservative white gospel music, which needed some soul flavoring.

The truth, of course, is that music is porous; it admits of all influences. The toned-down polish and clear enunciation of Sam Cooke's delivery, for instance, and his deliberately sparing use of melisma, which most certainly ran counter to prevailing black gospel singing, undoubtedly owes a debt to the stylings of white gospel music.

In like fashion, there are few references to black gospel music in the available sources on Southern, or white, gospel music. One of my own favorite songs of the Blackwood Brothers from their live RCA LP *The Blackwood Brothers in Concert* is "The Devil Can't Harm a Praying Man," a showstopper that features some phenomenal high tenor from Bill Shaw. While re-listening to the song in preparation for this book, it dawned on me that Shaw was deliberately imitating his black gospel counterparts during parts of the song. James Blackwood confirmed my observation.

"'The Devil Can't Harm a Praying Man' was one of our most popular songs in concert. It's a song the Dixie Hummingbirds did. We did several songs that I call black spirituals, and Bill Shaw incorporated that style into his part of the show. The crowds really loved it. We did that song during concerts and All Nite Sings when we were entertaining as much as ministering, but on Sundays we did the songs that we felt were more reverential."

When I asked Blackwood about the influence of black gospel music on their sound he unhesitatingly named the Golden Gate Quartet as one of the most profound influences on the early Blackwood Brothers. "When we were still living in Shenandoah, Iowa, in the early 1940s, the Golden Gate Quartet had a Wednesday night late-night program on CBS radio. We listened to them every time we could. We'd be coming back from a concert somewhere—back in those days we did a lot of live radio broadcasts in the morning and we'd do concerts at night—and we always made it a point to listen to the Golden Gate Quartet. They became real idols for us.

"In the early '50s after we moved to Memphis, the man out in Texas who promoted us in that area, W. B. Mallum, booked us with the Golden Gate Quartet for double-header concerts in Fort Worth, Little Rock, and in Southern Illinois. This was a real high point for us in our career because we had idolized them so much. One of the songs that was on our first album for RCA was called 'Swing Down Chariot,' which we had gotten from the Golden Gate Quartet. They are the ones who had made the song famous.

"At that time our audiences were nearly all white, and it seemed to me that the Golden Gate's singing, for some reason, appealed more to white audiences than black audiences. A little aside that I usually don't tell is that one night we sang at the Will Rogers Auditorium in Fort Worth and the next night we were to sing in the Robinson Auditorium in Little Rock. I was backstage that night before the program started and some of the Golden Gate members were back there also. One of the Golden Gate was coming back into the dressing room with me and the stage manager stopped him. He wasn't going to let him come in. Well, that really got to me. I said, 'Either he comes in here or I'm going to the front of the auditorium and get the manager.' Well, he relented. That's really the only incident of its kind I remember from back then.

"The Golden Gate Quartet were masters of stage presence and microphone usage. I can remember that on some songs they'd be standing back 10 feet from the microphone and within seconds would be within inches of the microphones—this created great effects in their dynamics.

"We were definitely influenced by black gospel music like the Golden Gate Quartet and I believe they were influenced to some extent by us too. It went both ways."

# Suggested Further Reading and Listening

**Books**

Blackwood, James. *James Blackwood Memories*. Brandon, MS: Quail Ridge Press, 1997.

Davis, Paul. *The Legacy of The Blackwood Brothers*. Greenville, SC: Blue Ridge Publishing, 2000.

Racine, Kree Jack. *Above All: The Fascinating and True Story of the Lives and Careers of the Famous Blackwood Brothers Quartet*. Memphis, TN: Jarodoce Publications, 1967.

**Recordings**

Blackwood Brothers Quartet. *Rock-A-My-Soul*. Bear Family five-disc boxed set (German import), 2002.

**Note on recordings:** Many of the classic RCA LPs of the Blackwood Brothers Quartet from their heyday, roughly 1950-1965, are now available on CD, including those recorded with country music performer Porter Wagoner. Beware of re-recordings and repackagings of their classic originals. The *Rock-A-My-Soul* imported boxed set contains all the RCA material up until 1959. The Bear Family label, renowned for their superb remasterings of classic recordings, does a flawless job with the Blackwoods material and include a must-have booklet with the set that contains an authoritative history of the group. Unfortunately, this boxed set, by stopping at 1959, omits some of the Blackwoods' best material, those RCA recordings from 1960 until J.D. Sumner left the group in 1965. As mentioned, some of these LPs are now available on CD. Original vinyl LPs can be purchased easily on eBay, but to get them in mint or near-mint condition requires more effort and expense. If you are not a sound buff, then you can purchase the LPs in less-than-pristine condition cheaply. However, the sound quality of the early RCA Living Stereo LPs is an audiophile's dream. They are well worth the investment for serious listeners who have audio systems of high fidelity quality.

# Sympathy for the Devil: A Kind Word for Albert Goldman

Sympathy for the Devil:
A Kind Word for Albert
Gothman

ALBERT HARRY GOLDMAN IS inarguably the most controversial music biographer of the last generation. His biographies of first Elvis, then John Lennon, have been spit on by the best and worst critics on both sides of the Atlantic. "Bio-porn" Gore Vidal called his writing. And when Goldman veered off into wild sensationalism, as when he referred to Elvis's uncircumcised penis as a "hillbilly pecker," who could argue?

Yet, I have a confession to make. I like the work of Albert Goldman, rotting carcasses and all, and I liked the man himself. To be philosophical about the Elvis book, I believe his scabrous take on the man was necessary, an antidote to the agitprop nonsense written about the man his whole career, and upon long reflection I feel it is a proper bookend to the balanced portrait presented in the definitive, and far politer, biographies by Peter Guralnick.

Goldman, to me, is the Yin to Guralnick's Yang, and when Guralnick was too gentlemanly to go down the ratholes of Elvis's final skid, Goldman relished the opportunity and came up with a morality tale and an American nightmare. I have been privileged to personally know three Elvis biographers, not to mention a score of other writers who have contributed masterfully to the Elvis canon. But no one explored the dark side of Elvis better than Albert Goldman.

My friend Dave Marsh, one of those three Elvis biographers, unsurprisingly detested Albert Goldman and in an interview with me suggested that if he met Goldman in a dark alley he would feel obligated to throttle the bastard. He also stated emphatically that Goldman not only had a welter of inaccuracies in the book (more on that in a minute) but that the book was full of outright lies. This accusation confuses the issue with Goldman's John Lennon bio which to me and others seemed calculated to create controversy by deliberately placed distortions (or outright lies). The most notorious of those about Lennon was Goldman's assertion that Lennon trolled exclusive sex parlors in New York City for boys. To my knowledge no one has ever found one shred of evidence to back up that preposterous claim. So why would Goldman say it? Answer: to sell books. My take on it is that Goldman felt so bloodied and beaten down by the hostility toward his Elvis book, which Goldman felt was truthful and accurate, that he had nothing to lose by exaggerating a few things in the Lennon book. He knew coming out of the gate that he would be reviled no matter what he wrote.

I was in my mid-20s when Goldman's *Elvis* came out. Being a Memphian, you can't imagine the reaction to the book in Elvis's hometown. Of course the fans went completely apeshit; none of them wanted their idol besmirched, particularly by some smirking, sneering New York Jew (Goldman was right when he said much of the reaction against him was rooted in anti-Semitism) who hated Elvis and everything about the American South. I was a part of the Memphis youth who had more or less rebelled against the Elvis faction when the Beatles stormed America. Elvis was old and déclassé, a greaser who still slicked his hair back with hair cream at a time when the rest of us kids were fighting our dads to let our hair touch our ears. Elvis and his Las Vegas lounge act were hopelessly out of date to many of us who were hip to *Rolling Stone* magazine, and when Elvis went off the grid to visit Richard Nixon in the White House we shut the door on him.

Goldman's book confirmed all those rumors that had circulated about Elvis for years. If you lived in Memphis you couldn't help but hear what was going on. He had become the Howard Hughes of the rock generation. One evening at a local café I bumped into a friend who was the brother of a local lawyer. This friend had a copy of Goldman's *Elvis* in his hand. We started discussing the book. He told me that his brother was one of Priscilla Presley's attorneys and that it was he who had discovered that Col. Tom Parker was born in the Netherlands under another name. This lawyer had passed the information on to Goldman. I told this friend that I had noticed about a dozen or so factual errors in the book, primarily small things about people and places in Memphis.

This chance comment set in motion a chain reaction of events that led me to the man himself, Albert Goldman. Goldman was preparing revisions for the paperback edition of the book, which was expected to sell in the millions, and wanted to weed out every mistake he could from the first printing. He asked me to go back through the book and note everything I could. I did and subsequently 14 minor changes were made to the manuscript. He also asked me to do some library work for him and verify a movie Elvis would have seen at a particular movie theater on a particular date. That was easy enough.

Goldman struck me as very funny (he had tried his hand as a standup comic, and failed) and obsessed with getting his book right. He was also very helpful in giving a budding writer some advice and encouragement and even sent an article of mine around to a few editors he knew, which is something no writer has done for me before or since. I told him I would be in New York within a few weeks and he invited me to his apartment that overlooked Central Park. I took him up on the invitation and spent a very pleasant afternoon with him discussing all kinds of things, but particularly the Elvis book.

I remember the conversation well. One thing I very nearly argued with him about was his insistence that Sam Phillips in private said, "If I could find a white boy who could sing like a nigger I could make a million dollars." His argument ran that ALL Memphians used the n-word universally, that changing the word was revisionist and political posturing. Undoubtedly the months Goldman had spent in Memphis convinced him of this because he was absolutely right that a majority of Memphians in the 1950s spoke just that way. What I feel he didn't get was how different Sam Phillips was from the Memphis norm. Phillips was weird by any definition and the fact he recorded black music at all set him far apart from day-to-day Memphis racism. Sam Phillips was exactly the kind of man who would refrain from racial invective.

I also remember that Goldman had the crappiest home stereo I've ever seen in an otherwise wealthy man's apartment. It was a beat up Pioneer system and, I swear, he had masking tape wrapped around one speaker to keep the grill cloth attached. When I asked him jokingly about it he replied blithely that he had an expensive European sound system "in the back." Needless to say, I got no tour of "in the back."

Goldman tired of me in later years; the young writer (me) wore out his welcome and usefulness to him. I read the Lennon book and shook my head. I heard he was working on a biography of Jim Morrison. Then I heard that he had become a member of a very exclusive mile-high club: He died of a heart attack en route to London.

I still read Goldman from time to time. At times his writing was brilliant, as in his acclaimed biography of Lenny Bruce that few dispute was a major work. At other times his writing was little more than hysterical piffle, a very bad imitation of Tom Wolfe and the other New Journalists. He was a champion of disco when others, like me, were dismissive and he wrote eloquently on the subject. He wrote a strange but insightful book about marijuana (he wrote a lot for *High Times* magazine and apparently enjoyed the effects of cannabis) and I'll never forget a story he told about smoking some hashish so potent that he believed he couldn't swallow. He went to the emergency room in a state of panic and was greatly embarrassed when the doctors laughed and assured him he would, in fact, get better.

He reported wrongly that Albert King was B.B. King's brother, a lie Albert told for years to unsuspecting journalists to bring himself closer to B.B.'s brighter flame. In that same piece he brilliantly evoked a head-cutting contest between B.B. and Albert and in another article brought the drum contest between rivals Elvin Jones and Ginger Baker to vivid life. Lastly, he wrote a savage piece for *Life* magazine comparing a Rolling Stones concert to the Nuremburg rallies. Robert Christgau later reported that as he and Goldman passed a joint between them one night, Goldman laughed and admitted that he never even attended the concert.

That's probably true. But I still liked him.

# 10 LPs You Probably Don't Have (But Should)

WE ALL HAVE SEEN THE lists of the absolutely greatest LPs, singles, movies, TV shows, books, etc. OF ALL TIME. I've done them myself and circulated them among friends and fellow music scribes.

They are fun, they show off your quirks, idiosyncrasies, and personality, and, let's face it, an awful lot of the selections in the big press get repetitive. Who could deny *Citizen Kane*, or *Sgt. Pepper* are great, or "Sittin' On the Dock of the Bay" or "Heard It Through the Grapevine"? So my idea here was why not go a whole different approach and list a few of those albums I am pretty sure other music lovers either don't have, haven't heard of, or will strongly disagree with? Well, that's what this list is all about—quirks, quirks, quirks and finding the occasional buried treasure.

# 1. Canned Heat – *Living the Blues*

Canned Heat did what no other '60s rock group can claim: They singlehandedly made the term "boogie" a national music joke. It became at least as corny as wannabe hipsters flashing the peace sign back in the day. Their second lead singer, Al Wilson, was so bad that alley cats still hold their ears. But this double-LP has got some fine moments and you know it has to be good because only one song on the whole thing ever makes it onto Canned Heat's greatest hits packages.

They do terrific remakes here of "Walkin' By Myself" and "Pony Blues" and a wow-inducing acid-drench-a-thon in the little heard "One Kind Favor." On LP number one the highlight is the nearly 20-minute "Parthenogenesis" which is a hodgepodge of solo spots by each band member and contains the most incredible blues jew's harp playing I have ever heard. "Parthenogenesis" is a visionary track, blues taken to a *Sgt. Pepper* level of creative *out there*. The only bad moment is the obligatory, but thankfully brief, drum solo. Also incredible is Wilson's raga-ish chromatic harp solo.

If that isn't enough, the entire second LP is one gigantic song—the dreaded "Boogie," the song that started the whole bad joke. But this version starts off with a primal wail of feedback-drenched elephant honk that is almost better than "Ball and Chain," Janis Joplin's only great song thanks to that criminally underrated garage band of hers, Big Brother and the Holding Company. When the band all comes in together on the down-boogie, they have left John Lee Hooker way behind. Understand John Lee Hooker cannot be topped, ever, but these boys know that and decide to instead blow the doors off the auditorium (did I say this was recorded live?).

Even the bass solo here is good. Once again a dreaded drum solo. Nothing's perfect. If you can pick this up cheap, go for it. I've got an expensive retooled vinyl copy. Bliss!!!!

### 2. Kraftwerk – *The Mix*

Many of you will remember this musical oddity from the mid-'70s, a quartet of nerdy engineer-looking Germans sitting deadpan in front of an intimidatingly large bank of synthesizers and playing a repetitive-themed song called "Autobahn" that in a long, slow, hypnotic pulse suggested the monotony of freeway driving. It was a clever piece, a novelty of its day, and these Germans spearheaded a small but influential music subgenre now termed "krautrock." They also created one of the funniest shticks of any group ever. Ralf and Florian, two for-real music engineers and nerds supreme, formed the group basically to tinker with computerized music. They took their nerdiness to showbiz level, wearing business suits when everyone else on the scene was sporting glitter. When they were accused of sounding "fascist" they donned blazing red shirts (Commie colors for you babies) with Nazi-youth looking uniforms, completely turning the accusations on their head. The late Lester Bangs wrote one of his most brilliant pieces on Kraftwerk and in his interview with them he egged on their Teutonic bluster and it was obvious they had a sporting time of it all and, more importantly, *all got the joke*.

This CD marked the first time in years Ralf and Florian recorded again as Kraftwerk. The reason is because the rudimentary noises of "Autobahn" became the foundation of much of hip-hop's sampling and their pioneering electronics exploded into a new worldwide technology. No wonder they didn't have the time to record much as Kraftwerk. What they do here is take some of their best-remembered tracks and give them a thorough updating. Their redo of "Autobahn" is sheer genius, taking that slow brontosaurus plod and giving it a T. Rex's bite. The weird humor ain't left 'em either, with a hilarious synthesized yodeling coda. And those zooming car sounds that livened up the original have been recreated to sound like a speedway in your house. The lead track here, "Robots," is maybe the most danceable German song to come out of the rock era, yet fully retains that goosestepping attitude that makes the Germans, well, the Germans. After listening to this song there should be no doubt that the future belongs to the robots and, like it or not, they will have a sense of humor.

### 3. Roger Miller – *Golden Hits*

There are several Roger Miller CDs and compilations, but trust me, this is the ONE. In the mid-'60s, during the reign of the Beatles and Stones, came this twang-talking peckerwood from the Deep South who had a string of the most unclassifiable hits ever. They weren't exactly pop, not exactly country, certainly not folk, or were they? Miller, like Woody Guthrie, Dylan, and hell, I can't think of 'em all at the moment, was an American original, a guy who could write just as well about hoboing around the country, with an admission he'd steal in a minute, as visiting England for the first time. What made Miller a great artist was his extraordinary wordplay, a love of words and the very *sound* of them. No other songwriter could have come up with this great couplet: "Roses are red/Violets are purple/Sugar's sweet/and so is maple surple." And make it all sound as natural as cornbread and molasses.

## 4. Lester "Roadhog" Moran and His Cadillac Cowboys (aka The Statler Brothers) – *Alive at the Johnny Mack Brown High School* (Mercury Records)

I once proposed a serious article on the making of this classic comedy LP to a very serious magazine putting together their very serious annual All Music Issue and was met with a collective "huh?" from the editors. Such is life.

Imagine if you will the entire Monty Python cast forced with shotguns at their backs to travel the rural American South visiting the worst imaginable backwater honky-tonks with their only time off being to watch *Hee-Haw* reruns. Then as a reward they were paid extravagant sums of money to come up with a comedy album based on these experiences. Well, *Alive at the Johnny Mack Brown High School* is it, only it was The Statler Brothers, and not Monty Python doing the work. It would be hard to tell the difference, because this is about the most surreal take on cornpone humor ever waxed, and the album circulated for years to audiences who had no idea it was The Statler Brothers.

Just like Monty Python's *Holy Grail*, I knew guys when the LP came out who could perform this entire LP with every guttural "Alll-right" spoken by the deep-voiced Roadhog imitated to perfection. What this hilarious fraud pretends to be is a live recording of an unbelievably bad country band at a rural high school dance, where fights break out, lyrics to country classics are mangled beyond recognition, guitars are wildly out of tune, and in the most politically correct of times the Cadillac Cowboys have the audacity to start naming a roster of country music greats and when Roadhog comes to the name of Charley Pride he pauses then says, "He's the only n..., the only n..., (long breath), the only *name* that ain't on our list. Alll-right."

The Cadillac Cowboys' take on "Sixteen Tons" simply must be heard to be believed. Words alone cannot begin to describe this vocal trainwreck. Likewise a version of "Hey Joe."

This is just side one. Side two is "The Saturday Morning Radio Show No. 2" where besides the Cadillac Cowboys we get a sampling of the "local" talent. If you have never heard a country radio station from waaaaay back yonder in the sticks, then this will be the only introduction you ever need. The liner notes and photos and cover art also are alll-right and howdy-howdy, doth quote the Roadhog.

### 5. Masters of Reality – *Sunrise on the Sufferbus*

As a long-time music scribe I have vented my spleen times a-plenty on the lack of good drumming in today's music. Oh, there are some inventive programmers out there who can tart things up a bit, but name three drummers in the last decade who were really anything more than glorified time-keepers. Many drummers nowadays cannot even accomplish that. Imagine my shock and amazement when I was driving in Memphis to nowhere in particular and this track comes on the radio where the drums are going off like a string of M-80s and the rhythm is not only nitro-fueled, but there are more drum fills, thrills, and spills than the days of Keith Moon and his monster drum kit. I kid you not, I literally pulled over to the side of the road so that I could hear the name of the band so I could find out who this four-handed drummer was. It had been years since I had heard drumming of such jaw-dropping virtuosity. And all to back up a minimalist power chord band.

The good news was that it was indeed a new band, the

bad news was that it was Ginger Baker, GINGER BAKER!!!!!, on drums. But that bad news was actually good news, except for the fact that it took a 60-something-year-old legend to make me pull over to the side of the road. Baker had recorded only sporadically over the years since his heyday with Cream and Blind Faith, and he obviously preferred jazz to rock and polyrhythms from his African jaunts to hanging out with long-haired boys with Marshall stacks. How the band, Masters of Reality, talked Baker into this one-shot album would probably make an interesting story in itself. As is, the album is as good as it is curious. There are killer hard rock tracks such as the aforementioned pull-to-the-side-of-the-road tune, "She Got Me (When She Got Her Dress On)," lovely ballads with some super-slick drum licks, and a song by Baker about his pet American peeve—that he can't get a good cup of tea out of us Yanks. The song is clever and funny, but the drumwork!—damn! After this album Baker went back to Arizona to play jazz and polo. (p.s. He now makes his home in South Africa.

**Author's Note in 2015:** He again lives in England.) Believe you me it is our loss and the horses' gain.

## 6. Jerry Lee Lewis – *Live at the Star Club* (Bear Family)

Maybe it's just a holdover from adolescence, but I always enjoyed those "who's better?" debates. You know, who's better, B.B. King or Albert King? The Beatles or the Stones? James Brown or Otis Redding? I even like those apples and oranges comparisons such as "who's the better guitar player, Chuck Berry or Jeff Beck?" Debates spark interest and interest sparks excitement.

Okay then, I've got one for you. Who's the better piano player, Keith Emerson (of Emerson, Lake, and Palmer for those of you born after that fad) or Jerry Lee Lewis? My opinion? Hands down it's Jerry Lee. Why? Well, Emerson can undoubtedly whip out a decent "Toccata and Fugue" by Bach that might even impress classical snobs, but honestly who would you rather see play a piano with his ass, Emerson or the Killer? If your answer is the former rather than the latter then don't ever go club hopping with me.

Jerry Lee Lewis is a category unto himself because no one else would dare to be like him. Right here in Memphis there is an excellent tribute artist who does a killer Killer named Jason D. Williams, but compared to the real deal Jason seems positively civilized. Which Jerry Lee isn't and never has been. His live recording in 1964 at the Star Club in Hamburg, Germany, the joint that the Beatles made famous, is all the proof you'll ever need that civility is overrated. Think about it, during the same year the Beatles were eating up the charts in America and Jerry Lee was reduced to playing prom dances, someone came up with the idea of putting this 20-something-year-old rock and roll has-been in the whore-saturated Reeperbahn club that was already attracting Beatles tourists.

There is much conjecture among Jerry Lee aficionados about what he was on when this recording was made. The playing is so hard, ferocious, and unrelenting that it seems as if Jerry Lee, and not Elvis, should be dubbed the atomic-powered singer, because nuclear fission seems to be about the only thing that could explain this much entertainment combustion. Or lots and lots of amphetamines (my guess).

The set is backed by the Nashville Teens, the British group that despite its wimpy-sounding name came up with a pile-driving hit cover of "Tobacco Road," and they do an admirable job trying to keep up with the rocket sled. Jerry Lee starts off with a growl then explodes into a version of "Mean Woman Blues." During his take on "Money" he goes off into a jaunt of singing "ha-ha-ha-ha" repeatedly and *makes it sound good*. Then he yodels a verse's worth or so, and on it goes. The crowd recognizes real rock and roll danger when it sees it and after about the sixth time of chanting "Jerry Lee, Jerry Lee, Jerry Lee" between songs, the Killer has had enough of the fan worship and snarls out "alright already!" On this one night in 1964 in Hamburg, Germany, it is hard to believe that anyone, *anyone*, could have topped this pompadored force of nature who makes sure he gets in at least one self-reference per song. And just think who all he has outlived.

### 7. Everything But the Girl – *Eden* (import version)

It's late, the lights are low, the mood is slightly boozy, and the hormones are on slow simmer because you are sipping on your third martini with that gorgeous somebody in that slinky dress, and you go to your hi-fi and slip on a little Guns N' Roses. No?

So, what's wrong with that picture? Suffice it to say that Sinatra and not Slash is much better at setting the, shall we say, *proper* tone for those late night dances when the shoes are off and the laughter is longer. That said, what else out there besides Ol' Blue Eyes does the trick for sexy mood-making? I can't speak for you, but *Eden* by British duo Everything But the Girl sure puts me there. The whole album has that slow, languid, early a.m. quality that makes me think of tiki bars, Caribbean-themed nightspots, beatnik haunts, lovers's quarrels, loose neckties, all that good stuff. Both of the members, Ben Watt and Tracey Thorne, have breathy voices that insinuate themselves into your central nervous system and make you want to sway to their tropical blend of jazzy heartbreak. Think Sade with leaner, more bop-sounding arrangements, some acoustic guitars, some ripe-toned low volume electrics, and an ocean breeze. The import version has the terrific song "Bittersweet" that for inexplicable reasons is left off the domestic version. This song, slow, and, yes, bittersweet, is one of the best songs I know of for getting her to slip out of those high heels. Pay attention lads.

### 8. The Cramps – *Off the Bone*

The year was 1977 and in Memphis the rumor went 'round like a rifle shot that the first ever punk rock band was to play in town, an unknown group called The Cramps, a name that had pretty much everyone scratching their heads.

Word was they had been doing some recording in Memphis, with Alex Chilton, of all people, producing. The Cramps were cloaked in mystery and menace and by the time they actually played this gig, people were whispering that they ate live children.

The day before their show, I was driving down a major midtown avenue and saw what had to be the strangest looking white couple I'd seen in a decade or two strolling hand in hand down the sidewalk. The guy was tall, lanky, with a rooster's comb of unruly and obviously dyed black hair; the other, the girl, had a permed electric frizz, kohl-rimmed eyes and seemed half the man's height. "Hey honey," I said to my then wife, "I'll bet that's those Cramps. What do you say we offer them a ride?" "Don't you DARE!" was the answer, thus spoiling at least one story I could tell the grandkids.

I've always been surprised The Cramps never rose beyond their hardcore cult following. I don't think I've ever seen them on a best-of list of any kind. But boy do they deserve something. Even in that early era of shock rock and shock jocks and shock everything else, The Cramps always went to the brink and jumped off. They were no pose.

To see what I mean check out one of the few available videos of them on *Urghhh! A Music War,* the punk documentary, and tell me they don't raise your eyebrows higher than anyone else. The late lead singer and front madman Lux Interior looks like what Elvis's twin brother might have had he been born completely deranged and hidden in a closet for most of his life, having been forced to listen to that pretty boy Elvis's music. In this video Lux, shirtless, does Jim Morrison's leather pants one better by wearing a pair that covers only half his ass and doesn't quite make it covering his pubic hair. He does just about everything but backflips and those leather britches miraculously still manage to stay up. Then he takes his microphone and performs fellatio on it, but does it in such a maniacal, exaggerated way that you will collapse on the floor laughing, as I did. And his main squeeze, Ivy Rorshach, impassive as the sphinx, watches and plays her guitar. Is she real or a mannikin? Only a window dresser would know for sure.

Okay, okay, the music. *Off the Bone* is kind of, sort of a greatest hits package, but a band this weird can't really fit completely into one compilation. But as an album standing on its own merit, this album packs more genuine rockabilly dementia and warpage than a hundred Stray Cats. Take their take of Charlie Feathers' "I Can't Hardly Stand It." Feathers was about the most out there of the rockabillies to begin with, with more vocal hiccups and spasms than all the early hitmakers put together. But Lux Interior takes Feathers and pushes the vocals so far into outer space that there's no oxygen left—and in space no one can hear you hiccup. But hiccup he does, incredible vocal belches that have everyone I've ever played this song for in stitches. Oh, and when he comes to the verse, he sings it with a perfect tremolo effect that is the work of his double-jointed vocal cords and not the recording studio.

The Cramps infused rock and roll with a *Creepy*-magazine ghoul flavor and found the most obscure covers imaginable to amp up beyond endurance. I could rave about this album for many more pages, but I'll leave you with an example of Lux Interior's poetic muse from the song "Human Fly": "I'm a human fly/and I don't know why/and I buzz, buzz, buzz/and it's just becuzz ... I got 96 tears/and 96 eyes."

As I say, they certainly deserve something.

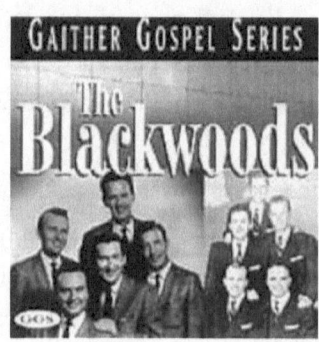

**9. The Blackwood Brothers –** *The Blackwoods*
***(Gaither Gospel Series)***

There is a CD out, finally, of what purports to be the Blackwood Brothers greatest hits, but the truth is no Blackwoods greatest hits package has ever done this unheralded great vocal group proper justice. The Blackwood Brothers, in case you've never heard of them, are the biggest gospel group in history. One could even say in all seriousness that they were the Beatles of the gospel world; such was the power and respect for them in their glory days. They became a national phenomenon in 1954 about a month before Elvis, who was thoroughly besotted with the group, recorded "That's All Right." They were already huge in the South and Midwest, but a succession of appearances on the highly-rated *Arthur Godfrey Show* catapulted them nationally. They were signed to RCA, the big time indeed, and were racking up record gospel sales. Disaster struck in July 1954 when the 10-seater Beechcraft they flew to their gigs—that's how big they were—crashed on a practice take-off in front of thousands of fairgoers. Two members were on the ground. Two died on impact.

The funeral for the two members who died in the plane crash was held at Ellis Auditorium (where Elvis soon thereafter performed) and is reported to have been the biggest funeral service in Memphis history until the King himself died. People who still believe that white gospel music did not cross over to black audiences should note that so many requests were phoned in to Ellis Auditorium that the balcony was reserved specifically for black mourners. And it was full.

After the crash, the Blackwoods regrouped and brought in one of the great bass singers to ever overshadow a stage, J.D. Sumner, who later toured with Elvis. Sumner was like no one before or since—a revelation as a singer, who brought a rhythmic, boogie beat to the staid gospel field, a superb songwriter (you've got to hear his vision of heaven as a Hawaiian Eden in "Paradise Island"), and he was a great entertainer who could bring down the house with his deadpan ad-libs. At the other end of the quartet was Bill Shaw, a high tenor as good as any competitor on the roster at Atlantic Records. Bear Family a few years back put out a terrific, if expensive, box set of the group's pre-1960 recordings. But the Blackwoods recorded many more treasures after that, up until the departure of Sumner for the Stamps Quartet (which was owned by the Blackwoods). One example of the group's vocal aerobics is their cover of the Dixie Hummingbirds' "The Devil Can't Harm a Praying Man" where they morph their style from black gospel to white and back again, all in homage to the black gospel groups the Blackwoods openly adored.

If there's one group America needs to rediscover before the historical rust obliterates this music form, it's the Blackwoods and their singular gospel quartet style.

## 10. *One From the Heart Soundtrack* featuring Tom Waits and Crystal Gayle

Everyone with a serious music collection should have at least one surprise album to amaze and confound their friends. Isn't bragging rights part of the fun? This is my pick. I've told people that there is an album of duets with Tom Waits and Crystal Gayle and received more than one, "yeah, right" in response. Well, here it is in all its weird glory, the strangest bedfellows in pop music singing their hearts out in this soundtrack to *One From the Heart*, one of those disjointed, slightly off-kilter, post-*Apocalypse Now* films from Francis Ford

Coppola, who, it must be said, has been responsible for more than one interesting soundtrack (see *Rumble Fish*).

I confess I've never been much of a fan of Tom Waits. His retro beatnik persona strikes me as more about shtick than music, and even his highly-touted *Swordfishtrombones* is pretty much earwash to me. Crystal Gayle was more country-politan polish than country for my tastes, and although she admittedly had the pipes her material never seemed to rise far above radio pap. Here, however, Waits tones down the barfly piano crooner act and actually sings, and Gayle is the perfect chanteuse foil for his gravel. They mesh well and the songs, all late hours lounge lizard moodiness and dazzle, have a rat pack patina with a post-modern Cocktail Nation edge. A good one to put on when the party's all but over and the laggards, who you really wanted to hang behind anyway, sip the last of the drinks and let their masks down.

# When the Sex Pistols Came to Memphis

WHEN THE SEX PISTOLS blitzed into Memphis on a very cold Friday night in January (the 6th) 1978, probably not one in 10 people in the audience had ever heard one note of their music.

Only days before the concert, Warner Brothers Records released their atom bomb of a record, *Never Mind the Bollocks, Here's the Sex Pistols*, stateside in a hot pink cover with the iconic torn graphics that came to symbolize everything about the British punk movement. Prior to that, the Sex Pistols had received no airplay in Memphis and an import version of their LP, which had a dayglo yellow cover instead of hot pink, was available at none of the Memphis-area record shops.

A tiny section in the back of Peaches Records on Park Avenue had some imported singles and it was there that I found "Pretty Vacant," as far as I know the only Sex Pistols anything that was available prior to the news that the most controversial band in history—way more reviled than Elvis, the Beatles, the Stones or anyone else you would care to name—was actually coming to Memphis and six other cities. I was 23 years old, newly married, and was by far the oldest person I knew with any interest at all in the band. I subscribed to *Rolling Stone* magazine and was as shocked as everyone else when I read a cover story by Charles M. Young about a new rock and roll movement in England called "punk" that was spearheaded by a spike-haired group of angry working-class misfits called the Sex Pistols. The name alone seemed calculated to outrage the status quo including the staid rock press.

I immediately wanted to check them out.

The *Rolling Stone* article didn't exactly endorse the band or their music, but it was a powerful advertisement for an indefinable *something* that they were selling in their attitude. I had no idea what to expect when I gave "Pretty Vacant" its first spin, but from its first repeated guitar signature followed by a thunder of drums then the nastiest-sounding power chords this side of the Who's *Live at Leeds*, I was completely hooked. My wife, predictably, hated it as did every friend I pigeon-holed into listening to the song. As I say, the music of "Pretty Vacant" could be compared distantly to other rock music I had heard and, indeed, loved such as *Live at Leeds*. But nothing prepared me for the raw, screaming, snarling mess that was the utterly unique voice of Johnny Rotten.

As a teacher, at various times I've tried to explain to my students just how revolutionary the Beatles were when they first appeared in America. I was in the fourth grade and because my parents were strictly-observant Southern Baptists, I never got a chance to watch *The Ed Sullivan Show*. (We attended church every Sunday morning *and* Sunday night.) I had no idea that a rock and roll group called the Beatles had even made an appearance on the *Sullivan Show*. However, the next Saturday I was at a friend's house; his sister was watching *American Bandstand*. The whole show was devoted to the Beatles and when I asked innocently who the Beatles were a whole group of kids turned to look at me and said in unison,

"You don't know who the Beatles are?"

Before I left that house I not only knew all the Beatles by name, but I was already practicing my sales pitch for getting Mom and Dad to buy me one of their records. The way they looked, their hair, their clothes, their sound, their photos, the graphics on their album covers—nothing about them was familiar ground. It was as if a flying saucer from Planet Cool had deposited four of its subjects on Earth to change all the young people. Elvis was instantly passé.

The Sex Pistols were similar in many ways. Their look was new, their sound different, and they brought with them a whole new aesthetic. Even their album graphics, as mentioned, were revolutionary. They brought danger back to rock and roll and we in Memphis knew they were going to be a force to be reckoned with.

As I recall, the tickets for the concert cost $3.50. I bought three—one for myself, one for my wife, and one for a friend. They still haven't forgiven me. The concert was going to be held in a dilapidated former ballroom (the Taliesyn) attached to the 20th Century Club on Union Avenue. I do not recall any rock concerts being booked there prior to the Sex Pistols. The ballroom supposedly held 900 people, but no one mentioned that this was to be the highly dangerous "festival" seating, where concertgoers are herded like cattle into an open room and made to stand without seating for hours. Police Director Buddy Chapman, already worried that the Sex Pistols might instigate some sort of riot, along with Fire Marshals, declared the festival seating arrangement unsafe (they were dead right about this) and required the promoter to put seats in the room. In so doing at least 200 people holding tickets—astoundingly, the concert was a sell-out—were left outdoors in the freezing cold drizzle and did not take kindly to the notion that they weren't going to be admitted inside. But more on that in a moment.

Being a lifelong Memphian, I knew it was best to show up early to get a good seat. As we arrived I heard the sounds of "Pretty Vacant" shaking the building; the Sex Pistols were inside doing a sound check. Not being able to yet enter from the front, we ran around back to try and catch a glimpse of them. A very small crowd gathered and suddenly there were shouts of "Sid! Sid!" "Johnny! Johnny!" They were hustled out quickly, enough so that only a few people sighted them and they were not to be seen again for several long hours. (**Author's Note:** Sid wandered away from his Holiday Inn room to try and score a heroin fix. It took his handlers several hours to find him.)

Fast forward: The ballroom was packed, cameras hovered everywhere, and a lot of the crowd obviously were from the media. Only one kid was dressed punkishly—he was the only one who got *that* memo apparently—and when he half-heartedly threw a piece of ice at some bright camera lights the cameraman WENT OFF and the kid, obviously no street fighter, slunk down in his chair and didn't stir again until the band came out. A warm-up band, Quo Jr., played first, and they got a very nasty and rude reception from a crowd that was totally amped-up for the Pistols. I have never felt such anticipation and electricity in a crowd before or since and it was both exhilarating and frightening. The feeling was as if we'd been soaked in some inflammable juju and were waiting for a match to ignite us. Quo Jr. was a local, all-black punk band led by the charismatic Roland Robinson (now deceased) who at one point screamed, "Man, we can't communicate!"

Then he launched into a high-volume song of the same title. However, the crowd was composed mostly of thrill-seekers (by the way, the crowd was entirely white) who seemingly didn't give a damn about the music, especially that of a black warm-up band. All night long the audience threw ice from soft drink cups—the only refreshment for sale—and the cups themselves. (**Author's Note:** Years later I had the pleasure of reminiscing with Roland Robinson about that night. He was amazed that I could remember the name of that song.)

After Quo Jr. left the stage, the wait seemed interminable. I went to the restroom and right above my head a window shattered and a rock tumbled to the floor. The ticket holders outside who weren't allowed in were nearly rioting and I could hear someone on a bullhorn (Police Director Buddy Chapman) trying to calm the crowd down outdoors. After about an hour and a half with the tension thick enough to slice, the lights dimmed and out strolled the band who quickly fired-up the stage. There were no giant video screens and I could lie and say how small they seemed from my seat midway back. But they seemed HUGE. The crowd seemed stunned. At one point Johnny Rotten even said, "Why are you all staring at me?" They had nowhere near the amplification firepower of someone like the Who, but MY GOD when Steve Jones and Paul Cook thundered down I thought the Talicsyn Ballroom would fall to pieces. Steve Jones looked as if he had stepped out of Don Pedro's hair salon. He had a sculpted coif that didn't look punk in the least, but his white Les Paul shredded all notions of a fancy boy. Paul Cook, a powerhouse drummer, rooted the band's sound to his rhythmic, solid pounding. The T-shirt he wore contained a close-up photo of a woman's bare breasts.

Sid Vicious, none of us knew at the time, could not play bass guitar at all. His sound was so thick and muddy you could not distinguish notes; all you could hear was a huge, earth-swallowing throb. Sid was shirtless and had red markings all over his torso that I originally thought were made by a red felt-tip marker. I didn't know until much later that he had carved a message into his chest with a knife: "I need a fix." He wore leather pants and his hair was spiked, as was Johnny Rotten's. Sid attempted to talk several times between songs, but his accent was absolutely impenetrable. Something else no one has mentioned previously is that Johnny Rotten's voice was heavily reverbed, so much so that in one particular instance when he began to speak to the crowd all you could hear was echo. He gave a deadly look to someone off-stage who corrected the problem and we could then hear him speak.

What did he say?: "I'm not here for your amusement, you're here for mine. So behave yourselves and don't throw things at me. I don't like it." I seem to also remember some quips about Elvis. Johnny wore a blue tartan suit and in the spotlights his blue eyes blazed like pilot lights on a stove. He mimicked some of the Shakespearean mannerisms of Sir Laurence Olivier, particularly Richard III, hunchbacked, rocking back and forth as he sang dementedly, appearing ape-like at times, deliberately of course. Sid's bass was slung lower than I had ever seen anyone play a musical instrument. At one point a member of the stage crew held a bottle of Heineken for him to drink while he played. He looked like a baby nursing.

Few people in the audience knew any of the songs, as I mentioned. But that didn't stop the crowd from wanting an encore when the Pistols left the stage. I've read that Memphis was one of the few times the band ever gave an encore, in this case "No Fun," a song originally by the Stooges.

My ears rang for days. My wife complained every time I played the Sex Pistols album, which I managed to finally buy a couple of weeks later. "It was history, baby," I kept telling her. She scoffed.

Some weeks later I met a worker for the telephone company, a big Southern bubba-type, who told me he and some friends had been hired as bodyguards for the Sex Pistols. "Yeah," he laughed, "that damn Sid guy. That scrawny little bastard kept wanting to fight everybody." "What did you do?" I asked. "Aw man, we just laughed at him and pushed him away. He wud'n gonna hurt none of us."

And you know, I was right. It *was* history.

# Folks I know for sure were there that night:

Me.

My now ex-wife, Denise Graves.

Friend Chuck McCall (where did you go Chuck?).

The late record producer Jim Dickinson, whose take on the concert was so wildly off-the-wall and different from my reality that I can only conclude he had a heaping helping of the record companies' drugs backstage.

The late songwriter and lead singer for Quo Jr., Roland Robinson

Writer John Floyd (author of a fine book on Sun Records).

Record man Ward Archer Jr. (who gave me his photographs of the event…thanks Ward).

And outdoors, unable to get in and mighty pissed about it (his rant was captured on film)…writer/songwriter/musician Rick Clark.

# Guilty Pleasures: Tennessee Ernie Ford

MY MOTHER TELLS THE story of a Bob Hope television special that aired in the 1950s. The comedian had just made a crack about the new summer swimsuit fashions that were "so skimpy the girls will have two sets of cheeks to powder instead of one," when the screen suddenly went blank then to an "Experiencing Network Difficulty" super that remained on until the top of the hour.

It was in the climate of these squeaky clean times—when to overhear the F-word in a lady's presence called for an instant showdown with the offender—that an unlikely character named Tennessee Ernie Ford with an offhand, easygoing brand of Southern humor became one of television's most beloved personalities and one of Capitol Records' biggest recording stars. Ernest Jennings Ford, from the mountains of East Tennessee, was singled out early in high school as having the makings of a great singer. His booming baritone was folkish and untrained enough to communicate almost effortlessly with his audience (not an easy thing if you have operatic potential), yet skilled enough to bend a song to his will and deliver a powerhouse performance.

His resonant speaking voice is what originally got him out of the hills of Bristol, Tennessee and into a prominent deejay spot on KXLA outside Los Angeles—the city's number one country-and-western station. He became a local celebrity by dint of his quick, natural wit, daily doses of "Ernie-isms," and by opening the mike and singing along with the records. While doing the latter, he was discovered by talent scouts and given a spot on the *Hometown Jamboree* show alongside country artists like Merle Travis and steel guitar great Speedy West.

It was here that Ford, who had developed a hillbillyish rube character for the show he called "Tennessee Ernie," began to delve into pulse-quickening country boogie numbers, which had grown in popularity after the Second World War. With his likeable persona and naturally funny demeanor, Ford was an instant hit and soon found himself with a daily network television show, a Capitol Records contract, and more engagements than he could fill.

Ford's first singles for Capitol did almost unbelievably well. With his stunning, big voice he took the widely-covered "Mule Train" straight to Number One on the country charts in 1949, followed by huge hits with "The Shot Gun Boogie," "Tennessee Border," and "I'll Never Be Free." His boogie-woogie numbers, such as "Catfish Boogie," "Blackberry Boogie," and "Rock City Boogie" were also enormously popular in England, where Ford was and still is considered one of the great pre-rock and rollers. But Ford's voice isn't the only thing to recommend these tracks: Capitol employed some of the most daring session men in the business, such as Jimmy Bryant and Speedy West, who could take even a bland number and rocket it into the stratosphere with breakneck guitar fills, great blasts of bass note twang, and Speedy's incredible "bar crashes" on pedal steel.

But it wasn't until 1955 that Tennessee Ernie Ford made

recording history with an obscure number written and recorded earlier by Merle Travis. The song, "Sixteen Tons," was initially performed by Ford on his television show, and over 1,200 requests poured in for him to sing it again. No fools, Capitol seized upon those requests and rushed out a single. Upon release the song sold over 400,000 units in 11 days. To date it has sold a minimum of four million copies–and probably much more than that if one could accurately assess the total of sales worldwide.

Even after 50 years "Sixteen Tons" remains one of the most unflinching, crystalline images of the common laborer ever recorded. Its bitter tone against the almost palpable evil of the coal company coupled with the pride expressed in the sheer physical strength required of a coal miner actually caused some in those McCarthy times to brand the song "Communistic." It is a song that has already become a part of American lore and embedded into the national consciousness. No one was surprised when the Soviet Union took the song to heart when Tennessee Ernie Ford toured there during the '70s.

Two recent CDs, *Sixteen Tons* on Bear Family and *The Best of Tennessee Ernie Ford* on Rhino, splendidly document the country boogie and country pop sides of Ol' Rockin' Ern, and thankfully leave out of the hymns and sacred music that comprise the bulk of his recorded legacy. After reading Ernie's autobiography in preparation for this piece, I'm more convinced than ever of the man's great humor, compassion, and humanitarianism. At heart a humble family man, he said this about his career in 1954: "I love show business, don't get me wrong. But I'd retire today, if I could, and I'm not kidding. As soon as I made enough money [sic], and it doesn't have to be a whole potful, I'm going to quit and retire to a farm."

Speaking for those of us who've ever owed our souls to a company store, I wish you, Mr. Ford, a pleasant farm life and many years of pea-pickin'.

# Woodstock Revisited

"IT'S A NEW DAWN," Grace Slick, lead singer for the Jefferson Airplane, told a swelling crowd of 400,000 at Woodstock, the most famous music gathering in American history. The Woodstock Music and Arts Fair of August 1969 proved to the world that nearly half a million American youth could live together, under conditions soon to be declared a disaster area, in love, harmony, and peace.

The festival was a for-profit venture. Michael Lang, who had produced the modestly successful Miami Pop Festival, wanted to build a recording studio in Woodstock, New York, where Bob Dylan and members of The Band lived. Believing that a studio in Dylan's hometown was sure to be a success, he enlisted the aid of a music industry friend, Artie Kornfeld, and the two put together a business proposal.

Lang and Kornfeld then approached two young, hip entrepreneurs, John Roberts and Joel Rosenman, who had placed a classified ad in *The Wall Street Journal* that read "Young Men with Unlimited Capital Looking for Interesting and Legitimate Business Ideas." As it turned out, Roberts and Rosenman had begun building Media Sound, soon to become a highly successful New York City recording studio, and weren't particularly interested in the risky proposition of opening yet another studio, especially in a small town such as Woodstock.

They were, however, intrigued by one point in the business plan. Lang and Kornfeld had suggested creating a three-day music festival in Woodstock, with profits to go to their proposed recording studio. Roberts and Rosenman struck a deal with Lang and Kornfeld to form a partnership known as Woodstock Ventures Inc., which would produce the music festival. Lang and Kornfeld could direct their profits to building the recording studio they originally wanted.

From the outset, Lang had an almost mystical vision of the Woodstock Festival. He felt strongly that there were magical properties to the Woodstock name and quickly trademarked it for his purposes. It soon became apparent, however, that no site for the concert could be found in Woodstock proper. Eventually, they settled upon one in Wallkill, New York, but Lang insisted on retaining the Woodstock name and logo—the image of a dove of peace resting on a guitar neck.

One month before the concert was to take place, authorities in Wallkill banned the festival. Fortunately, within days Lang found what he felt was the perfect, magical site in White Lake, New York on Max Yasgur's pastoral farm.

"Three Days of Peace and Music" and "An Aquarian Exposition" weren't just catchy advertising phrases dreamed up by Lang and his fellow producers for Woodstock; in effect, they were safety measures. Lang and the other organizers were extremely concerned for the safety of the concertgoers and worried that the rhetoric of violence from radical groups protesting the Vietnam war might incite a deadly riot. They crossed music groups and speakers advocating violence off the concert list, substituting pro-peace artists such as Joan Baez and Arlo Guthrie.

No one expected a turn-out of half a million people at Woodstock. New York state law enforcement agencies were so skeptical of the crowd that was estimated that they didn't bother to plan at all for traffic tie-ups. The result was a horrendous traffic jam that closed down a portion of the New York Thruway. Cars were abandoned all along the interstate and throughout nearby Bethel and White Lake. Emergency food, water, and medical supplies were flown in by National Guard and Army helicopters.

Lang, realizing that security of some kind was needed, developed a "Please Force" of unarmed policemen, including members of a commune called the Hog Farm, who were especially effective in dealing with LSD overdoses (acid freakouts as they called them). Whether it was the calming influence of the hallucinogenic drugs on hand or the peaceful tone set by the concert's promoters and the Hog Farmers, Woodstock is remarkable for what didn't happen.

Nearly one American in every 500 was in attendance at Woodstock. For three days half a million people congregated with little food (most vendors ran out) or potable water; poor sanitation; and too many drugs, yet only two attendees died, an amazing achievement if one considers the statistics and realities involved. One death occurred when a farmer hooked a tractor to a wagon and accidentally rolled over a boy in a sleeping bag. The other death was attributed to a heroin overdose. Although there are many tales of births at Woodstock (we will never know how many conceptions took place), none can be verified as happening at the festival site.

The pregnant women were all flown out to area hospitals. The number one health hazard at the event was cut feet; so many in the crowd were barefoot and there were so many discarded glass bottles that accidents were bound to happen—and did, by the hundred.

Although Woodstock is best-remembered for its music, the biggest artists of the day were not in attendance. The Beatles, who were then on the verge of breaking up, had not appeared in concert since 1966. The organizers purposely excluded the Rolling Stones from the festival for fear they would incite or bring violence to the event (a fear borne out at the Stones' disastrous Altamont concert later that same year). Bob Dylan, whom concertgoers expected to make a "surprise" appearance, was a conspicuous no-show.

Abbie Hoffman, the infamous 1960s radical leader, met with the Woodstock producers and threatened to shut down the concert with a staged riot unless they acceded to a $10,000 demand. To avoid the possibility of disaster, they reluctantly paid him. But Hoffman showed up anyway. When he jumped on stage during the Who's set to make a political statement, he was greeted with a flying guitar to the head wielded by guitarist Pete Townshend. Hoffman jumped off the stage, ran into the crowd, and wasn't seen again at the event. It was one of the few reported incidents of violence in the festival's three days.

After the event, which became a free concert when the fences were torn down, the producers were deeply in debt. The documentary film of the concert and the sound recording, neither of which the organizers owned outright, eventually paid enough in royalties to help them break even by 1980.

Many of the most important musical artists at the festival, for contractual reasons, never made it on the film or album and thus have been largely forgotten in the context of Woodstock. For example, the Grateful Dead, The Band, Creedence Clearwater Revival, and Janis Joplin were all there, but few today know it.

The Port-O-San man, perhaps the most fondly-remembered person in the Woodstock film, sued Woodstock Ventures, claiming that he was embarrassed by having been shown cleaning toilets. The case was thrown out of court.

Wavy Gravy, the genial head of the Hog Farm commune, summed up the events at Woodstock best when he said, "Let's face it: Woodstock was created for wallets. It was designed to make bucks. And then the universe took over and did a little dance." There were other festivals, some even bigger, but none had the Woodstock magic.

When the festival was over, literally tons of refuse remained behind. Where else but Woodstock would they have made a giant peace symbol out of the garbage?

# Interview: Frank Zappa

**Author's Note:** *This interview with Frank Zappa for* Rock & Roll Disc *magazine in 1987 coincided with the reissue on compact disc of the early Mothers of Invention albums on the Rykodisc label. These highly influential albums had been out of print for years due to Zappa's litigation to reclaim the rights and mastertapes to these works. This interview appeared in the second issue (I believe) of* Rock & Roll Disc *magazine, which was just finding its legs. As a courtesy to Mr. Zappa, I gave him a permanent subscription to the magazine. Some months later I received a call from an employee at the Zappa estate. Could I please send two copies per month of the magazine? I was, of course, glad to oblige and asked why they wanted two copies. "Every month went it comes Frank takes it up to the big house and we don't get a chance to read it." I don't know that I've ever received a finer compliment.*

FRANK ZAPPA IS NOTHING if not an American original. As American youth swarmed to record stores in search of Monkees and Archies records (it should be noted that Zappa actually appeared on a Monkees TV segment) in the 1960s, Zappa was honing his skills as a satirist of brilliance and as a major force in studio experimentation. On such early albums as *Freak Out*, *Lumpy Gravy*, and *We're Only in It for the Money*, Zappa singlehandedly expanded much of the language and direction of rock music by constantly testing studio and audience limits and boldly broaching new musical frontiers.

Never at a loss for an opinion or razor comment, Zappa made headlines in 1985 when he took on the Washington wives of the Parents Music Resource Center (PMRC) during the infamous Danforth hearings. Other targets of his poison jibes have included hippies, drugs, disco music, and television evangelists.

At 47, Frank Zappa is still in the forefront of rock innovation and remains as controversial as ever.

**Tom Graves: For a number of years I had considered *Freak Out!!* one of my back closet relics until I dusted it off and played it about five years ago. I was surprised at how viable it still seemed to me. Why do you think *Freak Out!!*, which is now over 20 years old, has retained its bite, wit, and innovation for this length of time?**

**Frank Zappa:** Because some things just don't change. The things that the songs are critical of in American society are still there today. So that is one of the reasons why the wit still works. It tells you two things: One, that the targets of the songs are still alive and kicking; and two, it shows you roughly how much humor is worth in the larger scale of things. Obviously, since I have been talking about the same topics for over 20 years and nothing has happened, it kind of proves that nothing ever will get changed.

**Graves: Many critics consider *Freak Out!!* to be the first concept album in rock music. How did you arrive at**

**some of the sophisticated studio techniques this early in your career? You had only done a couple of minor movie soundtracks prior to this.**

**Zappa:** As a matter of fact I did have studio experience because I owned a recording studio in Cucamonga, California before we even made that album. It was one of the few places in the world at that time where it was possible to do multi-track overdubs. Because of a man named Paul Buff, who is living in Memphis now, I believe. Paul learned his electronic skill in the Marine Corps, got out and decided he wanted to go into the record business. And he built this recording studio which I later purchased from him. He built a homemade five-track recorder which operated on half-inch tape.

You have to remember that in 1962 when I purchased this there was only one other multi-track recording situation, and that was Les Paul's. He had an eight-track machine, which was a custom device. And all the rest of the studios in Los Angeles were either stereo or at the most four-track. What Paul did was he built his own heads for the machine. At that time it was believed it was impossible to put any more than four heads that close together on one piece of tape. And so he laughed at everybody and set out and did it.

He was also one of the pioneers of 24-track recording, because of a subsequent job he had for a man in Los Angeles named Art Laboe [who has compiled oldies collections for LP and CD – T.G.] Art helped Paul get his job there and financed some of his inventions. One of them was a 10-track recorder where he built all the electronics for the machine and modified an Ampex half-inch recorder and had a brand new 10-track head stack put on the thing. Without Paul Buff a lot of the things that exist in the recording business today would not be there. He invented the Kepex. Do you know what that is?

**Graves: No, I'm afraid I don't.**

**Zappa:** It's a noise gate device. He also invented a compressor called a Gain Brain. Paul had built this rather unusual recording studio in a town called Cucamonga, California. Shortly after I met him he was in debt, and he owed various vendors money for different things. He also owed back rent to his landlord. So I made an agreement with him where I took over the studio and its debts lock, stock, and barrel for a small amount of money. So I virtually lived in this recording studio for a year before the *Freak Out!!* album was made. I learned all the tricks of the trade that I knew at that time from Paul Buff and from working with the equipment in that studio.

**Graves: You've been outspoken in your views of *Sgt. Pepper*. How did your earlier work portend the Beatles' experimentations on *Sgt. Pepper*, and do you feel that you have gotten the proper credit for the innovations you pioneered on those first albums of the Mothers?**

**Zappa:** Well, for one thing it was reported in a few interviews of the time that John Lennon had heard the early stuff that we had done, and probably because of that some of the things that the Beatles later went on to do, and actually at least one of the albums the Rolling Stones later did, was directly traceable to the kind of weirdness we were doing at that time.

**Graves: Which Stones album, *Their Satanic Majesties Request*?**

**Zappa:** Yeah, their psychedelic, quote, unquote, album.

**Graves: When I first became aware of the Mothers and *Freak Out!!* you had the wildest image of anyone in rock at that time. Everything about you seemed outrageous. How did you cultivate this image and what kind of trouble did it get you in?**

**Zappa:** The funny thing was in order for you to get a job in Los Angeles during that period of time, just to work in a bar for example, you couldn't walk in the door and even get an audition in that bar unless you had long hair or some kind of physical deformity. Because the bar owners were only booking bands that looked strange. I remember going to this one place in a suburb of Los Angeles in one of my nightly visits trying to find bars and clubs I could get our band to audition for. I walked in during the last set of this one group, and they had hair all the way down to the middle of their backs. And I went, "This is not possible." These guys really looked tremendous, you know. The secret was when they walked off the stage they all pulled these wigs off, and they were like blond-haired surfers underneath it.

**Graves: Some of the guys in the Mothers weren't really accustomed to long hair were they? Weren't some of them really doo-woppers who wore pompadours?**

**Zappa:** Well, a couple of the guys—Jimmy Black and Roy Estrada—lived in Orange County, which is another suburb of Los Angeles. It is a very right-wing kind of an area, with a big John Birch presence down there ...

**Graves: Richard Nixon lived there, right?**

**Zappa:** Right, you got the aroma. So every time they would drive home to Orange County they had to hide their long hair. The way they would do it was they would stick it inside their collar and stuff it down their shirt and ride around with their shoulders hunched up so nobody looking in through the window would think they had long hair.

**Graves: What was the public's reaction to your image at this time, on the streets and going into the grocery for example?**

**Zappa**: I managed to raise a few eyebrows, but as far as the audiences went for the concerts, I think it didn't make any difference to them what we looked like. They came there for whatever it was we were doing at the time, and we never advertised ourselves as fashion plates.

**Graves: What was it like in those early days playing for**

**tourists at the Whisky A-Go-Go who had come to see Johnny Rivers?**

**Zappa:** Well, that's pretty funny. You have to understand that the Whisky A-Go-Go at that time was one of the primary places in the United States where a group could play to achieve major attraction. The guy who was the resident entertainer at the Whisky-A-Go-Go at that time was Johnny Rivers. They had a sign outside the place that had never been changed because he had worked over a year at this place. Just about the time we came along Johnny decided he wanted to go on the road. He had booked a tour that was going to take him out for five weeks and they needed somebody to replace him at the Whisky A-Go-Go.

If you don't remember what Johnny Rivers sounded like, let me make it very clear that we didn't sound anything like Johnny Rivers. Our audience was hardly Johnny's audience. But somehow or another we wound up being his replacement for the five weeks at the Whisky A-Go-Go. But what they did was they left his sign up outside. So, they never changed the sign to put ours up because they didn't want to let anybody know that he wasn't there. People walking in there were in for a big shock when we started playing for them.

**Graves: How do you think digital technology could have improved the studio experimentations in *We're Only in It for the Money* and *Lumpy Gravy*?**

**Zappa:** In the case of *Lumpy Gravy* it would have been a real blessing. *Lumpy Gravy* is edited together out of hundreds, maybe thousands, of tiny pieces of tape which took a long time to collect. First of all you have to find just the right little noise and things that are going to go in there, and then you have to manually cut these pieces of tape together with a razor blade. Anybody who has ever edited tape knows how boring that can be. Digital editing with the system I have now would have been a breeze with *Lumpy Gravy*, and all the edits would have been seamless. You could match levels from cut to cut even with the smallest segment and everything could have been done real slick. That would have made that one a lot easier to do.

**Graves: What about with *We're Only in It for the Money*? Could digital sound have added a lot of nuance, for example to the whispers and speeded-up voices in it?**

**Zappa:** Well, it could have enhanced it more if all those things were recorded on multi-track tape and you could have gone in and dubbed them out at a later date or changed the track balances. But some of those things were not. They were recorded direct to two-track and then some things were eight-track mixed down and some things were recorded direct. There's no question that if all this technology had been available then better things could have been done, but that's pretty much the story of my career. Right from the beginning I knew certain things were technically possible but the gear wasn't available at the time to do it. And finally years later when the gear comes on line and it's available, what happens? The big groups get it for free and I gotta go out and scrounge and find ways to buy this stuff, and it's ungodly expensive.

**Graves: You have your own digital studio now, right?**

**Zappa:** That's right.

**Graves: And you have had it for how long, four or five years?**

**Zappa:** The studio itself was operational in 1980. We got the digital gear in there by about 1982. That's when I first bought the digital multi-track machines.

**Graves: How do you like it?**

**Zappa:** Well, if that's a yes or no question then the answer is yes, it's great. It makes things a lot easier.

**Graves: Do you think there has been a turning away from experimentation in rock music toward the basics like Springsteen and Bryan Adams seem to have done? If so do you think rock music is missing out by adhering so strongly to these roots? Is it preventing artistic growth?**

**Zappa:** One of the things that ought to be debated right here and now is whether or not—when you say "back to basics" whether the basics you are describing is something that ought to be admired. As far as I'm concerned the real essence of

American culture, the basics of being American is being an experimenter, being a pioneer. You can't be a pioneer if you stick your head in the sand and continue to rehash old stuff. I would point out to you that the beginning of the dark ages of rock and roll pretty much took effect when Reagan went into office. One thing that you ought to look at is the linkage in all the different art forms. Like, for example, in motion pictures where the reliance on remakes and rehashed old titles has been characteristic over the last seven years.

**Graves: You mean this whole craving for nostalgia.**

**Zappa:** Well, nostalgia is one thing. But the idea of not taking a chance, which is what you do when you make *Jaws 4, Jaws 5, Rocky 9*, and everything over and over and over again. When you are forced into that position and tell yourself that you are prudent because you are doing it, you're just kind of giving it all up. You've kind of reduced the whole concept of making entertainment to something really mundane. But on the other hand you can also look at that and say what the arts have done is to reflect the reality of life under Reagan.

**Graves: What about the disco era of the '70s prior to Reagan? Many people look at that as the dark ages of rock and roll.**

**Zappa:** I would disagree with that simply because of this: Disco was a functional type of music. We may be using the term "music" loosely here. Disco was designed for a specific function. It was wallpaper to be used in the background of the lifestyle of the people who inhabited those disco places. And those places were basically meatracks. The function of this music was to provide this rhythmic dance texture while people went to the meatrack. If you are going to have a meatrack why would you have anything more intelligent than disco? It seems to me to be perfectly designed for its usage.

**Graves: Does it bother you at all that your music is very demanding of the listener?**

**Zappa:** It bothers me that listeners find it demanding. I don't try to figure out how I'm going to be demanding in the music. What I write is natural to me, and if people have difficulty with it, it is not *my* fault. It is *their* fault.

**Graves: Do you think there are times when you have carried experimentation too far?**

**Zappa:** No. You can experiment and you can fail. But then even the failure is a success in itself. Because you took that direction, you got the answer, and there's the answer. You've presented the answer as a documentation. At least somebody took the step and found out what happens if you put this with this, that with that, and try it.

**Graves: Can you tell us a little about the litigation involved in obtaining your early recordings? They were gone from the shelves for a long time, and the collectibility**

of albums such as *Freak Out!!* climbed and remain quite high.

**Zappa:** There have been at least three lawsuits, maybe four lawsuits, between me and record companies leading to the point that I'm at now where I own those masters. I had to sue MGM Records, I've sued Warner Brothers, and I've sued CBS. In fact, I've sued Warner Brothers twice. The amount of time I've spent in court—with MGM it was eight years and another eight years for the Warner Brothers case. So think about it. The bulk of the time I have been in the recording industry I've had ongoing legal battles with the companies that have released this material.

**Graves: Isn't that mentally exhausting for you to be tangled up in legal matters for that long?**

**Zappa:** If I had my choice between going to court or writing a song, I think I'd rather write a song. There's a song on *You Are What You Is* called "Charlie's Enormous Mouth," and I actually wrote that song during a break in the depositions for the Warner Brothers trials. I was deposed for 40 days, and on one of these boring days the lawyers were arguing about something in the other room, and I just went into an office and wrote those lyrics on a pad. It helps keep your mind off some of these things. But the fact of the matter is most artists don't like their record companies. They wimp out when it gets down to the wire, and they don't sue often enough.

If there is anybody reading this who has got a career in

the music business, if you don't already know, the saying in the business is like this: nobody ever audited a record company and found out that they were *not* owed something more than what the statement told you. That's why they have auditors. But the fact of the matter is, the cost of suing a record company, and the time element of suing a record company, and the emotional drain of fighting one of those kinds of battles is something that most artists don't want to put up with. But in my case, I've never been a multi-platinum selling artist, and they were screwing me! What do you think they are doing to the guys who are really selling multi-platinum? If they're doing it to me, then they're doing it to everybody.

**Graves: The Beatles, I believe, are now tied up in litigation because Capitol Records allegedly unloaded truckloads of their records off the books.**

**Zappa:** That's an old story. They did the same thing to all the artists, as far as I could tell, at MGM. One of the things that was going on there was one of the most popular albums in the mid-'60s was the soundtrack to *Doctor Zhivago*. And they got caught shipping at least a quarter of a million of those things out the back door of the pressing plant in Terre Haute, Indiana. Apparently the stuff was going into the back of somebody's truck and being traded for roomfuls of furniture in another state. Weird stuff like this.

They would do it by a process called pressing overruns. In other words the record company would send the masters over to the plant, say "print 10,000 of this title." Of course they would print 15,000 and the 5,000 extra would go out the back door and be traded for something of value, and the artist would find on his statement that only 10,000 had been pressed. That's simplifying it, but that's one of the ways they would screw you in those days.

**Graves: Allen Klein has made a career out of going in and auditing record company books hasn't he?**

**Zappa:** Here's a good Allen Klein story. He used to handle the Rolling Stones. The Rolling Stones have a company called Nanker Phelge. If the group has jointly composed the song then the song goes into the Nanker Phelge company. So the story I heard was that Allen Klein had set up the deal with the record company for the Rolling Stones and had told the record company that the funds that are to be paid to Nanker Phelge should be sent to a bank account in New York City, when in fact it was his account in New York City. But the Nanker Phelge account that the Stones had was in London!

**Graves: *Lumpy Gravy* and *Ruben and the Jets* seem in retrospect to have been incredible artistic gambles in the '60s. Did they seem so to you at the time?**

**Zappa:** It just seemed like that's what I was supposed to be doing. I don't look at things as being a gamble or not. My basic philosophy is this: If I'm interested in a certain type of musical style or a topic during that period of time I follow my own trail, finish the project, and present it to the public. And those people who have the same interests as me will like it, and the ones who don't won't. And I'll just take my chances. But it's not making a calculated gamble to change my direction. I work on whatever I'm interested in that week or that year or that month.

**Graves: The song "Trouble Every Day" on *Freak Out!!* was an angry indictment of the times. After looking back at the releases of the day, it seems to be one of the first implicit social commentaries in rock music. Was it considered inflammatory at the time?**

**Zappa:** It was considered inflammatory at the time, but we're talking *explicit* not *implicit*. That song does spell it out. You have to remember what the Watts riots were. They were the first major race riots in contemporary history. People just didn't know how to deal with it. The television stations in Los Angeles were covering this thing like it was a real news spectacle ...

**Graves: Like the Super Bowl of riots?**

**Zappa:** Right. And the line [in the song] about the woman driver being machine-gunned from her seat, that really happened. It was a lady, and the news announced, "Yeah, this woman has been sawed in half by 50-caliber machine gun bullets by the National Guard." That's what the Watts riots were. It wasn't quaint, it wasn't cute, it was like "what in the world is going on here?" And it was only a few miles from where I lived.

**Graves: But was this song in fact a first of its kind? It was much longer than the average Top 40 hit and really blistering in its outlook.**

**Zappa:** One of the things that it derives from is there has been a tradition in blues lyrics to tell social stories. A lot of people in the pop music world are unfamiliar with the world of folk music or the world of blues lyrics. I had grown up listening to blues records, so that kind of form wasn't unfamiliar [to me]. But the things that were being spoken about in the folk songs and the blues records were not generally major news stories. There was a guy named J.B. Lenoir who had a couple of songs, "The Eisenhower Blues" and "I Am in Korea." If you can ever find those records and listen to those things they were made in the early '50s. That would be some of the roots the Watts riots songs would come from. Maybe it was unique for a white person's rock and roll to stick something like that in it, but in other musical forms that kind of style had existed to a degree.

**Graves: On *Uncle Meat* you again took what is considered to be a radical departure toward jazz and jazz fusion. Why did you decide to risk working in this more musically complex and demanding setting?**

**Zappa:** There are two reasons why the music I put out on a record at any given time will sound the way it does. Reason number one is whether or not that style is something I'm interested in during that period of time. And two, who's in the band. What are their assets, what are their liabilities. At that particular time of recording *Uncle Meat* we had Art Tripp, who is a conservatory-trained percussionist. We also had Ruth Underwood—she wasn't in the band but she was working on the sessions. We had Ian Underwood who was a conservatory-trained guy. And we had Bunk Gardner, who I don't know if he was conservatory-trained, but he was like a schooled musician. They were in the same band with guys like Motorhead Sherwood, Billy Mundi, Jimmy Carl Black, and Roy Estrada. It was a real strange mix of guys who could read and had been to school and guys who were just regular guys. Suppose you were me and you had these human resources to deal with, what would you make out of it?

**Graves: Not something nearly as interesting as *Uncle Meat*, I can assure you.**

**Zappa:** You know you take your chances with the material that is available to you at the time. The other thing that will determine what an album sounds like is how much money there is to make the album. That money translates into studio time, it translates into rehearsal time, things like that. All of the early Mothers albums were done on really low budgets. There wasn't enough studio time to go in and perfect anything. It wasn't until I got my own studio that I could take as much time to work on an album as I really needed. So the bulk of my career has been done under duress.

**Graves: What is the latest on the Tipper Gore, PMRC front?**

**Zappa:** I just debated Albert Gore's campaign manager on a radio station in Los Angeles. I don't know whether it's been reported here, but they came to Los Angeles to have a closed door meeting with big shots of the entertainment industry to kind of allay their anxieties that Mr. and Mrs. Gore really weren't interested in censorship. That was the supposed theme of this meeting. Now, I was not invited to the meeting. I read about it in the papers after it had happened. But generally speaking, the newspaper commentary on the thing was not favorable and most of the people in show business were not all that impressed with what the Gores had to say. They were kind of apologetic about the hearings that they had held in Washington in '85. They were trying to give the impression that they had gotten a bum rap about all this censorship business, that they in fact could be trusted if Albert did get elected and he wouldn't harm the show business world. Now you decide. Is anybody buying this or what?

**Graves: Do you think the PMRC may be losing steam at this point?**

**Zappa:** They just released their first video you know. It was reported in *Billboard* last week. The PMRC through a Christian distributing company has released a full-length video about rock and roll lyrics which features four-letter words and frontal nudity. I figure this is a major step forward for a Christian distribution company. That's what Tipper and the girls are into now.

**Graves: What do you think of the Gores' admissions to**

smoking dope? And especially Tipper's where she smoked dope just once?

**Zappa:** Well, let me put it to you this way: To me that is the best reason for people *not* to smoke marijuana. You see she smoked it just once and look what happened to her. He smoked it, how many times?, and look what happened to him.

**Graves: My God, he's wanting to run for President!**

**Zappa:** That's right (laughter).

**Graves: You met with Tipper and Albert Jr. for a drink after the Danforth Committee hearings? What was that like?**

**Zappa:** It was kind of interesting. I must say I don't dislike them as people. I think basically they are probably nice people. I haven't spent enough time with them to give you a complete character analysis or anything. We met in a kind of bar/restaurant in Washington, D.C. called the Monocle at about six o'clock in the evening. It was like happy hour in the bar and it was jam-packed with all these senators and all these people who do that nasty business in Washington, D.C., and we were at a table in the back.

We just talked about this whole record rating business, and I asked them some questions about things I had come across that I had experienced in California and asked them to either substantiate or deny what these things were. And I asked for some background information on the hearings themselves. For example, I said, "Why is Paula Hawkins ... what was she doing there?" And Albert Gore said, "Well, basically Paula was a Republican in trouble." She was having trouble getting reelected in Florida, and she prevailed on Senator Danforth to let her make an appearance at the committee because she thought that it might be good. So the whole thing was a show trial from the word go. Danforth went along with the thing. It was just a waste of the taxpayers' money and was a bunch of nothingness.

**Graves: The hearing seems like a subversion of everything America is supposed to stand for.**

**Zappa:** It is more than a subversion, it's an actual violation of Senate rules. My understanding is you don't have a hearing unless you are talking about legislation. And it was clear from that hearing that they were not talking about legislation. And in fact Senator Exon from Nebraska asked the question in the middle of the hearing, "If we are not talking about legislation why are we here?" And that didn't even get reported in the news. And when he said it it got a round of applause at the hearing. The other thing people have to remember is the committee that heard this matter had five members on it, five senators, who were married to women who belonged to the PMRC or signed the original PMRC complaint letter to the record industry. So it was a kangaroo court. If they were talking about legislation it would have been pretty unusual to have the husbands of the complainants sitting there judging the matter.

**Graves: What kind of hate mail do you get?**

**Zappa:** Little or none. We get some amazing fan mail. Well, here's one example of hate mail. During that PMRC business in '85 I got a greeting card from a man, and he said he was an Italian, but that he was born again. He was incensed that as an Italian I would be out there fighting against this. That's about the extent of it. I think it is an erroneous conclusion that you would think that a person such as myself would get masses of hate mail. That is not true. Most of the people who write to me—I'm talking about 99 percent of the people who write to me—are absolutely delighted that I'm doing what I'm doing, that I continue to do what I've been doing for the last 20 years, and to urge me to keep doing it and do more of it. There it is.

**Graves: Could you give us a quick appraisal of the talk shows you've been on? You had a rather high profile on television during the PMRC hearings.**

**Zappa:** First of all, name the ones that I *haven't* done. I haven't done *Donahue* and *Oprah Winfrey*.

**Graves: Why, because the powers that be don't want you to have a forum for that long?**

**Zappa:** (Laughs) Yeah, I know what you mean. I don't think I would enjoy *Donahue* just because of the style of the show, and I was actually invited to do *Oprah Winfrey* when she was still a regional show in Chicago, but I didn't make it. And the other one that I haven't done is *Sonya Friedman*, which I would not do because I don't like her show, and I don't like what it stands for. I kind of enjoy doing them if the interviewer can hold a good conversation, and that's not often the case. I thought Johnny Carson was a nice guy to talk with, and he surprised me when I went on the show because when I was brought on I was told that we were only going to talk about *Miami Vice*. He didn't want to talk about politics or anything else. He surprised everybody by talking about censorship, and he told me before the show that he had stayed up—you know those Senate hearings when they were broadcast live, they didn't broadcast them completely. Just before I went on to testify they switched to the Senate floor. Consequently they reran the whole thing on Saturday and Sunday at two o'clock in the morning. Johnny Carson said that he stayed up and watched them, which also surprised me. The idea that Johnny Carson sits around watching C-SPAN on the weekends is pretty fascinating.

**Graves: Speaking for myself, I was extremely annoyed that Carson relegated you to the last five minutes of the show in that Phantom Zone where they put anyone with opinions.**

**Zappa:** That's true on every talk show.

**Graves:** But they had some lady with an egg collection, of all things, who went on and on and on. She took up nearly the whole show.

**Zappa:** Want to know the story about the egg lady?

**Graves:** Sure.

**Zappa:** She had a vision that she was going to be on Johnny Carson and she called them. And it was so off the wall. She called them from some kind of phone booth in a shopping mall in New Jersey or something like that and they said, "Oh, this has got to be great." And they brought her out just because she got in contact with them. It was just off the wall, and it didn't turn out to be quite as good as they thought it was going to be. And they devoted this major segment of the show to it.

**Graves:** Which I thought was a big mistake.

**Zappa:** Well, don't tell me, tell them.

**Graves:** What about the Joan Rivers show. That one seemed a little amiss.

**Zappa:** First of all, she opened the show by making fun of my children, which I'm not going to be too enthusiastic about no matter who's saying it. You can only talk about what they want to talk about or what they'll let you talk about. Because a talk show host, if he's really afraid of his job, is always going to change the subject, or they can beep you or whatever. I did the Tom Snyder show years ago when he was on television, and I found that to be a really difficult interview. But I did his new radio show about a month ago and that was really good. It was his first broadcast of a new show. He had the ABC network executives outside the window watching what was going on, some of these middle management guys pacing back and forth. I happened to go on this tirade about Pat Robertson, calling him a fraud and saying the guy ought to be brought up for tax fraud and all the rest of this stuff, and they were pissing their pants out there in the hall. It is usually easier to get away with this stuff on radio than it is to get away with it on television. Television broadcasters are ... to say that they were chickenshit would be absolutely too kind.

**Graves: What do you think about the Jim and Tammy Bakker episodes of late?**

**Zappa:** I think it's great that it happened. It's unfortunate that it took so long to happen. You have to remember that the fundamentalist right in the United States is one of the main reasons why Reagan is in office. It is a little known fact that not only did Jim and Tammy attend the inauguration, but Reagan gave them a humanitarian award in '83. They are right in there together, you know. I think it's great that Jim and Tammy were exposed. I just wish the exposure had been more thorough. I think that the media pussyfooted around the issue of whether or not Jim Bakker was having sex with a man. I think they could have been a little more assiduous in following that up and getting some conclusive evidence out.

I think the word has yet to be delivered on the financial wrongdoing of PTL [PTL Ministries, or "Praise the Lord" Ministries]. I think they're not being as aggressive as they can with that. Let me give you one theory as to why the IRS has not been doing its job in terms of these television ministries. You have to understand that [television evangelists] make their money because they are tax exempt. And in order to keep the tax exemption they may not, according to the law, lobby for or against any political candidate or any legislation. They are supposed to be religions and not involved in politics. It gets into at the very least a grey area, and in my view it's all completely black and white, that religion is religion and politics is politics. If you have a tax exemption and if you're building empires with tax exempt money, then somebody should make you hold to the mark as to how you earn that money.

The IRS's job is to enforce this law. The problem of enforcing it is that the people who are auditors for the IRS are usually not the cream of the auditing crop. For example, the starting salary for an IRS auditor is about $14,000 a year. The same guy in the private sector gets $23,000. So usually they don't get the best talent at the IRS. The other thing is that auditing often takes place at regional offices. So if you are in the Bible Belt somewhere then an auditor for any of these pseudo-religious organizations is probably going to be a member of that community, who may even belong to that church. Do you think he's really going to go in there and look at the fine print in the books? I don't think so, and I think that's another reason why these guys have been able to get away with murder all this time. The other thing is this current administration owing its butt as it does to the fundamentalist right certainly has not been too strong in pushing for compliance with the regulations that lets them be tax exempt. I don't think there's been any effort by the Reagan administration to say yeah, go out there and do what the law says to do. Check their books and see whether or not they've lived up to this exemption. The reason they won't do that is when they violated their exemptions and got into politics, they got into Republican politics and actually helped to put Reagan in office. That's why they have flourished.

**Graves: In the book out now on *Saturday Night Live* it reports that you and the Prime Time Players did not work out too well together. Would you care to give your side of the story?**

**Zappa:** Well, the guy [who was quoted about me in the book] happens to be a person that I spoke to only briefly during the time that I was there, and I did the show twice. He was not the major writer or one of the major writers on *Saturday Night Live*. I think you know the guy and the kind of material that he and his partner would put on the show, absolutely the weakest element in the *Saturday Night Live* show. Nobody ever turned that show on to see Al Franken and his partner.

Here's what it was like at *Saturday Night Live* in those days: If I were from the DEA [Drug Enforcement Administration] and I wanted to make my quota for the year all I would have had to do was walk onto the 15th floor of Rockefeller Center. There were more drugs on that floor than I have ever seen openly displayed anywhere. In fact in the office of the aforementioned [writer] we are talking about plastic bags of every known form of pill in every color. And in another office with one of the major talents of the show the office consisted of a desk, two bunk beds, and a haystack of marijuana on the desk. That's *all* that was in the office. So that's the atmosphere of the times. Now, I don't exactly fit in with people who have that as a lifestyle. I don't use drugs. If somebody else wants to use them fine, but I'm not a party guy. I came there to work. If there was any friction between me and the people who worked there, let's just say it was an anthropological difference.

**Graves: While we are on the subject of drugs, it is well-known that you do not use drugs. Did you at any time ever experiment with them?**

**Zappa:** For social purposes in the early '60s I tried to smoke marijuana. And I say tried because every time I smoked it it made me sleepy and gave me a sore throat. I've never gotten high from it and I could never understand why people would smoke this stuff. But because I like tobacco I said, "Well, why don't I try this?" If I were to calculate there probably wouldn't be over 10 marijuana cigarettes in my entire lifetime that were ever passed to me. Not that I sat there and really smoked 10 joints, but if you're with a bunch of people and they hand you that ... It's not the world that I wanted to be in. As far as cocaine, never. LSD, never. Speed, never. Heroin, never. Anything with a needle attached to it, give me a break. Who needs it.

**Graves: For what it's worth I'm in complete agreement. I'm one of the few music writers who totally abhors drugs.**

**Zappa:** I find it unfortunate that drug use is so extensive in the United States, but let's be philosophically clear: It is not my position to be somebody's dad other than for my own children. If somebody wants to use drugs that is their right if they choose to harm themselves that way. The part that becomes a public concern is if that person under the influence of those chemical substances—I would include liquor in that—that person becomes a menace to other members of society then it's bad. If you're just sitting at home and you want to get yourself wrecked, or even if you want to commit suicide, I feel that you own your own body. You might as well do whatever you want with it. But you don't have the right to harm other people because of what you do to yourself. The extent to which Americans are willing to hurt themselves and then hurt other people by proxy is what is the worst aspect of the drug situation in the U.S. Because it has gone beyond recreation.

**Graves: If there had not been any such thing as drugs how do you think rock music would have been different?**

**Zappa:** I think it still would have been rock-like because a lot of it is based on alcohol. If you subtract the hard liquor from heavy metal then what have you got?

**Graves: Why is no one in rock music today willing to push the frontiers as you did in the '60s?**

**Zappa**: You couldn't even get a record contract today, because of the people who run the record companies. They have made the decision that to be successful you have to be like Michael Jackson. Let's face it, if you are experimental the chance that you will make millions of dollars is not good. Record companies only want things that make millions and millions of dollars. When we first got a record contract with MGM the advance we received for signing was $2,500 divided between five guys.

**Graves: I'll bet that didn't go very far.**

**Zappa:** You ain't kidding. Today if I had a group called the Mothers of Invention and I went out to get a contract I couldn't get a contract anywhere. There's not a company on the planet that would sign a group like that.

**Graves: Who out there today is doing something in music you find interesting?**

**Zappa:** I've seen a couple of videos recently that I thought were not only interesting videos but good songs and good performances. One is "Living In A Box" by Living In A Box on the album *Living In A Box*. I wasn't that impressed with their second video, but I think the guy is a good singer. I thought the track sounded great. The other is "Daddy's Coming Home" by Walk the Moon. Especially the guitar was interesting in that.

**Graves: What about some of the critics' favorites such as Bruce Springsteen?**

**Zappa:** I met Bruce one time. I was brought backstage to one of his shows when he was working at the Palladium in New York, and he seemed like a nice enough guy. But that is not my style of music.

**Graves: For someone who has accomplished as much as you have artistically, where do you go next? What can we expect from Frank Zappa in the future? Where will you be taking us?**

**Zappa:** Well, you can expect a tour which begins February with a 12-piece band and a five-piece horn section in it. I've got a whole bunch more CD product coming out next year, and of course there's all the Honker Home Video product of which the first two titles were released October 28. The next two will be in February, then there's two more that will be coming out around June next year. *You Can't Do That on Stage Anymore*, a live compact disc series, will begin in February. One double-CD set will be released each month, February through August, making a total of 12 CDs. Nothing else like it.

**Graves: How do you think the public will react to such a monumental CD set?**

**Zappa:** The people who like what I do will love it, and the people who don't like what I do will find it inconsequential.

# Interview: Mick Taylor

MICK TAYLOR INITIALLY CAME into the public spotlight as the very young (17 years old) replacement for the renowned Peter Green in John Mayall's Bluesbreakers.

Although his early work reflected a preoccupation with the blues guitar style set forth by Eric Clapton during his legendary tenure with the Bluesbreakers, Taylor quickly matured into one of the most melodic, articulate, and technically accurate of players. He rapidly gained recognition for his fluid soloing, but became equally celebrated for his brilliant slide guitar style.

Taylor did not become known to the mass rock audience, however, until 1969 when the Rolling Stones sent shock waves through their corps of fans by announcing Brian Jones' departure and replacement by the relatively unknown Mick Taylor. Only weeks later Brian Jones drowned in his swimming pool and the Stones began a tour of America that ended in the murder and chaos of Altamont. In addition to *Let It Bleed* and *Get Yer Ya-Ya's Out*, Taylor was a crucial musical cog in the Stones' most influential middle-period albums, *Sticky Fingers* and *Exile on Main Street*. He recorded two other albums with the Stones and unexpectedly called it quits, seemingly going into hiding. In 1979 he resurfaced with a self-titled solo album which sold poorly but was well-received by fans and critics. Reportedly sidelined by debilitating drug habits, he nevertheless toured and recorded with Bob Dylan, among others.

Taylor is currently working with a new band that includes Jeff Beck alumnus Max Middleton, and a record deal with a major label is said to be forthcoming. According to several sources, including Taylor himself, he has kicked his drug habits and is playing better than ever.

Taylor has rarely granted interviews since leaving the Stones, certainly none that were in-depth. A naturally quiet and reflective man, Taylor was not the ideal interview since he rarely opened up at length. If one reads his carefully weighed answers closely, however, they frequently speak volumes.

**Tom Graves: Did you have a musical upbringing? Were either of your parents gifted with an instrument?**

**Mick Taylor:** My mother had a younger brother who used to play guitar. That was kind of my inspiration and my starting point on the guitar, but my whole family liked music. I won't say they were overtly musical—they didn't play instruments or anything other than my mother who played a bit of piano—but I grew up in a house listening to music all the time.

**Graves: Were you too young to have been a part of the first wave of rock and roll in England, when Elvis, Bill Haley, and Buddy Holly had all become tremendously popular and influential?**

**Taylor:** Well, I suppose I would have been too young if my parents had not bought those records. They even took me to my first rock and roll concert when I was nine years old. They took me to see Bill Haley and the Comets in 1958, I think it was.

**Graves: When do you recall becoming seriously interested in music yourself?**

**Taylor:** Well, when I started making a bit of progress on the guitar. I got together with some school friends and formed a band, which was when I was 13 or 14 years old.

**Graves: Would this have been during the time of the British Invasion?**

**Taylor:** Yes, the Beatles were then becoming famous in England and all over the world.

**Graves: At this early age were you yet aware of the Rolling Stones?**

**Taylor:** Oh yeah, of course. They were certainly an influence on me in the sense they were playing rhythm and blues as was John Mayall's Bluesbreakers who I listened to a little later on. I kind of got to discover American rhythm and blues—black music—and started listening to that when I was a teenager. That's when I started taking the guitar more seriously.

**Graves: What was your first guitar?**

**Taylor:** It was called a Hofner President. It was like a semi-acoustic single cutaway with two pickups. I can't remember what kind of amp I started on.

**Graves: When you began to play the guitar was it rock and roll or rhythm and blues that first interested you?**

**Taylor:** I was aware of rock and roll before I was aware of blues, but by the time I became aware of blues I was playing guitar, so I became more interested in rhythm and blues.

**Graves: In reading about you I'm always struck by your youth when you got involved with John Mayall or for that matter the Rolling Stones. You were playing blues in your very early teens and that surprises me, because it was my impression that blues appealed to the older more collegiate musical sophisticate in England.**

**Taylor:** No, it wasn't like that at all. I suppose it would seem that way, but it was people who were 15 and 16 years old. Certainly there were people older than myself, but I'm not the only one of that era who was aware of rhythm and blues music.

**Graves: Were you more influenced by the original American rhythm and blues or by the blues scene that was beginning to happen in England?**

**Taylor:** I became aware of it all at the same time really. It was impossible to listen to the Rolling Stones playing Chuck Berry and not realize they were playing American rhythm and blues music, so one naturally wanted to hear the original, the real thing.

**Graves: Who were the blues players who most interested you?**

**Taylor:** I used to listen to a lot of the Chicago blues artists such as Buddy Guy, Junior Wells, and Muddy Waters, a guy called Jimmy Rogers. One of the first blues albums I remember buying was a record called *Live at the Regal* by B.B. King. That had a big influence on me.

**Graves: What knocked you out the most about him, his singing or guitar playing?**

**Taylor:** Both, but especially his guitar playing at that time.

**Graves: Did you listen to Albert King or Freddie King much at this time?**

**Taylor:** Yes, I was aware of both of those guys, or at least I was by the time I joined John Mayall because we used to play a lot of their songs in our show—we used to play "Oh, Pretty Woman" and "Crosscut Saw" and we did some Freddie King instrumentals. Those records were difficult to find in London, though. There were only a couple of places where you could buy rhythm and blues imports, so I found out where the shops were in London and I used to go there and buy them. They weren't widely available. You had to be quite dedicated and quite keen on that music to seek out those record shops where they stocked American imports.

**Graves: Did you order many direct from Chess records in the States like Mick Jagger did?**

**Taylor:** No, I just used to buy them at those specialty shops.

**Graves: When the music scene began to happen in earnest in England who did you first hear that made you decide then and there to get in a band?**

**Taylor:** I suppose something that was really interesting—apart from the Beatles, who I always liked and loved their music—would be Eric Clapton, who was the best blues guitar player around at the time that I had ever seen.

**Graves: Your first record was *Blues Crusade* with John Mayall's Bluesbreakers ...**

**Taylor:** Yes it was.

**Graves: Many critics believe that your playing at this time was very heavily influenced by Eric Clapton, that your guitar sound was patterned almost identically after his, and in a sense was derivative ...**

**Taylor:** But it was derivative. I had just turned 17 years old and hadn't been playing that long, so my blues playing at that time was very derivative. I was still very much a beginner. I wouldn't say I was more influenced by Eric Clapton than anybody else though, than any of the other blues guitarists that I had listened to, but it certainly was derivative. It took me four years of being on the road with John Mayall to really develop my own style.

**Graves: Of course you are celebrated now as much for your slide guitar as your lead guitar playing. Wasn't this something of an extreme rarity in England in the early '60s?**

**Taylor:** There weren't too many people who played slide guitar, no.

**Graves: How did you learn slide guitar? Was it from listening to Brian Jones in the Stones?**

**Taylor:** No, he wasn't really an influence, though he played a bit of slide as did Keith Richards. I suppose the first slide guitar playing I heard was Muddy Waters.

**Graves: But slide guitar is considered to be such a difficult style, and it wasn't until you and Duane Allman popularized it that you saw that many people play it. Wasn't it difficult to pick up all the slide techniques on your own?**

**Taylor:** Not necessarily. Not if you were brought up in a musical environment and you liked rhythm and blues and you knew lots of other musicians, then it doesn't seem so strange. But I know what you mean, because like I said before, that music wasn't widely accessible in England. So you had to really know a bit about it and know where to find the records...

**Graves: Who were some of these other musicians?**

**Taylor:** Well, there was Eric Clapton, there was Jeff Beck, there was myself, there were lots of other people really who played blues.

**Graves: But they weren't really known for slide playing then were they?**

**Taylor:** Not then they weren't, no. Eric Clapton does now.

**Graves: You didn't play slide guitar on *Blues Crusade* at all. Was this because Mayall, who hyped his own slide playing, was considered the slide player of the group?**

**Taylor:** No, I don't think so. I think it was just the choice of material.

**Graves: Have you ever stopped to think that of all the guitar players around only you and Duane Allman and perhaps Johnny Winter are considered to have been**

equally articulate as slide players and as lead players?

**Taylor:** What about Ry Cooder?

**Graves:** Yes, but his favor among critics and guitarists is weighted more toward him as a slide guitarist than a lead guitarist.

**Taylor:** Yeah, that's true. You're right. But no, I really haven't thought much about that. I know I don't consider myself a sort of specialist slide player or anything. I have done a few sessions lately where I've played slide guitar, but I've played lead as well.

**Graves:** When Eric Clapton was in the Bluesbreakers, he seems to have been celebrated throughout England. There was the "Clapton Is God" graffito and so on. Was he that highly regarded?

**Taylor:** Amongst musicians, yes he was. He was the best blues guitarist around.

**Graves:** When did it dawn on you that you had those same kinds of virtuoso abilities?

**Taylor:** I suppose when I joined John Mayall's Bluesbreakers, or maybe even before that.

**Graves:** Your schoolmates in your first band must have

**held you in awe.**

**Taylor:** Well, no, all of them went on to become professional musicians themselves. There was a bass player who used to play with Jethro Tull named John Glascock, who died a few years ago, and his brother, the drummer, and he now lives and plays in Los Angeles. I think the other guitar player in this group went on into the music business for a while too.

**Graves: How did you become a member of Mayall's Bluesbreakers?**

**Taylor:** I was chosen as the result of a phone call. He called me up and said he needed a guitar player and that was because, a couple of years before that, I had been to see a show he was doing in a community center in a college-type place in Welwyn Garden City which is near Hatfield. Eric Clapton didn't show up for the gig and I went backstage during the interval and asked if I could sit in with them and he said yes. He must have been *quite* impressed because he took my number and got in touch with me a couple of years later when Peter Green left.

**Graves: What was it like standing in for Clapton that first time?**

**Taylor:** It was great! I knew most of the songs by heart ...

**Graves: John Mayall was obviously the coach for three of**

the most important blues players to come out of England. You replaced Peter Green, who had become something of a legend in his own right, and he had a very different blues approach from you and Clapton. How would you characterize the differences in the styles of you, Clapton, and Green?

**Taylor:** I don't think they are that different actually. I think there are more similarities than differences.

**Graves: Was Peter Green as big an influence on you as Clapton?**

**Taylor:** I never knew Peter Green at all. He was very highly regarded, of course, but he wasn't really an influence on me, because as I said before, we all listened to the same music. We all were influenced together at around the same time by the source of that music rather than each other. The only new guitar player who came along that really influenced everybody and influenced me too was Jimi Hendrix.

**Graves: What about Jeff Beck? He was doing many of the innovations most people credit to Hendrix before anyone.**

**Taylor:** Yes, that's true. He's always been one of my favorite guitar players.

**Graves: Describe what it was like working on your first album, *Blues Crusade*.**

**Taylor:** It was great and we did it all in seven hours! The whole record. It was like playing on stage—we just set the equipment up in the studio and it was "one-two-three-four here we go." There were hardly any breaks between the numbers and, like I said, it was all recorded and mixed in seven hours.

**Graves: Why can't they do it like that anymore? Some groups now spend a year in the studio.**

**Taylor:** I know. It would be much more simple, wouldn't it?

**Graves: In spite of the rush, the engineering on those Bluesbreakers albums seems to be quite good.**

**Taylor:** It had to be because everything was done so quickly. There wasn't really any room for any mistakes. You just set up and the engineers got set up and they got good sound and you just did it.

**Graves: When you first went on the road with Mayall you were still at a very tender age. You were thrust into a spotlight few could handle following Clapton and Peter Green. How were you received by your audience at first?**

**Taylor:** Not too big to start with. I was probably considered to be too young and not quite good enough. But that soon changed in a couple of years, especially when we started touring America.

**Graves: What kind of following did Mayall have in America at the time?**

**Taylor:** It was pretty much in England to start with, but we started to do some pretty big shows with people like Jimi Hendrix and Albert King, and we played at the Fillmore East and Fillmore West, we played everywhere really. We did very long tours. It was the beginning of John Mayall building up a big following in America too. A lot of people [in America] had heard of John Mayall's Bluesbreakers because I think by the time we toured America Cream was around as well, and people knew about Eric Clapton playing with John Mayall's Bluesbreakers.

**Graves: *Bare Wires*, your second album, marked quite a departure for the Bluesbreakers. We find your playing maturing quite a bit, you are playing slide here for the first time, and Mayall has changed the sound by adding a horn section ...**

**Taylor:** Yes, there was more of a rhythm and blues jazz influence on that one. He, like the rest of us, listened to jazz too, and he wanted to incorporate some of that into his music as well.

**Graves: At this point were you featured playing more slide guitar in your live shows?**

**Taylor:** No, at that time it was still something that I played very rarely. It wasn't until I got with the Rolling Stones that I started to play a lot of slide guitar.

**Graves: You did an instructional video with Arlen Roth a few years ago discussing some of your guitar techniques. I find it interesting that most slide guitarists use "open" bottleneck tunings of E, A, and G, yet you normally use the standard guitar tuning, which most people find far more difficult in playing slide.**

**Taylor:** Well, I do use the standard tuning, but I also use the open bottleneck tunings too. I believe Duane Allman used open tunings—most guitar players do. I think it is more interesting to play slide in the standard tuning and try to do what you can and switch from slide to regular lead guitar. You can't do that in an open tuning. It's much more versatile, because you're not restricted to an open blues tuning. An "A" tuning more or less confines you to an Elmore James style and a "G" tuning more like a Delta blues kind of thing. I don't consciously avoid it, but I do often play slide in a regular tuning unless it's a sort of Mississippi Delta blues song, which requires an open tuning.

**Graves: What about a song like "Alabama" that was on your solo record?**

**Taylor:** That's in an open tuning, done in an open E.

**Graves: In the mid-'60s nearly every guitar player used**

a Gibson Les Paul. You used one, so did Clapton, Peter Green, and Jeff Beck. Now the trend seems to be toward Fenders. Robert Cray, Stevie Ray Vaughan, Jimmy Vaughan, and Albert Collins all use Fenders.

**Taylor:** Well, they are good guitars. The Fender turnaround comes from the Jimi Hendrix influence, I think. I use a Fender Stratocaster nowadays with slightly different pickups and a Les Paul.

**Graves:** *Blues from Laurel Canyon* **is considered by many to be a minor classic blues record. It features all-original writing from Mayall and some of your best and most versatile playing. What are your recollections of this album?**

**Taylor:** It was a very popular album, I know that. It coincided with John Mayall's move to America and that's why all the lyrics are about Laurel Canyon and Sunset Boulevard and Los Angeles, California. It was about that period in his life when he decided he wanted to move to America. As far as my work with John Mayall, I suppose this is my best work. I have to agree with you there.

**Graves: How do you feel about the two live albums you are on of Mayall's?**

**Taylor:** I thought they were OK. The sound quality is not very good because of the method they used to record, which was a simple cassette machine-type thing with a condenser microphone in it on top of John Mayall's Hammond organ, without even an ambience mike or anything like that. But of course they are an accurate representation of what was happening because they are sort of live historical tapes of what was going on at the time.

**Graves: Do you know if there is much unreleased Bluesbreakers material still lying around in the vaults somewhere?**

**Taylor:** I don't think there is too much, but there is some rather interesting live stuff that he has—I know that.

**Graves: Why did you leave John Mayall's Bluesbreakers?**

**Taylor:** Well, I wanted to leave for one thing. But John decided to change his format once again and decided to use just an acoustic guitar player, saxophone player, bass player, and no drummer. This was not what I wanted to do at all and we just sort of went our separate ways at the same time. But I did not know that the Rolling Stones had been looking for a guitar player for two or three months, and I suppose John Mayall must have mentioned to them that I was leaving him and I might be a good person to replace Brian Jones. So that's kind of what happened.

**Graves: You were more or less asked to audition for the Stones weren't you? You were invited to record for a few**

**sessions so they could size you up, am I correct?**

**Taylor:** Well, I went down to the studio and they were doing a couple of tracks for *Let It Bleed*, which I played on, and later on that night they asked me to join the band. It all happened in the same evening. I said, "Well, I'll think about it for a couple of weeks." (Laughs) I became a member of the band the next day. (Laughs again)

**Graves: Had you known Brian Jones and were you intimidated at all about having to step into his shoes?**

**Taylor:** I didn't know him at all, nor did I ever meet him before he died. On a musical level I wasn't intimidated at all. I felt I was their equal as a musician ... in fact I ended up feeling superior, but that's another story. As I've said before, they were just an R&B band until they began writing hit singles. So we all had the same roots—I was a bit younger than them. I wouldn't say I was intimidated, but I was nervous for a while when I joined. Not so much because I was stepping into Brian Jones's shoes, but just because the whole experience of playing with a band that big was so different than playing with John Mayall.

But in some ways it might have been easier for me to do that first tour in 1969 than the rest of the band, because they hadn't toured America for several years. At least during that period they were off, I was on the road working the whole time. Once I got on stage with the Rolling Stones I came into my own.

**Graves: What was it like going from a respected ensemble like John Mayall's Bluesbreakers to the most infamous rock and roll band in the world?**

**Taylor:** (In typical British understatement) Well, it certainly was different. Like you said, it was joining a legendary rock and roll band with a bunch of rock stars instead of a traditional blues band. But it all came down to the same thing. One thing that always impressed me about the Rolling Stones was how much they were into the blues and rhythm and blues. It was and probably still is their inspiration.

**Graves: On just a personal basis, what were those first few months like for you as a Rolling Stone?**

**Taylor:** They were very hectic. We were rehearsing all the time, we did that Hyde Park concert, and then shortly after that we did a tour of America.

**Graves: Given that you were only about 20 years old at the time, weren't you sort of frightened by the Stones' circus-like atmosphere, high-powered accountants, and all that entourage mentality?**

**Taylor:** No, I soon got used to it.

**Graves: Were any of them helping you along during your first year?**

**Taylor:** How do you mean "helping me along"?

**Graves: Well, did they try to shelter you from some of the harsher aspects of being a Stone?**

**Taylor:** (With a touch of bitterness in his voice) No, absolutely not! They didn't shelter me from *nothing*. They didn't "gimme shelter" at all. (Laughs)

**Graves: Musically this must have been a change for you, going from the blues purism of Mayall ...**

**Taylor:** It was an exciting change musically, actually. I developed a lot as a musician and as a person and as a guitar player when I was with the Rolling Stones. I was with them for six years, during which time we toured the world and made five or six albums, which are now considered to be some of their finest. A lot of things happened. Six years is a long time—at least it seemed like a long time then.

**Graves: In the Bluesbreakers you were probably the main visual attraction of the group. Mayall has said that kids came from all over and sat on the front rows to watch your fingers as you played. What was it like to go from being this kind of focal point to taking a back seat to Jagger and Keith Richards in concert?**

**Taylor:** I think the thing with kids coming down to watch me play used to go on in the Rolling Stones, too. I think I became sort of widely recognized as a good guitar player in my own right. Other people didn't just come for my guitar playing, obviously, but I think it was kind of like a highlight during that period. Onstage, anyway.

**Graves: There was a concert movie that came out in the '70s called *Ladies and Gentlemen, The Rolling Stones*. Mick Jagger and Keith Richards entirely dominated this film and I bet there weren't 10 shots of you ...**

**Taylor:** But they didn't make the movie, it was whoever made the movie, that's the way they saw it. It didn't bother me at all. In fact, it would have bothered me a lot more if they had been concentrating on me. Me, Bill Wyman, and Charlie Watts greatly appreciated the relative amount of privacy we had. We were glad all the attention was on Mick and Keith, and after all it would have been anyway because they were the Rolling Stones. They *are* the Rolling Stones, basically. They wrote all the songs, it was their band.

**Graves: What were the musical ingredients you feel you added to the Stones?**

**Taylor:** Apart from my talent as a guitar player? I don't know, I mean Keith Richards and me, although we both had different kinds of styles complemented each other in a very natural instinctive way and made the group sound interesting and different sometimes.

**Graves:** In the film *Gimme Shelter*, which documented the disastrous Altamont concert, we see a very frightened Mick Jagger who doesn't know what to do and a Keith Richards who is very angry and wants to continue to play. The Mick Taylor we see is someone who seems bemused and doesn't quite know what's going on. Am I right?

**Taylor:** No, I had an absolute awareness of what was going on. I think we all did. There was a certain point in the show where we said to each other, "We had better keep on playing, otherwise this could get even worse." Of course it *did* get worse, but we all felt that to stop playing would have been even worse. There could have been a bigger riot and even more trouble.

**Graves:** Were you guys scared out of your wits up there?

**Taylor:** Well, it wasn't one of my more memorable or enjoyable gigs (laughs). I think they would all say that—we just had to get through it.

**Graves:** What was your reaction when you found out someone had been murdered?

**Taylor:** It was very depressing—you can just imagine.

**Graves:** What was your relationship like with the other various Stones members?

**Taylor:** We were good friends, all of us were. I suppose Keith was who I hung out the most with.

**Graves: When you first joined the Rolling Stones you were a health food convert ...**

**Taylor:** (interrupts) No, I wasn't, but that's what got reported, but it's not true.

**Graves: Everyone knows about Keith Richards' many problems, from his numerous drug busts to his very visible deterioration from heroin. It has been rumored that when you left the Stones you had a few of these kinds of problems yourself. Did you find it impossible to keep away from that whirlwind of vice that goes hand in hand with the Stones?**

**Taylor:** Yes, I did find it impossible. I went through similar things to Keith myself, but it didn't end when I left the Rolling Stones. It was part of my lifestyle too, I guess ...

**Graves: Keith, it would appear, has gotten somewhat back on track. Is it true that you've been able to get some of your problems behind you?**

**Taylor:** I have, yes.

**Graves: The rumors I've heard are that addictions to alcohol, cocaine, and heroin are all part of your past**

problems. True?

**Taylor:** I will answer you by saying that, yes, they were a problem, but now they are not. I'm not going to illuminate on my personal life, not tonight. Maybe some other time. (Laughs an unnaturally long time.)

**Graves: Do you at all miss being a part of this huge thing that was the Stones?**

**Taylor:** No, I don't really anymore. I did for a long time, but I don't anymore because I have my own band together and I'm touring around playing in clubs and playing in theatres. I just got back from a tour of Europe. I'm actually enjoying playing more than I ever have and I'm singing and playing really well.

**Graves: What about the social life of the Stones—the Truman Capote, Lee Radziwill, Margaret Trudeau jet set climate? Were you at all a part of that?**

**Taylor:** No, not really. Bianca used to be a good friend, but that had nothing to do with the social life of the Rolling Stones. I know what you're talking about but those people used to just come around for a few gigs on one tour, but there was no real social life as such or lasting friendships that were formed.

**Graves: Probably the two most important albums you worked on with the Stones were *Sticky Fingers* and**

*Exile on Main Street. Sticky Fingers* **seemed to be a very well-planned record, very calculated.** *Exile,* **on the other hand, is known and loved for its looseness, rawness, and haphazard feel. Would you care to comment on them?**

**Taylor:** Well, they were both Rolling Stones records and they were both good. I don't see them that intellectually or anything, as one being more orchestrated and one being more raw. *Exile on Main Street* was done in a much rougher sort of way. We did it in a basement in Keith's house in the south of France and it took a long time. Lots of songs were made up as we were playing. I think *Sticky Fingers* was a bit more planned in the sense that most of the songs were together before we started recording.

**Graves: Following your tenure with the Stones, what did you do afterward?**

**Taylor:** Immediately after the Stones I played with Jack Bruce for about six months. We did a tour of Europe and did a bit of recording in England and hung out together a lot, but we didn't accomplish very much. We didn't stay together very long.

**Graves: There wasn't a record that came together was there?**

**Taylor:** No, there wasn't one. It was basically because we just didn't stay together long enough to make one.

**Graves:** Musically, wasn't this quite a departure for you. Bruce was into a more avant-garde jazz thing at this time wasn't he?

**Taylor:** We were playing his music, and his music is jazzy, bluesy, all kinds of things. It was a departure, yeah, but I didn't really think about it. It was just something to do.

**Graves: You did a solo album in 1979 on the Columbia label that received good notices but did not sell well. There has been some controversy about going far over budget, wasting an inordinate amount of time in the studio, and a lot of wasted musicians ...**

**Taylor:** There was no controversy. It happened just the way you say. I won't argue with your statement at all. It was a pretty good first attempt, I think, and I learned a lot from it. I'm hoping to do a new record very soon, actually, with my own band, which I'm looking forward to a lot. I've been playing with a band now on and off for about three years and I'm really ready to get back into the studio and do something. So it won't be a solo project in the same sense as the other one was. I got offered a great record deal by CBS in 1979 and they basically said, "Do whatever you want, take as long as you want." And so of course I did. It's good to have deadlines and limits, especially when you don't exactly know what you are doing.

**Graves: In the interim period there have been no more albums, but you have played impressively on several**

other people's albums including Joan Jett, Joe Henry, and Bob Dylan. Has this been fulfilling to you?

**Taylor:** Very fulfilling, especially the one with Bob Dylan. That was great. It came about after he came to a show I was doing at a place called the Roxy on Sunset Boulevard in Los Angeles in 1982 with John Mayall's Bluesbreakers, during the time we got back together for a couple of years, and I met him backstage and he asked me if I would be interested in recording with him when he was ready to make an album. Of course, when he was ready to make *Infidels* in New York I went to New York and was involved in that record. About a year later he went on the road in Europe and he asked me to put a band together. I enjoyed that.

I think I'm playing the best stuff I've ever played right now but I haven't got anything on record just yet. Max Middleton [the celebrated pianist on Jeff Beck's *Rough and Ready* and other albums] is someone I've known for a long time. We've done some good instrumentals together and various things we've written together that are good. When we first played together it was more of a fusion kind of thing, but over the years we've become more of an R&B band, with me singing a lot. I enjoy singing a lot now even though I didn't do it much in the past. It's a necessary part of what I want to do.

**Graves: Who are some of the younger guitar players who you find interesting?**

**Taylor:** I can't think of anybody.

**Graves: Well, why don't I run down a few names? Stevie Ray Vaughan?**

**Taylor:** He's OK. I like him.

**Graves: What about Jimmy Vaughan?**

**Taylor:** (With more enthusiasm) I like him a *lot*. I think he's a very tasteful blues guitar player. He's great. I like the Thunderbirds.

**Graves: How about Albert Collins?**

**Taylor:** I heard him a long time ago when I was listening to my first blues records.

**Graves: Changing the subject here, I would like to ask the Million Dollar Question. Exactly why did you leave the Rolling Stones? There doesn't seem to be a definitive answer.**

**Taylor:** That's really too complicated for me to go into right now. My reasons were many and varied and that's all I can say. They were mostly personal reasons, not musical reasons, no artistic differences or anything silly like that. I suppose I did have a musical vision I wanted to pursue, but it's taken me a long time to realize that. I had no clearcut vision when I left the Rolling Stones. It was mostly personal problems, my own mostly.

**Graves: I found it interesting that you were invited to the Rock and Roll Hall of Fame ceremony with the other Stones to collect an award. How did that come about?**

**Taylor:** Because I was included, that's why I was invited to the reception. I don't know whose idea it was, I don't know who the nominating committee [members] are for that, but I suppose I was with the Rolling Stones long enough to have made a difference to what they did during that period. Everyone else was getting one so I was included, too. It was fun but I didn't get a chance to speak to the guys.

**Graves: I suppose you know that the awards show has given rise to rumors that you will be rejoining the Stones?**

**Taylor:** I've heard those rumors, too, but I don't think there's any truth to them at all. I think they are busy making a record at the moment and they are hoping to get it down so they can go on and tour by the end of the year. I haven't been asked to play on the album or to go on tour, but if I were asked to play I'd play.

**Graves: Final question. How would you like to be remembered when all is said and done?**

**Taylor:** Just as a good guitar player.

# Have Mersey: An Interview with The La's Driving Force and Angriest Member, Lee Mavers

(front left: Lee Mavers)

JUST WHEN YOU THINK you've seen or heard everything that could happen in the music business, something like the La's imbroglio comes along. The La's in 1988 and '89 practically owned the music scene in their hometown of Liverpool, where there hadn't been so much excitement for a new Mersey band since four mop-topped lads created a mania of their own nearly 30 years previously.

Record company executives flocked to their sold-out club gigs, and Polygram's London label quickly snapped them up, ready to promote the La's as their major new artists of the year. London had enough confidence in this untested band to hire famed producer Steve Lillywhite (U2, among many others, to his credit) to be at the helm for their debut recording, and he was obviously impressed with the talents of the band and in particular their singer, songwriter, and driving force, Lee Mavers.

Then the fun began. The band chafed under Lillywhite's studio direction, feeling that he was intentionally subverting their aggressive approach in favor of a lighter pop sound. Toward the end of the session the band—all studio greenhorns—walked out on Lillywhite, leaving him to mix and master the 12 tracks himself without their input or consent. Stranger yet, the album when released became a hit, getting almost constant rotation on college radio stations and MTV.

The first single from the album, "There She Goes," attracted almost universal critical acclaim and Mavers was compared favorably to rock lions such as Pete Townshend and Ray Davies.

A worldwide tour was organized to capitalize on the album's success, but in the face of fame, recognition, and plaudits Mavers actively disavowed the album in print.

As an early admirer of the band and an admirer of the album, I was shocked that Mavers would seemingly commit commercial suicide by badmouthing his ticket to success. I thought to myself that Mavers either must be the most naïve megalomaniac in recent music history or an artist so sure of his vision that he would do anything to preserve it—to the point of attacking anything he felt was non-representative.

I caught up with Mavers toward the end of the La's' American tour. Polygram had tried to get me an interview with one of the less volatile members of the band, but I knew Mavers was the one I wanted and I told them I would only speak to him. The P.R. gang at Polygram obviously told him this and he thanked me for insisting that I speak to him only. Passionate and articulate, Mavers left no doubt that he was a man committed to his artistic principles first and foremost. Taken out of context, his comments here could be mistaken for the arrogance of youth (he's in his early 20s), but in context they can be seen as the opinions of a supremely confident and gifted young artist, an individual who allows no second-guessing when it comes to his music goals.

**Author's Note:** After this interview was published in 1991

I took a lot of guff from my fellow critics in the U.S. for my belief that the La's were going to be the next supergroup, the next Big Thing, out of England. It didn't work out that way. The La's disbanded shortly after the American tour referenced here and never released another album of new material. (There have been releases of outtakes, etc., and an album of their appearances on the BBC, which sound very close to the Steve Lillywhite-produced studio versions that Mavers complains about here.) However, the band became a cult favorite all over the world, particularly in the U.K. and Japan, and their songs have been covered by untold numbers of other bands. "There She Goes" has become a rock staple. So, in 2015 I feel vindicated and note that this is one of only a handful of interviews Mavers ever granted. The La's have regrouped for performances a few times in the past few decades, but Mavers invariably disappears again and closes himself off from the rest of the world. I have no doubt that Mavers had a great deal more great music to give us, but for some of the reasons he outlines here decided to keep it all to himself. It is our loss.

**Tom Graves: How do you think the current tour's gone over so far in the States?**

**Lee Mavers:** Yeah, it's OK now. Now that we've got our sound man things are looking up.

**Graves: At one time Britain's art schools were a training ground for musicians, especially in Liverpool. Did that have anything to do with how you formed?**

**Mavers:** No, man. Our school is the school of the universe, y'know. The universe is my university, y'dig. My school is the streets, my school is the world, the universe. I've got me own point of view about things, not somebody else's.

**Graves: How did the La's get together?**

**Mavers:** Out of necessity. It just sort of happened and we hit on somethin'. There was nothing particularly special, y'know, no fuckin' magic thing that happened. It just happened.

**Graves: Am I right that you've been together four years now?**

**Mavers:** Well, since 1986, which is close to five years now, i'n it? In '86 we just started jumpin' up on stage and playing after other bands, y'know, shouting out for bass players out of the audience, shouting out for drummers, etc., until by that October we had the nucleus of the band. We had no place to really play, we needed the extra time to get tight and get together—y'know what I'm sayin'?—to get more seasoned.

So we approached the public house and just asked 'em if we could play for nuthin'. They let us do it, and a few weeks later we were bringing in such a big following that they started giving us, y'know, 15 pounds, 30 pounds, 60 pounds. Then there was a shake-up within the band, the guitarist went, another guitarist came in, then we took Liverpool by storm, record companies came over, took us into a storm ...

**Graves: The record companies started courting you when word of your following in the clubs starting getting out, right? And did your following branch out into the rest of England at this point?**

**Mavers:** No, it was concentrated in Liverpool. Since we had no tapes or records out the following was just concentrated around there. So the record companies approached us, put us in their studio *thing*, and they got what they wanted out of us. But we don't like [the album], and we'll get our chance next.

**Graves: Did the La's have out four singles before signing to London/Polygram?**

**Mavers:** No, you're talking about what happened *after* we signed. I have no idea how many singles they've put out on us at this time. Y'know we were in their studios seven times before the album came out, but we turned our backs on the nonsense we've been made to do, and they mixed it over without our consent, so that's why I'm not interested in it, basically. There've been times when I've come home and me Mum's had [the album] on and I just don't like it.

**Graves: I'd like to ask you about this music scene in Manchester that's been discussed ...**

**Mavers:** It's been and gone in England. It might be coming over to America now, but belatedly so.

**Graves: Well, how would you characterize the differences you see between your music and the music of the critically successful bands from England like The Charlatans U.K. and Inspiral Carpets, and so forth?**

**Mavers:** Ours is soul, theirs is fashion.

**Graves: Was the La's the outgrowth of any musical movement in Liverpool?**

**Mavers:** There are a lot of bands from up around our way but they're all into fashion and we've got the soul.

**Graves: How has Liverpool's music history, with the Beatles and the Mersey Sound, affected what you are doing?**

**Mavers:** The Mersey Sound, no, it hasn't affected us, but the Beatles certainly had an impact on all of music. But we're not playing their stuff either first-hand or second-hand. The Beatles wouldn't even be in our list of top ten favorites.

**Graves: Yeah? Who would be some of your favorites?**

**Mavers:** Bo Diddley, Chuck Berry, James Brown, Captain Beefheart, early Who, stuff like that ... Louis Armstrong, Count Basie, Duke Ellington, Ella Fitzgerald. There's loads of other stuff, but they're not consistent enough to be named.

**Graves:** In the '80s acoustic music seemed to really take a backseat to electric music and only folkie die-hards seemed to play it, but that seems to be changing now. How do you feel about the acoustic parts of what you do?

**Mavers:** We keep getting lumped into a kind of indie, acoustic folkie thing, but no that's not us. But all music is "folk," isn't it? All of it is for *people*. We're not folk, we just occasionally strap an acoustic guitar on, but that doesn't make us a folk band. But look at "Substitute" by the Who. Is that folk?

**Graves:** What I was getting at is that it seems acoustic music isn't being categorized like it used to, don't you think?

**Mavers:** But we are fighting being categorized, I mean we play all types of music. It's like being categorized shouldn't have to exist today—they keep wanting to categorize music, and they keep getting it wrong.

**Graves:** Explain how you came up with the name the La's What does the name mean?

**Mavers:** When we formed the band we just named it the La's, I don't know why.

**Graves:** It doesn't have some sort of British meaning we Yanks don't understand does it?

**Mavers:** I could tell you one meaning, but it would mean only the one you say, and that might be the wrong one. I mean the word "la" is a musical term—you know do-re-me-fa-so-*la*-ti-do. It's also the most commonly used word in almost every language in the whole world. In Ireland and Liverpool it's also an abbreviation for "lad," like people here saying "alright lads" would say "alright la'."

**Graves: What goals do you have in mind when you sit down to write a song?**

**Mavers:** I don't know. I just don't know, man. If I knew what I was lookin' for it would be found. But what I believe in is music that's absolutely timeless; you know what is very ancient is also very futuristic and very now because *now* is always now.

**Graves: John Power in the La's is quoted as saying the La's is the only group around "making music properly." What did he mean by that?**

**Mavers:** The La's are the only ones who are making music, the others are just manners and things. Keep music *alive*, you know. Other music is nothing but sampled beats so everything feels and sounds the same.

**Graves: Of course we've been reading about your dissatisfaction with producer Steve Lillywhite on the album and you mentioned it earlier. Would you care to talk some more about that?**

**Mavers:** Well, that's why we turned our backs on the album and just left it with them and they did that mix without our consent. I feel that the album is duller than it should be and our bad time in the studio shows. I mean parts of it are just crap.

**Graves: If we heard the La's the way you meant for the La's to be heard, what would we hear different?**

**Mavers:** The La's the way I would have wanted you to hear it. I mean, you'll have to just hear it, I can't speak it, y'know. It's silly that that's the way it works, but live we are *exciting*. I want our records to show and feel that.

**Graves: If we saw you live would that clue us in to your real sound?**

**Mavers:** Well, we're still gettin' together live if truth be told. We've been playin' through somebody else's medium for the last five years. Now we've got our own sound boys and we're working on that. It's gettin' more like it.

**Graves: When can we expect to hear something new from you?**

**Mavers:** Once we get back home we hope to have something ready by New Year's Day or so.

**Graves: Who's going to produce the next album?**

**Mavers:** We're going to produce it ourselves as we play. I don't know what the fuck a producer can do, except produce bullshit from his mouth. I don't talk to Lillywhite, but that doesn't affect me. That pain that they've inflicted doesn't affect me because I know the score and them other people don't. On the next album we want to take the record company's fingers out of it so that we can do it.

You know we are the talent, they are the salesmen, and that's the way it should be. At the moment I'm just workin' through the business because we've got to get over the battle.

Also, just wait until the next time, because when we're up at bat we're going to hit a home run. This album, though, is largely dull and unentertaining. Don't buy the album, just give us the money.

**Graves: How do you like the video that's out?**

**Mavers:** I don't like it. You're referring to the one from '88 that was made on a Super 8 for 50 pounds in Liverpool in half a day. Not the one that was made for thousands of dollars in L.A. The reason we had to make that was they said, "If you don't have an American to make it, we're not going to show it." All that bullshit.

**Graves: So are you going to do your own videos in the future as well?**

**Mavers:** We're going to do our own records, our own record covers, and our own videos, absolutely everything to do with the album.

**Graves: Did you like the graphics on the album cover of a close-up of a girl's eye?**

**Mavers:** I thought it was pathetic. What does it signify? I hate it.

**Graves: How has the record company responded to your charges? I must admit I've never seen anything quite like this before.**

**Mavers:** They tell us to keep our mouths shut. Most of the time it's John Powers gettin' interviewed because he's diplomatic, and I'll tell the truth otherwise. So I'm kept down. I'm glad you wanted to speak to me. You know you've got to look after y'self because no one else will. We're tired of dickheads tellin' us what to play and how to play it. Now that they've used up the backlog of our recordings, the ball's in our court and it's our turn to bat, and they'll only get what we give them and they'll get it in such a way that they won't be able to tamper with it. They'll get it in such a way that they'll only be able to sell it, which is the whole point of a bleedin' record company. Y'know the art guides the artist, the artist guides the art, and the salesman sells it.

# Take Me Seriously! An Interview with Mark Lindsay of Paul Revere & the Raiders

WHAT MARK LINDSAY WANTS most is a little respect. And in his own polite way he is waging a one-man war to see he gets it. He is proud of the contributions Paul Revere and the Raiders made to the pop music swell of the '60s, but he also wants people to know he hasn't jumped on the nostalgia bandwagon to cash in on the "oldies" tours the way some of his ex-bandmates have.

At age 48, Lindsay is as trim, fit, and handsome as ever, and only his eyeglasses and a new hair style prevent him from being instantly recognizable. A thoroughly engaging conversationalist, Lindsay is an interviewer's dream, spinning colorful yarns and anecdotes from whichever direction he is pointed. Although careful to avoid offense, Lindsay painted a bleaker picture of his teen idol image than one would imagine. The music is what he cares about, and he seems genuinely surprised and flattered when this interviewer tells him he thinks Lindsay is one of the most underrated singers of his time.

**Tom Graves: It seems to me that Paul Revere and the Raiders could almost be divided into three distinct groups. The first was a tough, screaming, really raucous white R&B band. The second was a British Invasion-influenced great singles band, and the third was a more**

commercial-oriented pop band …

**Mark Lindsay:** I'd say that's a pretty astute observation, pretty accurate really …

**Graves: Getting into the earliest phase of the band, I was struck by how young Paul Revere must have been when he owned the hamburger stand that was the focal point of how it all began for you. How did he come to be a business owner at such a tender age?**

**Lindsay:** Paul had gone to barber school, I believe, after dropping out of high school, got married at a very early age, and he and his wife invested in this hamburger stand. There was a competitor in Boise right across the street from his hamburger stand, The Quik Kurb. So being a salesman—Paul has always been a good salesman—and trying to increase his business, with rock and roll being big at the time, he figured if he had a rock and roll band then kids would think he was hip and come to *his* hamburger stand. So that's why he started playing music and got a group together.

When he got this group together, the first night they played was when I walked up and asked to sing a song. But I didn't really know him at the time.

**Graves: How did you and Revere hook up?**

**Lindsay:** I was working at McClure's Bakery in Caldwell, Idaho, and we made the buns for both Paul and his competitor and a lot of other people. On Sundays McClure's didn't deliver, so Paul had to come down and pick up his buns. I had seen Paul rehearsing a few times, because I was working with a group called Freddy Chapman and the Idaho Playboys, which may have been called the Fireballers by that time, but they were both kind of country groups with a rock and roll segment; country music was very big in Idaho. I was the rock and roll singer for the group. When I heard Paul Revere and his band rehearsing and this rock and roll pounding coming from across the street, I thought, gee, a *real* rock and roll band, not a country band that sings rock and roll. That would be a great band to get with.

I didn't know Paul or any of the guys he was playing with, but that first night that he played, at the Elks Hall, I walked in and asked to sing a song. I had very poor eyesight—still do as a matter of fact. I'm legally blind—and I didn't have my glasses on because I kind of thought it was uncool to wear glasses. They didn't have contacts at that time. So I walked in and couldn't really see anything. I could see that there was a stage out there and I started walking straight to it. I remember the crowd parting like it was the Red Sea—everybody must have thought I was nuts. So I walked up and asked to sing a song. Paul said, "Well, what do you know?" And I said, "Anything by Jerry Lee Lewis." And he said, "What about 'Crazy Arms?'" And I said, "Sure." He said, "What key is it?" I said, "I don't know, any key will do." I didn't know what a key was.

So they struck it up and I sang the song and left. The next day was Sunday and Paul came in to get his buns. I was very slow that morning, having been up very late the night before. Paul started telling me this story, "You know the craziest thing happened last night. I was playing right across the street from the Elks Hall, and this crazy, skinny kid came walkin' in and asked to sing with the band." And when he finished the story I asked, "Well, how was the guy?" He said, "Well, he wasn't bad." So I whipped off my hat and my glasses and said, "It was me!" So that's how we met and started working together.

**Graves: When did you begin singing?**

**Lindsay:** I always sang as a kid. I always liked music. When I was a freshman in high school in Cambridge, Idaho, I was going to a basketball game and was on the bus, and I was singing. This girl said, "Hey, you aren't bad. You should enter our talent show." So I did, and lo and behold I won first prize. I sang "Don't Be Cruel" in a kind of impersonation of Elvis Presley. We didn't have a television set at that time—Idaho got TV very late and we were a little bit in the hills—and I hadn't seen Elvis on TV or anything. But I had heard he moved around a lot. And I had a band—piano, guitar, bass, and drums—and the drummer and guitar player, believe it or not, were so shy that they stood behind the curtain. So all I had on stage was the piano player and the bass player and me. Everybody thought I was miming, you know lip-synching, the record. So when I got through and won the prize, all my classmates would come up to me and say, "Hey, Lindsay, that was pretty good the way you mimicked Elvis." And I said, "No, it was *me*."

Of course I was trying to sound like Presley as much as possible, and when I couldn't convince anybody that it wasn't really Presley but me, I thought, "Well, wait a minute here. If they think I'm the guy that's on the top of the charts, maybe there's a future in it for me in this business." So I decided at that point in time that I wanted to become a professional singer.

**Graves: Do you think your talents as a singer have been underrated?**

**Lindsay:** I don't know about my talents as a singer. I never thought of myself as a great singer. I thought of myself as a rock and roll singer who was a pretty good entertainer, but I do think the Raiders didn't get taken seriously as a band too much.

**Graves: Did this bother the band very much?**

**Lindsay:** I don't think it bothered Paul very much, because—and I'm not trying to be critical here—as long as we were working and making good money, that was what Paul was interested in because he was first and foremost a businessman. He started the band as a business enterprise to begin with. So if we were making good money, as far as he was concerned we were very successful.

But *I* was the one, I think, who took the music critiques, or lack of same, to heart, and it really bothered me. We couldn't seem to shake the image. And I understand how people would see the costumes and skits on TV and stuff and remember those because a picture is worth a thousand words. But the Raiders made some great rock and roll music and I would like to be remembered as doing that as well as the comedy bits.

**Graves: The Northwest had a thriving music scene prior to the British Invasion. Groups like the Wailers [not Bob Marley's band] and the Kingsmen were hot and in the mid-'60s bands like the Sonics were popular regionally. This area had a reputation for loud, snotty garage band R&B. What was the scene like there in your early days?**

**Lindsay:** The Wailers came from Seattle and around Tacoma up in the Washington area and the Kingsmen were from around Portland, where we were living at the time our early records were released. But we were really from the Boise Valley area of Idaho, and there wasn't a lot of competition there. The band took a two-year hiatus while Paul was in the service, and we restarted the band in Portland, Oregon and we were playing frat parties and dances and whatever we could play. We got our first gig at Parker's in Seattle and I told Paul, "We can't go there." And he said, "Why not?" And I said, "Well, there's this line of guys in the front row who criticized the bass player's fourth finger technique, and I don't want to put up with that. We're not good enough to go there." And he said, "Nah, we're just a rock and roll band, we'll go up and have fun."

And that's what our saving grace was, I think. We were just a kick-ass rock and roll band. We wouldn't have been taken seriously in the *Down Beat* poll (laughs). But there was a certain toughness in Seattle—there were always a couple of fights that would break out—but since the Raiders were such a good-time band and we were up on stage, we were never really a part of that. We would stage some really raucous music when we saw something like that to kind of choreograph the fight till they stopped it. The Raiders were just a party band, a good-time rock and roll band.

**Graves: The Raiders had the wildest stage act of any band in its time. How did the act evolve?**

**Lindsay:** In the very early days in Idaho we didn't have much of an act. We just got up on stage and played and jumped up and down and did whatever we did. There really wasn't an act per se. When the band broke up when Paul went into the army, and I went to Hollywood to make my fame and fortune, the song "Like, Long Hair" had become a hit. The record company said, "You guys have got to go out and tour." And of course Paul was tied up at the time. So we talked about it, and I went out on the road as Paul Revere's Raiders. In that group was Leon Russell as the piano player. Of course, he was a consummate showman even in those early days and we had several other guys filling in on other instruments, but I remember going into these strange crowds where nobody knew me and I didn't know them, and I had terminal stage fright. I just sang the songs and it was terrible. And Leon said, "Hey kid, kick it to me and I'll show you what to do." And I did and he would say, "Ladies and gentlemen ..." So I saw how it worked. You have to talk to the people, you have to have a show. On that short tour and hanging out with the musicians in the Los Angeles area I could see how it was done. So when we started the band back in Portland I told Paul we had to have a show. We couldn't just be five guys standing up there singing songs.

So, the show just kind of evolved. The steps came with Drake (Levin) and Phil (Volk). We had seen the black groups do a lot of steps and we were doing a lot of R&B stuff. In fact that was one of the things that made us different—we were probably the first white R&B group in the Northwest, especially around Portland. In Portland it was all folk music; the Brothers Four were the hottest thing going. And here were these nuts doing "Ooh Poo Pah Doo" and "Over You" and all these screaming songs. That's where part of my vocal style came from, listening to all those old R&B records.

That made us unique. I don't think there were three black people in all of Idaho.

**Graves: Who specifically were some of those early R&B inspirations?**

**Lindsay:** Oh, Ernie K. Doe, anybody who had a hit that was kind of rockin', Aaron Neville, Jessie Hill, Ray Charles, all the good R&B guys.

**Graves: Do you think you picked up part of your vocal technique and stylings from those guys?**

**Lindsay:** I don't know what my vocal *style* is. I don't know if I really have one, I just kind of sound like me. In the early days we tried to do a lot of R&B and I screamed a lot. In fact about the time we signed with CBS records I had gone and had a throat nodule operation, because I had screamed my voice into oblivion. I read a recent overview of the Raiders in another magazine where some of the other guys said when I got my nodule operation it changed my style. It didn't really change my style because when we cut our first records for CBS, like "Over You," I was still screaming then. But what happened was we started having more commercial hits with a more breathy style, plus when we got on TV we had to tone it down. A lot of the Raiders' early act—I wouldn't call it "blue," but it wasn't really family fare either. It wasn't something you'd see on Dick Clark's television show. So when we got on TV we had to develop a lot of different things and that's where a lot of the skits came from. Because those were more palatable for TV and we couldn't do some of the outrageous things we would do onstage. I mean we would do anything. I mean, I had a 100-foot cord on my vocal mike and if I wanted to go to the john while I was singing, I would walk off the stage and drag the cord into the men's room and relieve myself and drag it back out. That was how we got our reputation ... I got a reputation for just doing anything. Using this long cord I would climb to the top of a gymnasium, hang from a basketball net, anything for a spectacular finish. We had this old blunderbuss, this old muzzle-loading pistol that I would load with flash paper as wadding. During the last note of the show, pow!, I would fire this thing, and hopefully the flash paper would burn out over the heads of the audience. We stopped doing that, nobody ever got hurt, but we stopped because somebody mentioned something about *insurance*.

We would set a piano on fire every night. We would rent the cheapest piano we could find, a real junker next to the good one we used, and on the last song Paul would play that piano and squirt lighter fluid on it and set it on fire. I'd be on top of the piano dancing up and down with this pistol waving it around ... it was pretty spectacular.

**Graves: So you had to eliminate all this for TV?**

**Lindsay:** When we got to TV we had to drop *all* that stuff. Every night I would split my pants. It's funny because reading about the Beatles, John Lennon would do this all the time too. We wore tight pants and if you do the splits a certain way you're gonna rip your pants. And so at a well-timed moment I would jump off the piano and do the splits and rip my pants. Purposely, of course, for effect. That's one reason why later we wore tights (laughs.).

**Graves: I was going to ask you about that. Adam West of *Batman* claimed the network censors made them do all kinds of things to their costumes so they would not, shall we say, betray any hint of their anatomical correctness. You guys wore those tights. Did you have those kinds of problems?**

**Lindsay:** Inside of the tights we wore on TV we had to wear two of what they call "dance belts." They're things that male ballet dancers wear to keep everything in place, and we had to wear *two* of 'em. I remember in the early days at ABC, the censorship in the middle '60s was horrendous. I remember one time we were doing a pirate skit and I had this long belt hanging down. And we had to reshoot it again because the woman from Standards and Practices said, "That looks very suggestive to me." (laughs) It was just a long belt hanging down, *ma'am*.

So we couldn't do anything we had done live. That's how the skits developed because we had to do something that was entertaining yet viewable on afternoon TV.

**Graves: The story is well known that you almost beat the Kingsmen to "Louie, Louie." Tell us how the CBS contract came about and the genesis of "Louie, Louie."**

**Lindsay:** We had cut "Louie, Louie" and the local CBS guy heard it and took it to a disc jockey, Roger Hart, who became our manager. He took it to CBS and we got signed, which was a miracle, because Mitch Miller was head of A&R at Columbia at that time, and he hated rock and roll. He thought it was a passing fad. We were, in fact, the first rock group to be signed to CBS. They probably thought, "Well, what'll it hurt. We've already got this master out."

[Whatever you may have read] I believe the Kingsmen cut their version first. In fact the records pretty much point this out, too. There was a two-week period between theirs and ours. I remember when we cut the thing, a guy in the studio said, "You know, this song is familiar. Yeah, a group was in here a couple of weeks ago and cut the same song." I'm taking my cue from that. It really doesn't make any difference since the Kingsmen had the big hit. Both versions came out simultaneously, and ours was a big hit in three states: Washington, Oregon, and Idaho where we were known as well as northern California as far down as San Jose. Everywhere we had played it was a hit. But CBS had no distribution facilities for rock and roll. They didn't know how to promote us. And I can't blame them, we were a new thing to them. In Portland, Oregon, the Kingsmen's hometown, their version sold approximately 600 copies, and our version sold 6,000.

**Graves: What is your take on the supposed dirty lyrics to "Louie, Louie?" Like everybody else I can't understand them.**

**Lindsay:** There are no dirty lyrics. The reason the lyrics are mumbled on the Kingsmen's version is because Jack Ely was wearing braces at the time he did the song, plus the engineer, if he used the same technique he used for us, had the vocal mike suspended from an overhead boom, and he had it up high so you had to sing up to it. I guess the engineer had found that rock and rollers would "pop the mike" when singing straight into it. So here's Jack Ely singing "Loooeeegghh Looooiiiigghh," trying to get his lips over his braces. It was a great marketing ploy, and look at the sales 2 Live Crew is getting just because of their controversy. It was the same thing then.

**Graves: So the mumbled lyrics became a sales tool?**

**Lindsay:** Oh, absolutely. It was like, "Hey man, play 'Louie, Louie' on 33 rpm and it sounds like …" If your imagination is running wild you can make something out of anything. Like these guys who play records backwards and find hidden messages … I've never played any of our records backwards, but I'm sure if I did I'd find something. Like if you get a group of monkeys typing in a room for 1,000 years one of them will probably hit on some Shakespeare sooner or later. Just the way words are formed, if you spin a record backwards you're going to find something that sounds like something weird if you listen long enough. And I'm not saying some groups don't actually put backwards things on or haven't in the past, but "Louie, Louie" was innocent. There are so many versions of "Louie, Louie." I was listening to a couple of CDs of just "Louie, Louie," and listening to the Angels' version of "Louie, Louie." It sounds just like the B-52's doing it. I think they got a lot of their stuff from the Angels.

There's even a mistake in the Kingsmen's version of "Louie, Louie" where he sings "Me see" then two bars later sings "Me see." He started to sing the verse two bars early, caught himself and started again. In those days a lot of mistakes were made and they would say, "Nobody will ever hear that, let it go." And the Angels copied that mistake in their version.

Speaking of copying songs, something interesting came up recently. "Louie – Go Home," which we wrote as a follow-up to "Louie, Louie," is copied on the Who's album, *Who's Missing* and there's a version called "Lubie – Go Home." If you listen to it it's "Louie – Go Home" word-for-word. Roger Daltrey even does the ad-lib, "miss her so much, tell you what I'm gonna do, gonna buy you a monkey and a new dog, too." And it's credited to Pete Townshend. So, about three years ago we called them up—on the liner notes it was referred to as "an obscure American cut."

The way I figured that happened was there was a girl who was a publicist who was a big Raiders fan in Los Angeles, who shall remain nameless. The Who were in town in Los Angeles, and I remember I was dating a girl who lived in some apartments. I was taking her home and it was early in the morning, and Pete Townshend was coming out of the publicist's apartment carrying the first cassette recorder I ever saw in his hand—it was a Philips. What I think happened, and I may be wrong but I'm trying to reconstruct the crime, was he probably taped some of her records and she had probably played "Louie – Go Home." It sounds like a black group on that cut, so he probably talked to the band and they liked it and cut it and couldn't find out who it was by. Because "Louie – Go Home" wasn't a big national hit for the Raiders. The record company probably thought Townshend wrote it and gave him credit. As a matter of fact our publishing company wrote their publishing company and they straightened it out and we got some back royalties. I find it kind of interesting that the Who covered the Raiders at one time and didn't even know it—or maybe they did.

**Graves: Getting into the period where you had the big hits. Did you grow to resent the costumes?**

**Lindsay:** Yes, I did. Paul and I probably differ on this, but by the time we were trying to be taken seriously musically—about '67 or '68 when music really began to change and the San Francisco music scene started to happen—CBS released five singles simultaneously of Moby Grape, but the Raiders, who had had a pretty good run, weren't taken seriously. It had nothing to do with the music—well, maybe partially—but mainly it was the image. So I convinced Paul that we needed to get out of the Raiders outfits, but we went to other costumes—we might as well have stayed in the George Washington outfits. If you're in matching jumpsuits it's really the same thing.

**Graves: What about the ponytail hairstyle you guys wore?**

**Lindsay:** When we got the costumes, we all decided to grow ponytails since the costumes could be rented with the powdered wigs. At first we all thought we would wear the wigs. We were in Sacramento, California playing with the Beach Boys—I remember this because Glen Campbell was sitting in for Brian Wilson at that time—and some Raiders fans happened to work in a beauty shop. And they said, hey we could give you a great deal on some of these wigs, so we went down and got some, and that night we put them on. I cannot tell you how hot it was. If you've ever been on stage in a wig under lights it is incredible—I mean sweat was just pouring off us. Finally after the show we went *zzziiinnnggg* (motions as if he's throwing the wigs in a garbage can)—no way would we wear them again. We put them on the car antennas and had fun with them for a few days. We liked the idea, however, and all started growing our hair. And you had to go through a real ugly period where your hair wasn't quite there and nobody had hair that long. Drake and Smitty both had kind of curly hair, so even when they grew it long it looked like S.O.S. pads were stuck on the back of their heads. Paul's got just so long and then broke off. I'm the only one who was stubborn enough to stick with it and it became kind of a trademark. Now they've kind of come back. I think Mel Gibson is wearing one in his latest movie.

**Graves: You guys must have been a hell of an act to follow. Didn't you kill your competition on stage?**

**Lindsay:** We were. We have a poster, in fact, of us playing in Memphis. It's sponsored by Shoney's and the tickets were $2.50. And for $2.50 you got to see the Byrds, We Five, the Raiders, Bo Diddley and the Duchess, and one more that I can't remember. And the Byrds were headlining. They insisted on it. I remember Paul said, "O.K." After about four days they went to the guy who was managing the tour and said, "Look, we want to go on before the Raiders." So, we closed the show because we were an impossible act to follow.

**Graves: What kind of immediate impact did the British Invasion have on the Raiders, because you were one of the only rock and roll groups to go head-to-head with them?**

**Lindsay:** It was the best thing that ever happened to us

because we were touted as "America's answer to the British Invasion." What better imagery could there be than Paul Revere and the Raiders with the outfits? We were the only real rock and roll band that had the exposure to be taken seriously as contenders against the British Invasion. When the British Invasion happened suddenly the teen magazines had something to write about—the Beatles, Herman's Hermits, and so on. And it didn't hurt that for whatever reason I got picked as the teen idol or whatever …

**Graves: Well, Mark, it's because you were the cute one (laughs).**

**Lindsay:** (blushes) Well, we were on the covers of all the magazines and so we fell right in line with it.

**Graves: It made you more marketable. You got on the Dick Clark show, *Where the Action Is*. Did you have any idea the exposure would rocket you to success the way it did?**

**Lindsay:** I had no idea, and I don't think anyone else in the group had any idea, of what television exposure meant. If anybody today doesn't understand it just look at MTV. I don't think you can get a record played today without a video.

**Graves: There's a lot of parallels with MTV and what the Raiders did on TV, isn't there?**

**Lindsay:** Oh sure. You can look at the Raiders' chart positions and the times we were on television and it's almost a parallel curve. We were attractive to Dick Clark because we were very visual and we were good enough musicians to cut backing tracks for Steve Alaimo and Linda Scott, who were the male and female lead singers for the show. The format of the show, for those who weren't around in the '60s was kind of like *Solid Gold* or *Video Jukebox*. We were the house band, and there were male and female lead singers; it was like a modern day *Your Hit Parade* in a way. They would sing the hit songs of the day. We would do the group-type songs by the Stones or the Beatles in addition to our own things which came soon, and then there was the day's special guests, like Donovan, the Zombies, or somebody.

We would go in the studio and cut the tracks for us and Linda and Steve and lip-sync it live on the air. We worked in this little studio above a garage and we would go in there a couple of days a week and cut tracks *all day*.

The third reason we were attractive to Dick Clark is that we worked cheap. Dick, I think, thought that if the show really took off he could afford a *real* band. But what happened was once we got the exposure everybody liked us.

**Graves: Your image was the calculated, conscious decision of several people, and I would like to get into that. What role did Gloria Stavers of *16* magazine have in your rise to success?**

**Lindsay:** She approached us, I guess, because she saw we

were hot on TV. She was a smart businesswoman and she wanted something that would promote her magazine and sell magazines. So when she saw the Raiders she jumped. She would come out to L.A. for two or three days and do pictures and pictures and pictures and interviews, and so she scooped everybody. Of course we did interviews for other magazines, but *16* was *the* big magazine at the time. As far as the biggest magazines I think they were in this order: *16*, *Tiger Beat*, *Flip*, and there were several other smaller ones like *Teen Scene* that didn't happen too big. I believe *Tiger Beat* and *16* magazine are still out there today, aren't they?

**Graves: What about this teeny-bopper image? There seems to be a discrepancy between this cutesy image and the tough, bare-knuckled songs you recorded early on.**

**Lindsay:** Like I said, a picture is worth 1,000 words. It was both fortunate and unfortunate that we were on TV and in so many magazines.

**Graves: Obviously it made you famous.**

**Lindsay:** It sold lots of records and it made us very famous. However, it categorized us to such a degree, plus when we got on TV the corny skits evolved, the slapstick and all. You asked how it was to be typecast in this role. After a while it got very wearing, and I became very resentful because no matter what the Raiders did we weren't taken seriously. So at one time when FM radio was just becoming big, the so-called *underground* scene, which started a whole new trend in album-oriented rock, a friend of ours at CBS as an experiment took an acetate—two cuts off our latest album, *Revolution*—and told the station guy it was by a new group called Pink Puzz. The disk jockey played the song two or three times and said, "This is something on Columbia by a new group called the Pink Puzz. I think we'll be hearing a lot more from these guys." Some listeners who had just gotten the new album called up and said, "That's not the Pink Puzz, that's Paul Revere and the Raiders." The disc jockey takes the needle and goes *zzziiipppp*, "No more of these guys."

So as Pink Puzz it was cool and as Paul Revere and the Raiders it was junk. The music didn't change at all. But when he heard the Raiders it was like, "God, I can't play this."

**Graves: Back to being a teen idol. What were the positives and negatives of that?**

**Lindsay:** The positives were it sold records and it was a great ego booster. The negatives were it put me—this little kid from Idaho, probably with a background very much like everybody reading this magazine and probably less than most. My folks were not well-to-do at all. My father was a school teacher and I had five sisters and two brothers. We weren't a two-car family, we were half-a-car family—growing up without a lot of material things and all of a sudden everything in the world is at your feet. It's great, but it's really not. I came from that background and all of a sudden you can go down and buy a Ferrari with that first royalty check. It's positive in the fact it sells records, but it's negative in almost every other way. I didn't have a chance to grow up … I didn't grow up until I left the group. It took me about 10 years to realize where I was. It was both fascinating and devastating.

There's a picture that I wish I had—I can see it in my mind's eye, I don't know if anybody ever snapped it or not—it was in Little Rock, and instead of parking the bus by the back door the fire marshal made us move the bus 50 yards away. Of course we got mobbed, and people were grabbing at me and I was forging ahead. By the time I got to the bus door this girl was hanging on to my ponytail and a police dog was hanging onto the *girls'* butt, and the cop was hanging onto the dog's leash. Me, the girl, the dog, and the policeman. It must have looked hilarious because everybody inside the bus was rolling.

**Graves: Wasn't this dangerous at times? Didn't getting your hair pulled out hurt like hell?**

**Lindsay:** That's why we made those quick escapes. I remember before the escapes were arranged, we came off the stage sometimes and went through the crowd and it became very ugly. All they wanted was a souvenir, like your hat, or your coat, or your sleeve. They didn't really want a piece of flesh, but they sometimes got it. You get a mob frantic and there's something about the psychology of a crowd … It's like a shark feeding frenzy.

**Graves: Did you come to dread all that?**

**Lindsay:** Oh yeah. I was so paranoid that for years I would go to a restaurant and sit in the corner with my back against the wall, because I remembered all that. And you just automatically put yourself in a position where you can fend 'em off. It affected my life vastly. It took me years before I could go into a restaurant and be comfortable. I still get recognized, but it's a whole different thing than fans wanting to grab you.

**Graves: You were someone every teenage girl wanted to cuddle with at night before she went to bed. How does something like that affect your real-life love life? Did that make it difficult for women your own age to regard you seriously?**

**Lindsay:** As far as a serious love life, I mean, I had a lot of affairs and a lot of one-night stands. We were on the road all the time. But I didn't really have time to get involved with anybody. I didn't even date anybody steadily. We were gone. Talk about a transitory state of being, I was constantly in motion. I'm just glad AIDS wasn't around at that point in time. I mean, I was pretty promiscuous and it was an era of so-called free sex, free love, and it was OK. It was condoned behavior at the time, but it was pretty heavy stuff, there wasn't anything of lasting value there. It looks great on the surface. It was nice sometimes, but I kept reminding myself that it all really happened because of timing ….

# Photo Credits

Louise Brooks circa 1928 courtesy of Margaret Brooks; signed copy of *Lulu in Hollywood* by Tom Graves; Linda Haynes in film *Rolling Thunder* courtesy of Paramount Pictures; Linda Haynes in Bonita Springs, Florida circa 2010 by Tom Graves; Harry Crews in Gainesville, Florida, 1979, by Tom Graves; Elvis mosaic on Memphis street by Tom Graves; D.L. Menard courtesy of Rounder Records; Blackwood Brothers Quartet courtesy of James Blackwood; Albert Goldman, public domain, courtesy of Wikipedia; Johnny Rotten in Memphis, 1977, by Ward Archer; Tennessee Ernie Ford outside Capitol Records Building in Los Angeles, courtesy of Capitol Records; Woodstock picturing Country Joe McDonald public domain courtesy of Wikipedia; Frank Zappa courtesy of Rykodisc; Mick Taylor, public domain, courtesy of Wikipedia; the La's courtesy of Polygram; Paul Revere and the Raiders, public domain, credited to Associated Press, courtesy of Wikipedia.

# About The Author

TOM GRAVES RECEIVED HIS first recognition as a journalist in 1976 when he won a Sigma Delta Chi (the journalism student organization) regional award for best feature article for a profile of a local eccentric, Prince Mongo, for *Memphis Magazine*. At graduation that same year he received the National Observer Award for journalism graduate of the year from Memphis State University. He began to publish reviews and articles for national periodicals while still in his early 20s and became the editor and publisher of the critically-acclaimed small circulation magazine *Rock & Roll Disc* from 1987 until the magazine ceased publication in 1992.

Graves wrote for *Rolling Stone, Musician, American History, The Oxford American, The New York Times, The Washington Post*, and many other magazines and newspapers before his first novel, *Pullers*, was published in 1998. The novel received glowing reviews, but it was nine years before Graves's next book, *Crossroads: The Life and Afterlife of Blues Legend Robert Johnson*. This meticulously-researched biography received praise from a wide variety of sources and won the author the Keeping the Blues Alive Award for Literature in 2010.

Beginning in 2010 Graves travelled with filmmakers Robert Gordon and Morgan Neville to interview the subjects for the documentary film *Best of Enemies* (released in 2015) about the 1968 debates between Gore Vidal and William F. Buckley Jr., a subject he had been working with since his freshman year in college. Graves was credited as the consulting producer for the film, which continues to play in theaters and is predicted to win future awards.

In 2012 Graves and his friend Darrin Devault formed a book publishing company, The Devault-Graves Agency, that specializes in re-publishing promising books that have gone out of print. The company made world news in 2014 when it published *Three Early Stories* by J.D. Salinger, the first legitimate Salinger book in over 50 years. They also published three Jack Kerouac novels, the celebrity profile collections of Rex Reed, Weegee's autobiography, and crime fiction by Jim Thompson, James M. Cain, and David Goodis.

In 2015 Devault and Graves published a book of their photography, *Graceland Too Revisited*, about the infamous Elvis-themed roadside attraction in Holly Springs, Mississippi.

Graves has lived his entire life in Memphis, Tennessee, and is a professor at LeMoyne-Owen College where he teaches English, humanities, and journalism.

# Other Books by Tom Graves

**Fiction**

*Pullers*

**Nonfiction**

*Crossroads: The Life and Afterlife*
*of Blues Legend Robert Johnson*
(winner of the Keeping the Blues Alive Award for Literature, 2010)

**Photography**

*Graceland Too Revisited*
(with Darrin Devault)

# Other Books You Might Enjoy from Devault-Graves Digital Editions

*Three Early Stories* by J.D. Salinger
*Big Sur* by Jack Kerouac
*Tristessa* by Jack Kerouac
*Maggie Cassidy* by Jack Kerouac
*Do You Sleep in the Nude?* by Rex Reed
*Conversations in the Raw* by Rex Reed
*People Are Crazy Here* by Rex Reed
*Valentines & Vitriol* by Rex Reed
*Weegee: The Autobiography*
*Black Man in the White House* by E. Frederic Morrow

**DEVAULT-GRAVES**
**DIGITAL EDITIONS**
www.devault-gravesagency.com